Quicken® 2000

fast&easy™

Rave reviews for PRIMA TECH's *fast & easy series*

"Excellent book! Easy to read, easy to comprehend, easy to implement!"
Cheryl Johnson
Reno, NV

"Fantastic! Remarkably to the point, yet not once does it neglect vital information."
Joshua Loop
Cincinnati, OH

"Excellent book. Easy to understand!"
Cay Colberg
Albuquerque, NM

"The best book I've found!"
Bertha Podwys
Iverness, FL

"Great for fast reference!"
Janet White
Orlando, FL

"Well presented, concise, and extremely helpful!"
Julia Kogut
Arlington, VA

"So well illustrated that one couldn't possibly fail to profit from its content."
Charles Bendal
Surrey, England

"Very thorough and easy to use."
Cathy Mercer
Clifton, TX

"This book dispels the myth that computing is complicated."
Iain Clark
Durham, England

Send Us Your Comments

To comment on this book or any other PRIMA TECH title, visit our reader response page on the Web at **www.prima-tech.com/comments**.

How to Order

For information on quantity or corporate discounts, contact the publisher: Prima Publishing, P.O. Box 1260BK, Rocklin, CA 95677-1260; (916) 632-4400. On your letterhead, include information concerning the intended use of the books and the number of books you wish to purchase. For individual orders, visit PRIMA TECH's Web site at **www.prima-tech.com**.

Quicken® 2000

fast&easy™

Coletta Witherspoon
and
Craig Witherspoon

PRIMA
TECH

A DIVISION OF PRIMA PUBLISHING

A Division of Prima Publishing

Prima Publishing and colophon are registered trademarks of Prima Communications, Inc. PRIMA TECH and Fast & Easy are trademarks of Prima Communications, Inc., Rocklin, California 95677.

Publisher: Stacy L. Hiquet
Associate Publisher: Nancy Stevenson
Marketing Manager: Judi Taylor
Managing Editor: Dan J. Foster
Senior Acquisitions Editor: Deborah F. Abshier
Acquisitions Editor: Stephen Graham
Project Editor: Estelle Manticas
Assistant Project Editors: Brian Thomasson, Melody Layne
Copy Editor: Judy Ohm
Technical Reviewer: Franni Ferrero
Interior Layout: Marian Hartsough
Cover Design: Prima Design Team
Indexer: Katherine Stimson

Intuit, Quicken, QuickBooks, TurboTax, and EasyStep are registered trademarks and/or registered service marks of Intuit Inc. Billminder, Quicken.com, QuickenMortgage, Insuremarket, EasyQuote, Investor Insight, Intuit marketplace, QuickFill, QuickTabs, Quicken Financial planner, and Financial Newsstand are trademarks and/or service marks of Intuit Inc. or one of its subsidiaries.

Important: If you have problems installing or running Quicken 2000, go to Quicken's Web site at **www.quicken.com**. Prima Publishing cannot provide software support.

Prima Publishing and the author have attempted throughout this book to distinguish proprietary trademarks from descriptive terms by following the capitalization style used by the manufacturer.

Information contained in this book has been obtained by Prima Publishing from sources believed to be reliable. However, because of the possibility of human or mechanical error by our sources, Prima Publishing, or others, the Publisher does not guarantee the accuracy, adequacy, or completeness of any information and is not responsible for any errors or omissions or the results obtained from the use of such information. Readers should be particularly aware of the fact that the Internet is an ever-changing entity. Some facts may have changed since this book went to press.

ISBN: 0-7615-2314-6
Library of Congress Catalog Card Number: 99-64756
Printed in the United States of America

99 00 01 02 03 DD 10 9 8 7 6 5 4 3 2 1

For A.H. and "Goodie" T.S. Witherspoon
for always being there when we needed them.

Acknowledgments

We would like to give special thanks to Intuit for allowing us to play a part in the testing and development of Quicken over the past few years. As always, we want to thank everyone at Prima; especially Debbie Abshier, our Acquisitions Editor, for all the opportunities she gave us to write books at Prima. We wish her the time of her life as she moves up to her new job. Also, we wish Stephen Graham the best of luck filling her shoes. Estelle Manticas deserves enormous credit for her patience and hard work to keep the book on track. It was a pleasure to work with her. Our thanks to Judy Ohm and Franni Ferrero for their great editing job.

About the Authors

COLETTA AND CRAIG WITHERSPOON are freelance writers and consultants who have authored more than a dozen books about software applications, Internet tools, operating systems, networks and networking tools. They also provide writing services and multimedia materials to corporate clients through Clare Stanley Productions.

Contents at a Glance

PART III
CONTROLLING YOUR ANNUAL FINANCES 163

PART IV
PREPARING FOR AN EMERGENCY 247

PART V
PLANNING FOR THE FUTURE 289

PART VI
APPENDICES 341

Contents

PART III
CONTROLLING YOUR ANNUAL FINANCES 163

PART V
PLANNING FOR THE FUTURE 289

Introduction

This *Fast & Easy* guide from Prima Publishing will help you master Quicken Deluxe 2000 so that you can take charge of your personal finances. Quicken Deluxe 2000 is a popular financial management program that provides a complete and easy way to keep track of your financial records. Quicken has been popular with users for many years, and with each new version of the software, new features and abilities have been added. This makes Quicken easier to use; it also means that even more information is available to help you make intelligent decisions about your finances.

Quicken Deluxe 2000 is a comprehensive financial management program that makes it easy to maintain checking and savings accounts, investment accounts, and inventories of your belongings. It also contains tools that calculate your financial outlook and help you plan for future events.

Whether you want to keep track of your checkbook or plan for a college education, you'll find the information you need in this book.

Who Should Read This Book?

This book is directed toward the novice computer user who needs a hands-on approach. Every step in this book is accompanied by an illustration of what you will see on your computer screen. You can follow along and check your results easily. The generous use of illustrations makes this an ideal tool for those who have never used a financial management program. This book is also for those who are familiar with previous versions of Quicken and are upgrading to Quicken Deluxe 2000.

This book is organized so that you can quickly look up tasks to complete a job or learn a new trick. You may need to read an entire chapter to master a subject, or you may need only to review a certain section of a chapter.

Added Advice to Make You a Financial Wizard

You'll notice that this book keeps explanations to a minimum to help you learn faster. Other features in this book provide more information on how to work with Quicken Deluxe 2000.

- Tips offer helpful hints about Quicken that make your job a little easier and help you manage your finances more efficiently.

- Notes offer additional information about Quicken to enhance your learning experience with the software.

Also, the first appendix shows how to install Quicken Deluxe 2000 on your computer and the second appendix lists some of the keyboard shortcuts that can be used with Quicken if you are looking to reduce your mouse usage.

Enjoy!

PART I

Getting
Organized

1

Starting Quicken for the First Time

It's never too late, or too early, to begin making plans for tomorrow. When you keep detailed financial records you can more easily work out budgets and savings plans, and by properly using these plans, you can make your dreams a reality. Financial management programs, such as Quicken 2000, make it easy to keep your financial records. Once you have entered financial transactions in Quicken, you can use its other tools to analyze the information and begin the planning process. Before you begin, though, you'll need to set up a checking account and spend some time getting familiar with the program. In this chapter, you'll learn how to:

- Open and close Quicken 2000
- Enter checking account information
- Work with Quicken screen elements

Opening the Quicken Program

Like other Windows programs, Quicken can be accessed from the Start button or by clicking on the desktop icon that Quicken installs.

1. Click on the **Start button**. The Start menu will appear.

2. Move the **mouse pointer** to Programs. The Programs menu will appear.

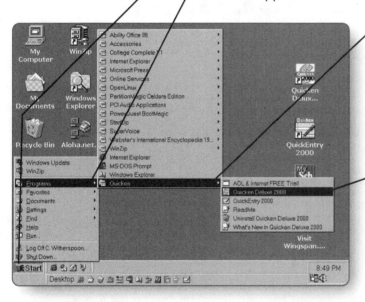

3. Move the **mouse pointer** to Quicken. The Quicken menu will appear. This menu contains some additional items that you may want to explore (such as the ReadMe and What's New in Quicken Deluxe 2000).

4. Click on **Quicken Deluxe 2000**. The Quicken program and the Product Registration dialog box will open.

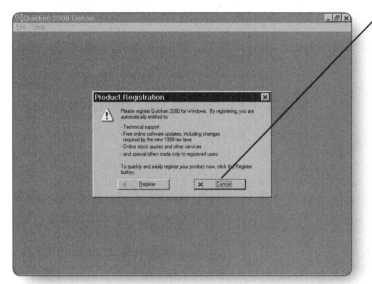

5. **Click** on **Cancel**. The Quicken New User Setup wizard will begin.

NOTE

You'll learn how to register Quicken over the Internet in Chapter 2, "Taking Quicken onto the Internet."

Setting Up Your First Account

The first time you use Quicken, the New User Setup wizard will start. This wizard needs some basic information about you and how you'll be using Quicken to customize the program to your needs. Follow the wizard to set up your first checking account.

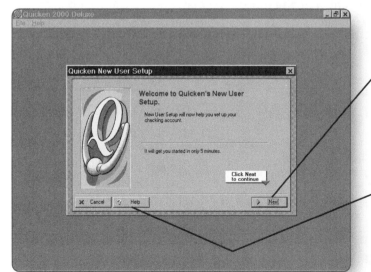

1. **Click** on **Next**. The Please tell Quicken about yourself screen will appear.

TIP

If you need help with any of the screens in the wizard, just click on the Help button. A window will open that contains more information.

2. Click on the **Yes option button** or the **No option button** in response to each of the four questions. The option for each question will be selected.

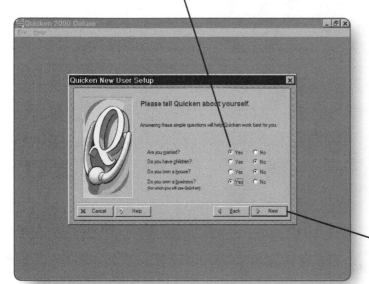

NOTE

Your responses to these questions will help set up categories that you can use to track what you spend. You'll learn more about categories in Chapter 5, "Categorizing Your Spending Habits."

3. Click on **Next**. The Let's set up your checking account screen will appear.

4. Type a **name** to identify the checking account in the Account Name text box. You may want to use your bank's name or maybe the purpose of the checking account (such as Joe's Allowance).

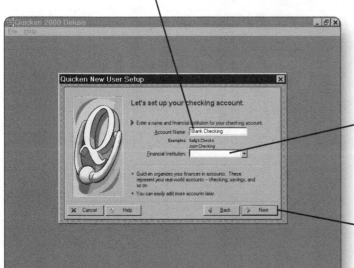

TIP

If you want to use online banking, select your bank from the Financial Institution list box.

5. Click on **Next**. The Use your last bank statement as a starting point screen will appear.

6a. **Click** on the **Yes option button** if you want to enter a beginning balance for your checking account. Use the bank statement that ends just prior to the date of the first transaction you enter into Quicken. The option will be selected.

OR

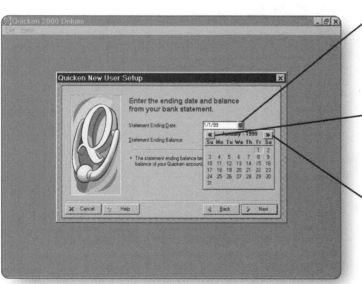

6b. **Click** on the **No option button** if you don't want to give Quicken a bank balance with which to start. The option will be selected.

7. **Click** on **Next**. The Enter the ending date and balance from your bank statement screen will appear.

8. **Click** on the **Calendar icon** to the right of the Statement Ending Date text box. A calendar will appear.

9a. **Click** on the **Back button**. The previous month will appear.

OR

9b. **Click** on the **Forward button**. The next month will appear.

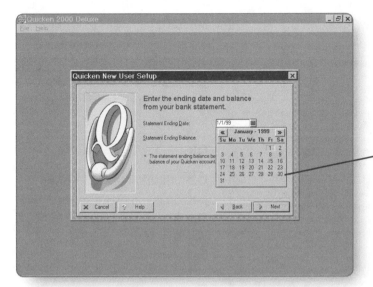

10. **Click** on the **Back** and **Forward buttons** until the month that corresponds to the ending date on the bank statement displays in the calendar.

11. **Click** on the **date** that corresponds to the ending date on the bank statement. The number will be selected, the calendar will disappear, and the ending date of the bank statement will appear in the Statement Ending Date text box.

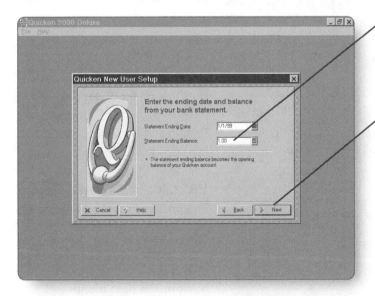

12. **Type** the **ending balance** from the bank statement in the Statement Ending Balance text box.

13. **Click** on **Next**. The You've just completed New User Setup screen will appear.

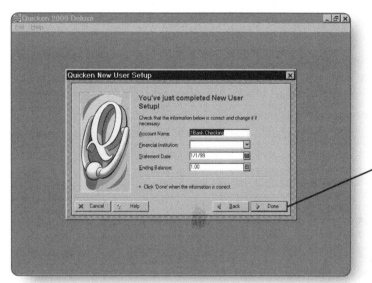

All the information that you entered during the wizard will appear in the four text boxes. You'll want to make sure that the information is correct. If not, you can make any corrections in these text boxes.

14. Click on **Done**. The Quicken program window will appear and you can begin to explore Quicken.

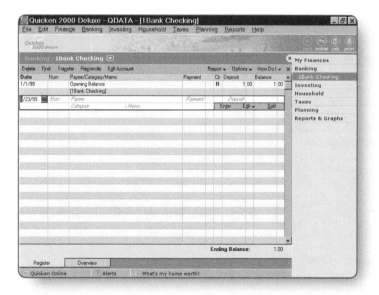

Quicken will open and display the account register for the checking account you just created. You'll see that a transaction has been created for the opening balance. The register is also ready for you to enter your first transaction for this account.

Exploring Quicken

After Quicken opens, it displays the account register for your first account. The program window contains menus, command buttons, and tabs. The register window is where you enter any checks, cash machine withdrawals, and deposits. The account register uses buttons and list boxes to help you enter these transactions with ease and tabs make it a snap to find other Quicken features.

Using the Program Menus

Quicken's menus are found at the top of the program window. Each menu contains a group of related commands. These menus contain all the commands that can be performed by Quicken.

1. **Click** on a **menu item**. A menu will appear.

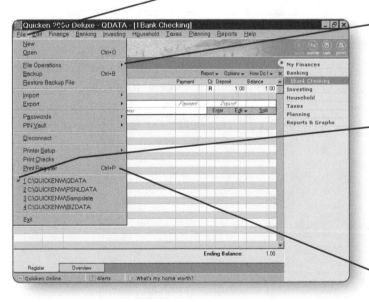

- When a right-pointing arrow follows a menu command, a second menu will appear as the mouse pointer moves over the command.

- When a menu item is preceded by a check mark (✔), it means that the item is currently displayed in the program window.

TIP

Keyboard shortcuts are listed to the right of menu commands. Type these keyboard shortcuts to execute a command.

● When a menu command is grayed out, the command is not available. You may first need to perform some function to make the grayed-out command accessible.

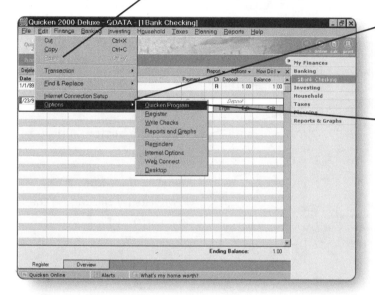

2. **Place** the **mouse pointer** over a menu command with a right-pointing arrow. A second menu will appear.

3. **Click** on a **command**. The Command will be executed.

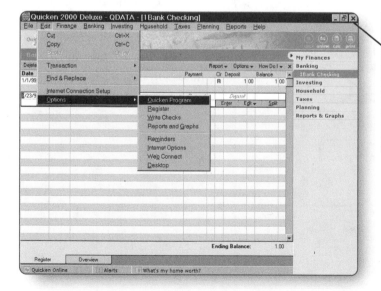

NOTE

It's easy to close dialog boxes without making any changes. Click on the Close button ([X]) at the top right of the dialog box.

Working with the Register

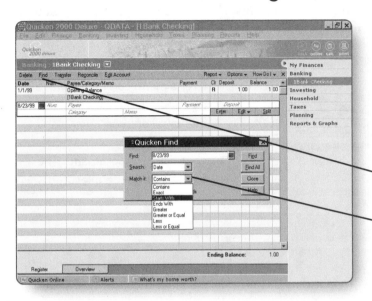

A menu bar along the top of the register contains buttons that execute commands and control the look of the register. These register buttons either open a dialog box or display a list of choices.

1. **Click** on a **button**. A dialog box will open.

- Select options from drop-down lists by clicking on the down arrow (▼).

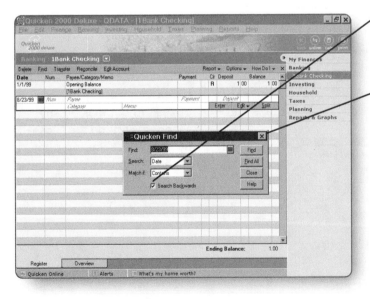

- Turn features on and off by clicking on the check box to the left of the feature name.

2. **Click** on the **Close button**. The dialog box will close.

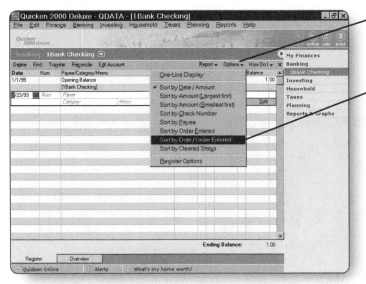

3. **Click** on a **button** with a down arrow. A drop-down menu will appear.

4. **Click** on a **menu command**. The menu command will be executed.

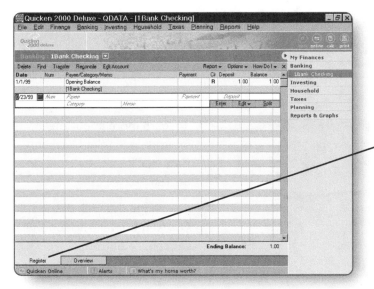

Along the bottom of the register, you'll see a number of tabs. These tabs make it easy to switch between accounts and to look at an overview of each account.

5. **Click** on a **tab** at the bottom of the register window. The tab will come to the top of the stack.

Shuffling Around with QuickTabs

QuickTabs are found along the right side of the Quicken program window and allow you to switch between the different Quicken Centers.

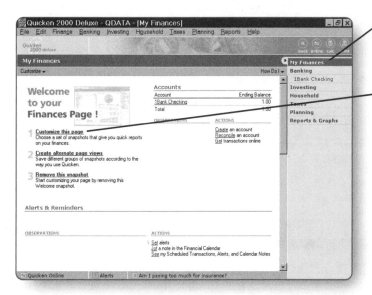

1. **Click** on a **QuickTab**. The related Quicken Center will be displayed.

● Click on the blue, underlined text to go to a page that contains more information about a topic.

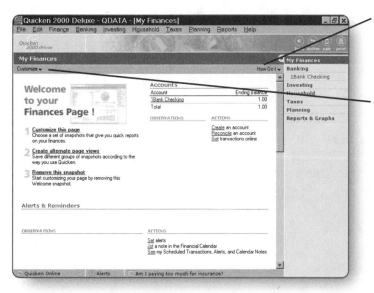

● To learn more about the information in the Quicken Center, click on the How Do I button.

● To change the look of the Quicken Center, click on the Customize button.

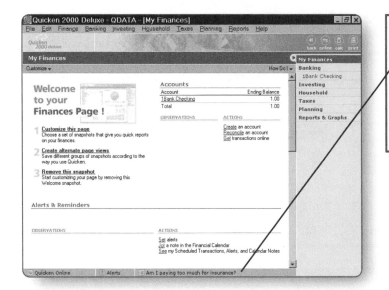

TIP

If you want to see the answer to the question at the bottom of the window, click on the question.

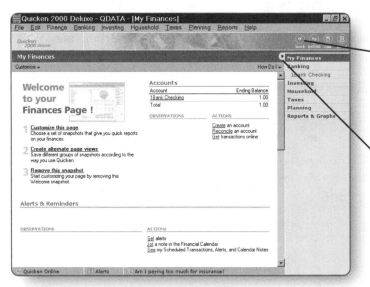

NOTE

Click on the Back icon to see previously viewed pages.

2. Click on the **arrow** at the top left of the QuickTab bar. The QuickTab will disappear and provide more working room within the program window.

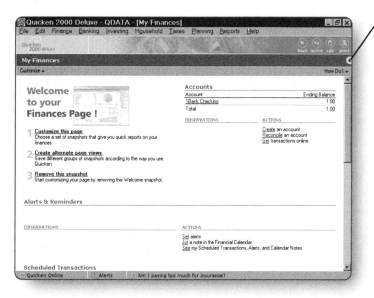

3. Click on the **QuickTab arrow**. The QuickTabs will reappear.

Working with the Calculator

No financial management program would be complete without a calculator. Whenever you need to add up a few numbers, use Quicken's handy calculator.

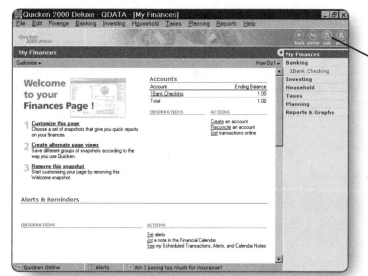

1. Click on the **calc icon** on the Quicken toolbar located just below the menu bar. The Quicken Calculator will appear.

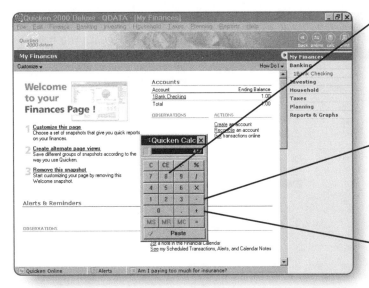

2. **Click** on the **number keys** that correspond with the first number in the calculation. The number will appear in the display area at the top of the calculator.

3a. **Click** on the **– key** if you want to subtract the next number from the first.

OR

3b. **Click** on the **+ key** if you want to add the next number to the first.

OR

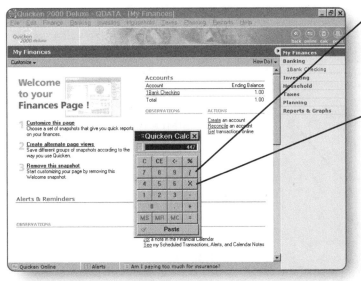

3c. **Click** on the **/ key** if you want to divide the first number by the next number you enter.

OR

3d. **Click** on the **X key** if you want to multiply the first number by the next number you enter.

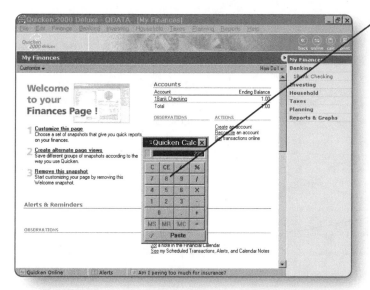

4. Click on the **number keys** that correspond with the next number in the calculation. The number will appear in the display area at the top of the calculator.

5. Add, subtract, multiply, or divide any **remaining numbers** in your calculation. The numbers will be computed in the calculation.

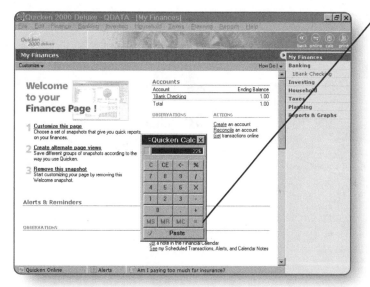

6. Click on the **= key**. The total for your calculation will appear in the calculator display.

NOTE

If the Num Lock key is active, you can also use the numeric keypad on your keyboard.

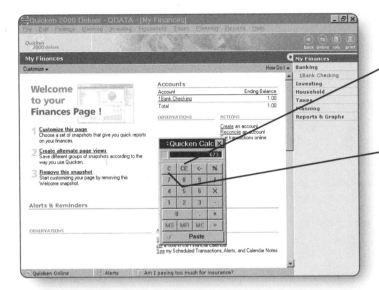

Here are a few tips to help you work with the calculator:

- If you notice you've entered the wrong number and want to clear the number, press the CE key.

- If you want to clear the display to start a new calculation, press the C key.

- Click on the Close button when you are finished with the calculator.

Exiting Quicken

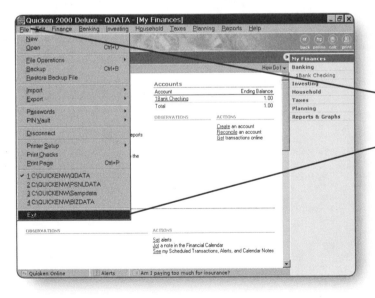

When you've finished with Quicken, exit the program. This automatically saves the data.

1. Click on **File**. The File menu will appear.

2. Click on **Exit**. The Quicken program will close and you will return to your desktop.

2

Taking Quicken onto the Internet

To conduct online banking or learn more about financial planning on the Web, you need to let Quicken know how you will be accessing the Internet. This is a straightforward process. Quicken will walk you through the steps and gather all the needed information. In this chapter, you'll learn how to:

- Set up Quicken to access the Internet
- Find financial information on the Web
- Close your Internet connection

NOTE

You can use either Dial-Up Networking or the Internet Connection Wizard to create a dial-up connection. If you are using Windows 98, you'll find both in the Communications submenu under Accessories in the Start Programs menu. If you are using Windows 95, you'll find Dial-Up Networking in the Accessories submenu and the Internet Connection Wizard in the Internet Explorer submenu.

Connecting to the Internet

You can use the Internet to help track and manage your personal finances. Quicken comes equipped to use the Internet for just these tasks but it first needs to recognize your dial-up connection to your Internet Service Provider (ISP).

Setting Up an Internet Connection

Before you can use Quicken on the Internet, your account needs to be set up with an ISP. The ISP will provide the information you need to create a dial-up connection between your computer's modem and the ISP's servers. Once you have a working Internet connection, you're ready to go online with Quicken.

1. Click on **Edit**. The Edit menu will appear.

2. Click on **Internet Connection Setup**. The Internet Connection Setup wizard will start and the Are you connected to the Internet? screen will be displayed.

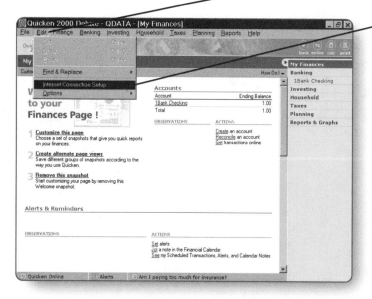

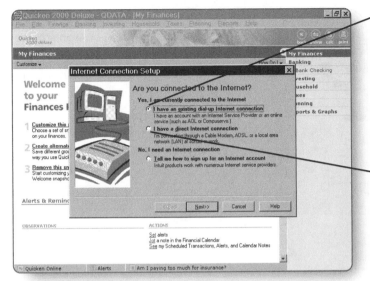

3a. Click on the **I have an existing dial-up Internet connection option button** if you connect to the Internet through an ISP. The option will be selected.

OR

3b. Click on the **I have a direct Internet connection option button** if you have cable or network access to the Internet. The option will be selected.

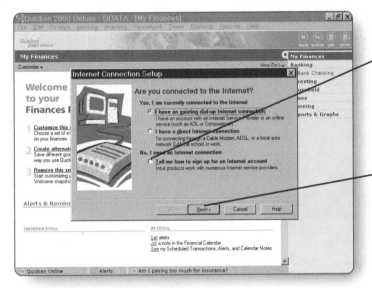

TIP

Quicken can help you find an ISP. Click on the Tell me how to sign up for an Internet account option button.

4. Click on **Next**. The Which dial-up Internet connection do you want to use? screen will appear. You can use this screen to select a dial-up connection that is already created on your computer.

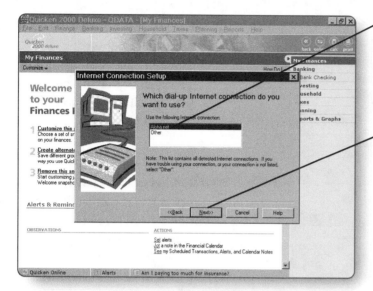

5. Click on the **Internet connection** that you want to use to access the Internet with Quicken. The connection will be selected.

6. Click on **Next**. The Browser Preference screen will appear.

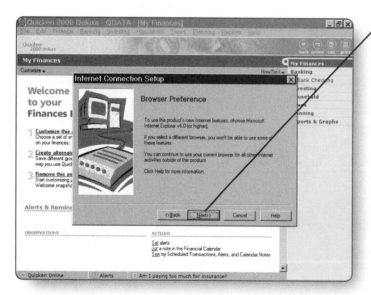

7. Click on **Next**. Quicken will search the programs on your computer and display a list of Web browsers that are installed on your computer.

8. Click on the **browser** you want to use when accessing the Internet. The browser will be selected.

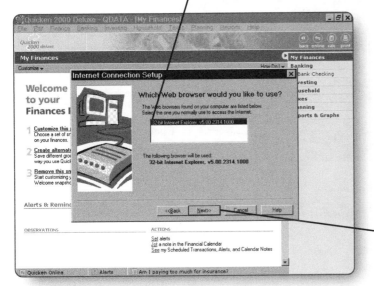

> ### NOTE
> You can install the 128-bit version of Microsoft Internet Explorer when you install Quicken. It is suggested that you use this browser if you'll be using the Internet for online banking and bill paying.

9. Click on **Next**. The Would you like to send diagnostic data? screen will appear.

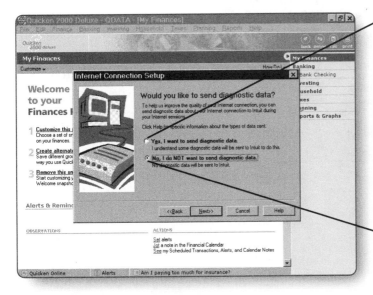

10a. Click on the **Yes, I want to send diagnostic data option button** if you want to send data (such as failed Internet connection attempts and connection speed) back to Intuit (the creator of Quicken) and your ISP for their use. The option will be selected.

OR

10b. Click on the **No, I do NOT want to send diagnostic data option button** if you do not want to contribute data. The option will be selected.

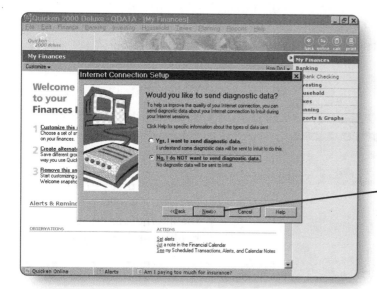

NOTE

Intuit and your ISP use this information to help improve the accuracy and speed of your Internet connection.

11. Click on **Next**. The Summary of your Internet Connection Setup screen will appear.

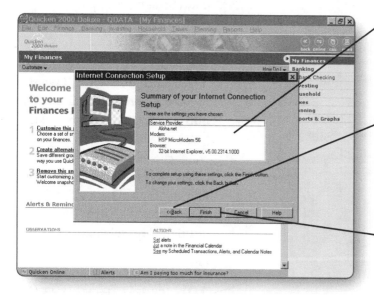

12. Verify that the **information** you supplied is correct.

NOTE

If you notice any errors, click on the Back button and make changes to the appropriate screens.

13. Click on **Finish**. The Customize Quicken 2000 Download dialog box will open.

14a. **Click** on the **Disconnect from the Internet option button** if you want to close your Internet connection after Quicken has finished downloading data to your computer. The option will be selected.

OR

14b. **Click** on the **Stay Connected to the Internet option button** if you want to keep your Internet connection open after Quicken is finished accessing the Internet. The option will be selected.

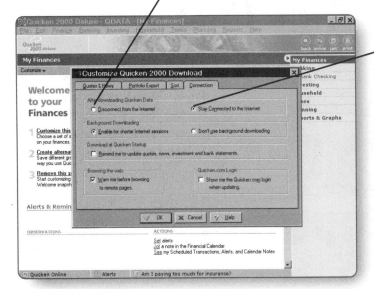

NOTE

The Quicken Download Agent automatically downloads any information you requested from the Internet whenever you have an open Internet connection.

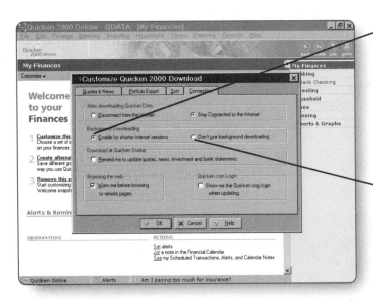

15a. **Click** on the **Enable for shorter Internet sessions option button** if you want to activate the Quicken Download Agent. The option will be selected.

OR

15b. **Click** on the **Don't use background downloading option button** if you want Quicken to download information only when you request it. The option will be selected.

16. Click in the **Remind me to update quotes, news, investment and bank statements check box** if you want to be reminded to download information to keep your data up to date. A check mark will appear in the check box.

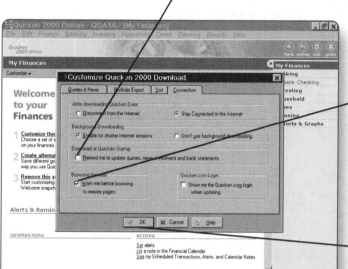

17. Click in the **Warn me before browsing to remote pages check box** if you do not want to see a warning dialog box whenever you move from Web site to Web site. The check box will be cleared.

18. Click on **OK**. Quicken will be set up so that it can access the Internet using your existing dial-up connection.

Getting Online

Now that Quicken is set up to use your Internet connection, it's easy to get online. Any time you click on an item in Quicken that needs information from the Internet, Quicken will automatically dial your ISP. Here's a quick example of how this works.

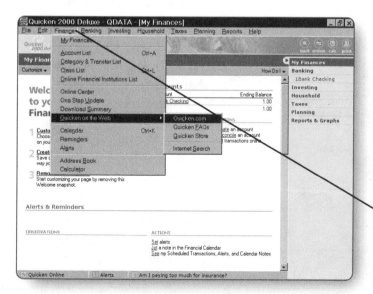

1. Click on **Finance**. The Finance menu will appear.

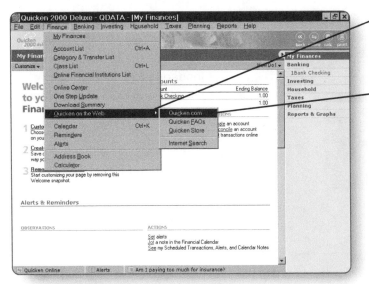

2. Move the **mouse pointer** to Quicken on the Web. A second menu will appear.

3. Click on **Quicken.com**. A confirmation dialog box will open.

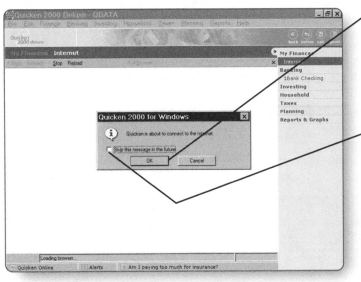

4. Click on **OK**. The Connecting dialog box will open.

TIP

If you don't want to be warned each time that Quicken connects to the Internet, place a check mark in the Skip this message in the future check box.

5. Wait while your computer connects to your ISP. When it connects, the browser will be loaded inside the Quicken window and the Quicken.com Web site will appear in the browser. The Quicken.com Web site contains a wealth of information that can help you manage your finances.

6. Click on a **hyperlink**. The linked page will appear in the browser window.

7. Click on the **Back button**. The previous Web page that you visited will appear in the browser window.

8. Click on the **Full Browser button**. The Web page will no longer appear in the Quicken window, but from the default browser. You can then use browser features, such as bookmarks or favorites, while surfing the Quicken Web pages.

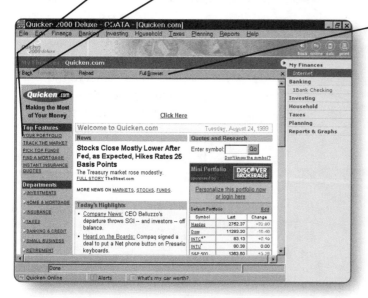

Taking Care of Business

When you first get on the Internet with Quicken, you should look into a couple of business items. One of the first things you should do is register your copy of the Quicken software. Then, if you think you'll want to do your banking over the Internet, check out what's available in online services with your local banker.

Registering Your Copy of Quicken

After you register your software, you qualify for product support, receive new product news, and have access to more Internet features. The Software Registration wizard walks you through the registration process.

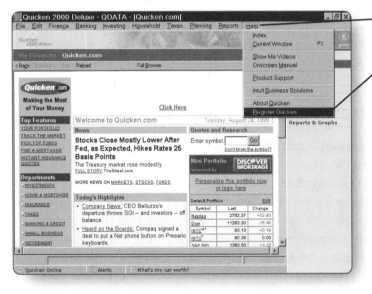

1. Click on **Help**. The Help menu will appear.

2. Click on **Register Quicken**. The Software Registration wizard will start.

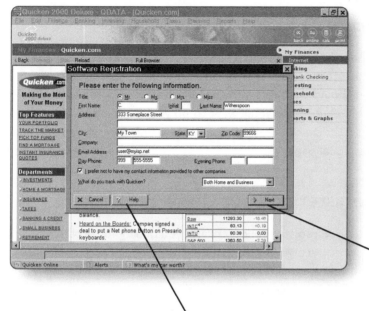

It's a simple process to follow the wizard and register your Quicken software. After you read the information in each screen, provide the wizard with the requested information. When that is done, you'll need to proceed to the next screen. At the end of the wizard, the information will be sent directly to Intuit and you'll receive a confirmation.

● Click on the Next button when you want to move on to the next screen in the registration process.

● Click on the Help button if you are unsure of the information requested in the screen. A Help window will appear with further directions.

Applying for Online Services

There's a plethora of financial services that you can access over the Internet. You can open a checking account with a participating bank, download your monthly statement, and transfer money. You can make paying your bills an automated process. You can also make investments over the Internet. Quicken provides a one-stop place to find some reputable financial institutions and even compare rates and services between them.

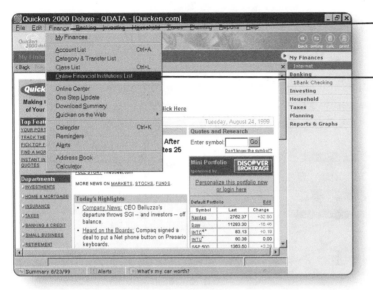

1. Click on **Finance**. The Finance menu will appear.

2. Click on **Online Financial Institutions List**. The Financial Institution Web page will appear.

3. Click on a **financial service** listed in the Online Financial Services frame. A list of financial institutions that supply that service will appear in the Financial Institution Directory frame.

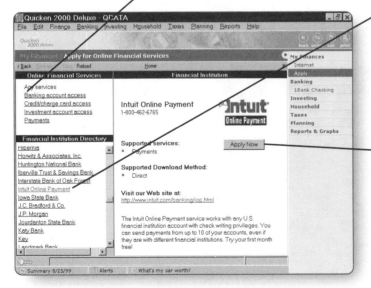

4. Click on an **institution** to learn more about its online financial services. An information screen for the financial institution will appear in the Financial Institution frame.

5. Click on the **Apply Now button** when you are ready to apply for an institution's service. The application form for the financial institution will appear. You'll need to read the instructions from the institution. This will contain all the information you need in order to open an account and begin the desired online financial service.

Finding Financial Help on the Web

You'll find plenty of financial information on the Internet. All you need to do is look around. Quicken starts you off with quite a list of Internet resources. You'll also find hidden clues to Web sites as you're working with the program.

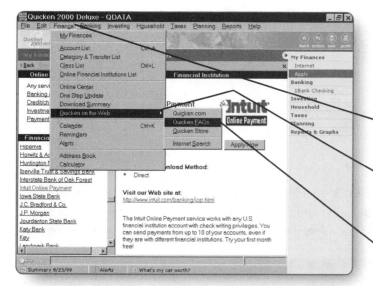

Visiting Quicken's Favorites List

1. Click on **Finance**. The Finance menu will appear.

2. Move the **mouse pointer** to Quicken on the Web. A submenu will appear.

3. Click on any **Web site**. The Web site will appear in the browser window.

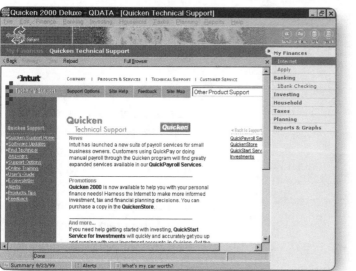

Take some time to explore the different Web sites. They contain valuable information that can help you make better decisions. They also contain tips to help you work more efficiently with Quicken.

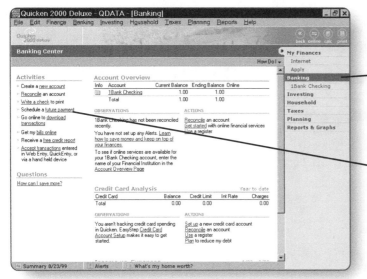

Exploring the Quicken Centers

1. **Click** on the **QuickTab** for the Center that you want. The Center will appear in the window.

2. **Click** on a **topic** in the Activities or Actions area that is Internet related. Here's a hint, you'll probably see the word "online" in the description.

Disconnecting from the Internet

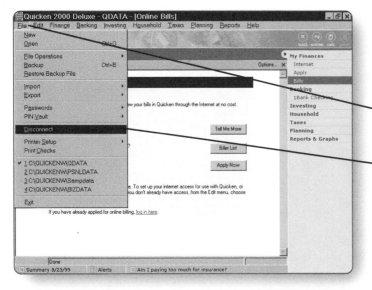

When you're finished working with Quicken's online features, you can disconnect from the Internet without exiting Quicken.

1. **Click** on **File**. The File menu will appear.

2. **Click** on **Disconnect**. A confirmation dialog box will open.

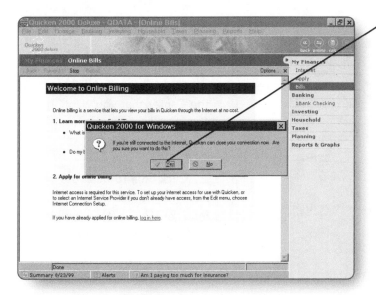

3. Click on **Yes**. You will be disconnected from your Internet service provider.

3

Learning about Quicken and Your Finances

Whether you're new to Quicken or if you are using a feature for the first time, you may need some extra help using the program. Spending some time browsing the help tools will help you gain greater control over your finances and plan for future events. Besides the manual, Quicken comes equipped with quite an arsenal of help tools. You'll find everything from the familiar Windows Help system to interesting videos that show you how to use the program. In this chapter, you'll learn how to:

- Find information in the Quicken Help system
- Read the Onscreen Manual
- Get more help on the window you are viewing
- Customize the Quicken Help windows

Finding Program Help

Quicken contains the same Windows Help system that you find in most Windows software programs. This familiar interface is a simple way to find the information you need.

Searching the Help Topics

When you want to search for a specific word or phrase, use the Find tab.

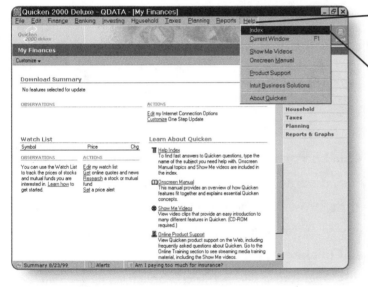

1. Click on **Help**. The Help menu will appear.

2. Click on **Index**. The Help Topics dialog box will open with the Index tab at the top of the stack.

TIP

You'll find links to many help topics on the My Finances QuickTab.

---

3. Click on the **Find tab**. The Find tab will come to the top of the stack.

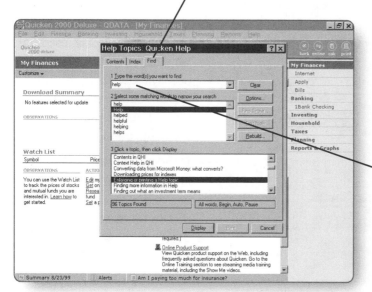

4. Type a **word** that describes the information that you need in the Type the word(s) you want to find text box. As you type, the list of matching words in the Select some matching words to narrow your search list box will be reduced.

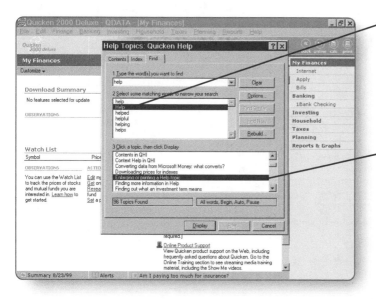

5. Click on a **word** that better describes the information for which you are searching. A list of topics will appear in the Click a topic, then click Display list box.

6. Double-click on a **topic**. The associated help file will appear in a separate window.

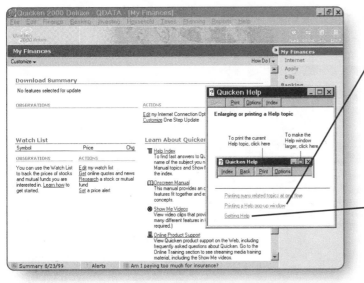

7. Find further **information** about the help topic.

• Click on text with a dotted underline to display a screen tip. These screen tips are usually a definition or explanation of the underlined word. To close the screen tip, click outside of it.

• Click on text with a solid underline to go to a different help topic. Use the Back button to return to the previously viewed help topic.

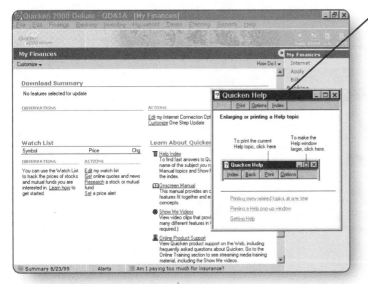

8. Click on the **Index button**. You will return to the Help Topics dialog box and the Index tab will be at the top of the stack.

Reading the Help Book

The help files are also organized into a book format. If you like to browse pages, read through the table of contents for the Quicken help system.

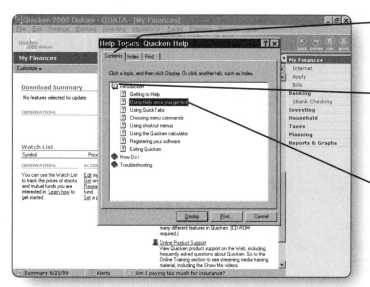

1. Click on the **Contents tab**. The Contents tab will come to the top of the stack.

2. Double-click on the **book icon** next to a topic. The topic will expand to show the contents.

3. Double-click on a **help topic.** The associated help file will appear in a separate window.

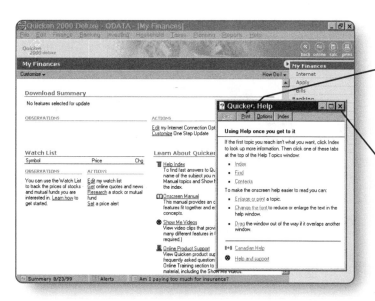

TIP

To keep a paper copy of a help topic, click on the Print button.

4. Click on the **Close button.** The help topic window and the Help Topics dialog box will close.

Reading the Onscreen Manual

The Onscreen Manual is another valuable information source to help you work with the Quicken program and learn how to manage your finances.

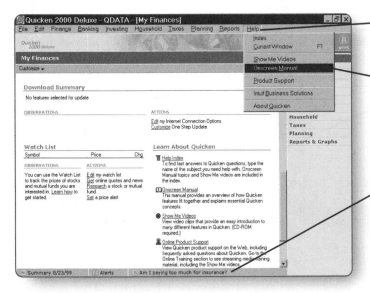

1. Click on **Help**. The Help menu will appear.

2. Click on **Onscreen Manual**. The Onscreen Manual will display in a window.

TIP

Click on the question located on the right of the status bar at the bottom of the screen. A new window will open to provide answers to the question.

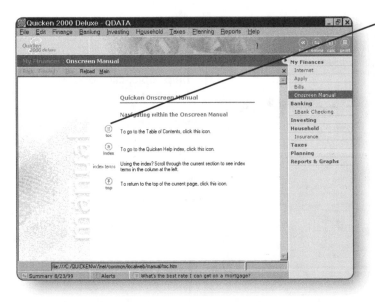

3. Click on the **Table of Contents icon**. The Table of Contents for the manual will appear in the window.

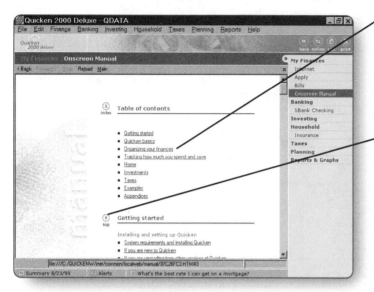

4. Click on a **section** in the manual. The window will scroll down to the selected section.

NOTE

Click on the Top icon if you want to return to the top of the page.

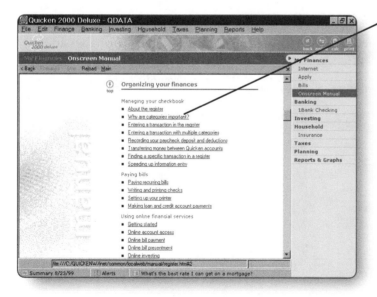

5. Click on a **topic**. The topic will appear in the window.

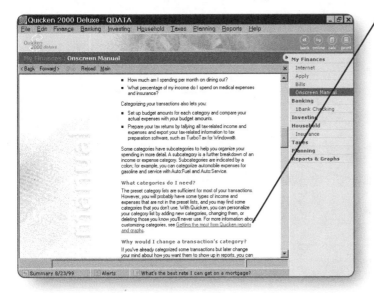

6. Click on the **blue, underlined text** to read about that subject. The associated page in the Onscreen manual will appear in the window.

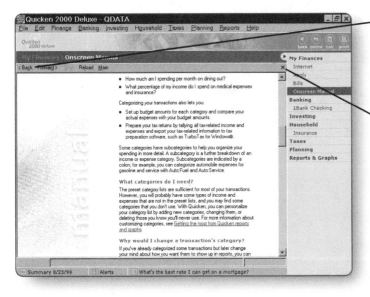

7. Click on the **Back button** when you are finished reading the help topic. You will return to the previous page.

8. Click on the **Close button** when you are finished reading the Onscreen Manual. The Onscreen Manual window will close.

Playing the Show Me Videos

Now it's time to sit back and learn while being entertained. Quicken contains many short videos that show you how to use the program and how to better manage your finances. Roll 'em!

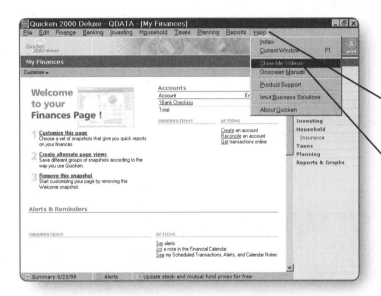

1. Place the **Quicken 2000 CD** in your computer's CD-ROM drive.

2. Click on **Help**. The Help menu will appear.

3. Click on **Show Me Videos**. The Show Me window will open.

4. Click on a **topic** in the left pane. The opening frame for the video will display in the right pane.

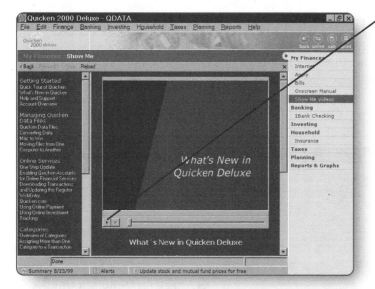

5. **Click** on the **Run button**. The video will begin playing.

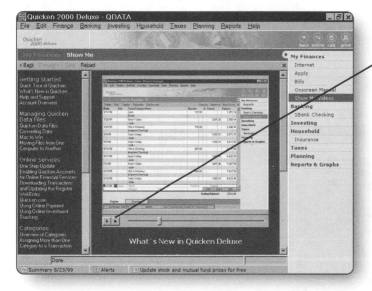

NOTE

If you don't want to watch the entire video, click on the Stop button. The video will quit and you can select another video.

6. **Watch** the **video**. When the video is finished, the video will stop and display the opening frame.

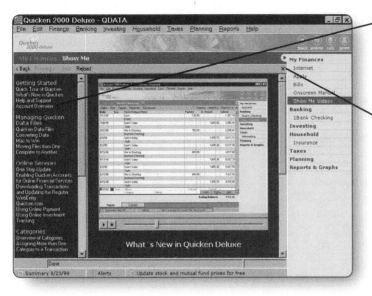

7. Click on another **topic** in the left frame if you want to watch another video. The video will appear in the right frame.

8. Click on the **Close button** when you are finished. The Show Me window will close.

Getting More Help

When you need help on the active window, you can find it in a couple of places.

Going to the How Do I? Files

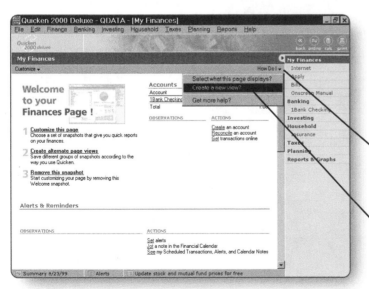

Clicking on a question in the How do I menu opens a Help dialog box that answers the selected question and gives further information about related topics.

1. Click on the **How Do I button**. The How Do I menu will appear.

2. Click on the **question** that you would like answered. The Quicken Help window will open.

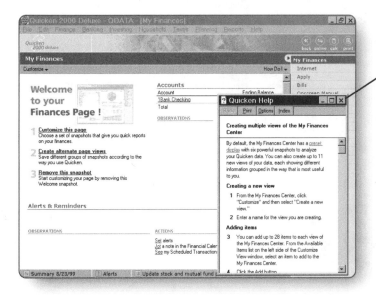

3. Read the **instructions** for performing the selected task.

4. Click on the **Close button** when you are finished. The Help window will close.

Getting Help on the Current Window

When you want to know more about the displayed Quicken program window, try this handy help tool.

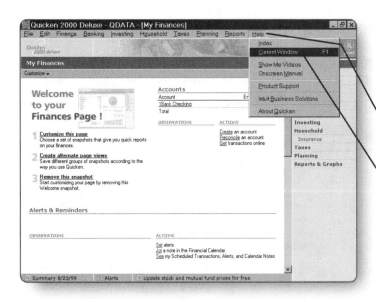

1. Display the **window** with which you need help. The window will appear in the Quicken program.

2. Click on **Help**. The Help menu will appear.

3. Click on **Current Window**. The Quicken Help window will open.

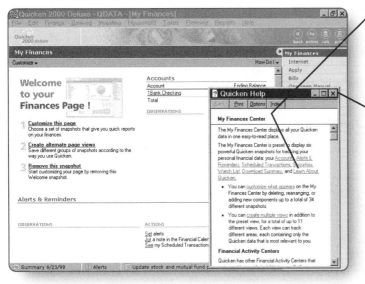

4. **Click** on the **underlined text** for any additional help topics. The help file will appear in the window.

5. **Click** on the **Close button** when you are finished reading the help files. The Quicken Help window will close.

Customizing the Program Help Window

There's more that you can do to the Quicken Help window than just read the help topics. You can customize how the text in the window looks or even add notes.

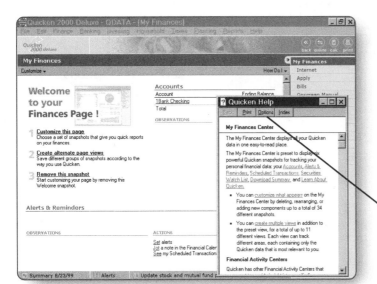

Changing the Font Size

If the font size used in the Help window is too small or too large, you can change the size.

1. **Click** on the **Options button**. A menu will appear.

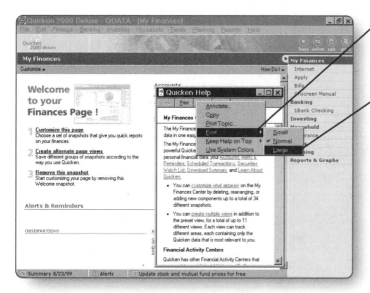

2. Move the **mouse pointer** to Font. A second menu will appear.

3. Click on a **font size**. The text in the help window will be resized.

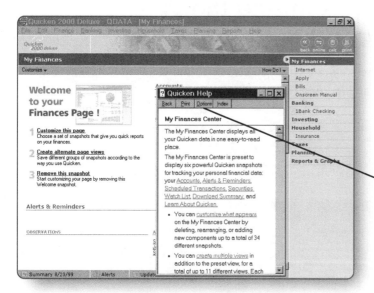

Making Notes in Help Files

You can keep notes to yourself or any additional information related to the help topic in the help files.

1. Click on the **Options button**. A menu will appear.

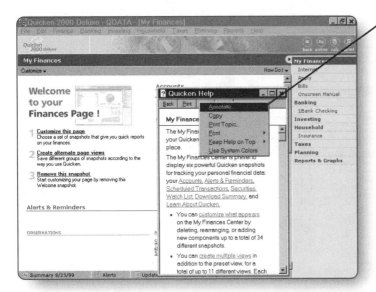

2. Click on **Annotate**. The Annotate dialog box will open.

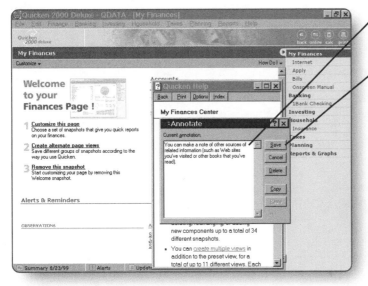

3. Type the **note** that you want to attach to the help file.

4. Click on **Save**. The note will be attached to the help file.

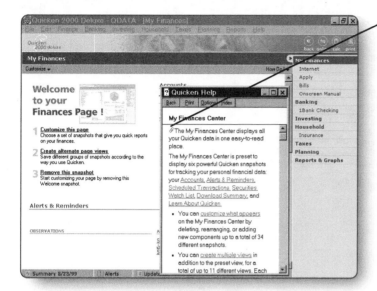

The annotated note appears as a paper clip icon at the beginning of the help topic.

NOTE

If you want to read or edit the note, click on the paper clip icon.

4

Working with Accounts and Files

In the first chapter, you set up your first bank account in the default Quicken data file. If you have other bank accounts, such as savings or money market accounts, you can also set these up in the same Quicken file. Then, as you progress and begin entering transactions for these accounts, this information will also be added to the default Quicken data file. But, what if you want to keep separate financial records for another member of your family or for a club to which you belong? It's easy to set up another file in which to store another set of financial information. In this chapter, you'll learn how to:

- Set up additional banking accounts
- Work with inactive accounts
- Create additional data files
- Copy and rename data files

Working with Accounts

You may have more banking accounts than the one you set up during the New User Setup. If you have additional checking and savings accounts, you can add these to Quicken and keep track of these account balances. You can also set up accounts for any investments that you may have. After you've been working with Quicken for a while, you may need to make changes to these accounts. Perhaps the bank information has changed, or maybe you're not using that account any longer.

Adding Accounts

You can keep track of many different types of accounts. If you set up your checking account in the New User Setup, you may want to add savings or credit card accounts. If you want to keep track of cash purchases, create a cash account. Setting up an account is similar for each type of account. Just follow the EasyStep instructions.

1. **Click** on **Finance**. The Finance menu will appear.

2. **Click** on **Account List**. The Account List window will appear.

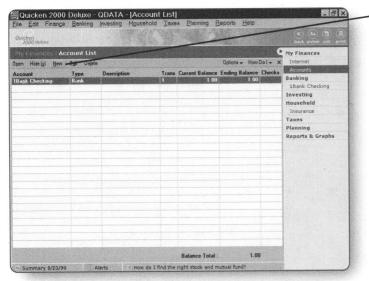

3. Click on **New**. The Create New Account wizard will open and display the Choose the type of account to create screen.

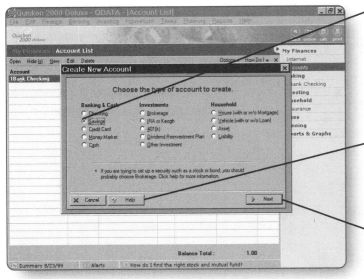

4. Click on the **option button** that corresponds to the type of account you want to create. The option will be selected.

TIP

If you need help with a screen, click on the Help button.

---

5. Click on **Next**. The EasyStep setup for the account type will start and display the Enter a name and optional description for this account screen.

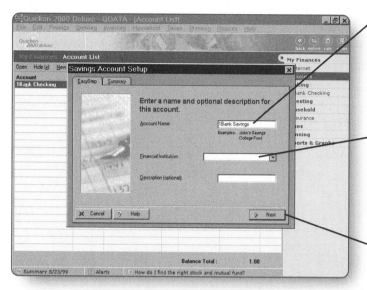

6. Type a descriptive **name** for the account in the Account Name text box.

NOTE

If you will be using online banking, select your bank from the Financial Institution drop-down list.

7. Click on **Next**. Quicken needs a starting point for this account screen to appear.

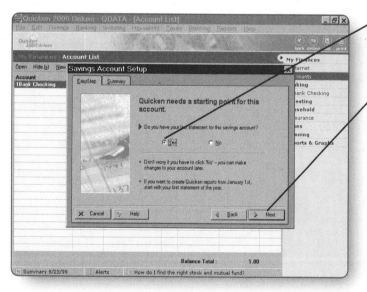

8. Click on the **Yes option button**. The option will be selected.

9. Click on **Next**. The Enter the starting point information screen will appear.

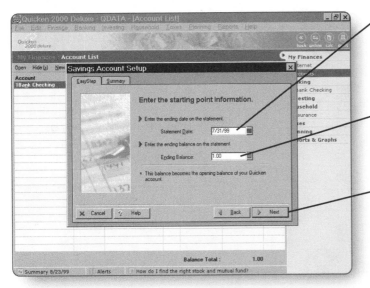

10. **Type** the **ending date** of the statement you will use as a starting point in the Statement Date text box.

11. **Type** the **ending bank balance** found on the statement in the Ending Balance text box.

12. **Click** on **Next**. The setup will be completed and the Summary tab will come to the top of the stack.

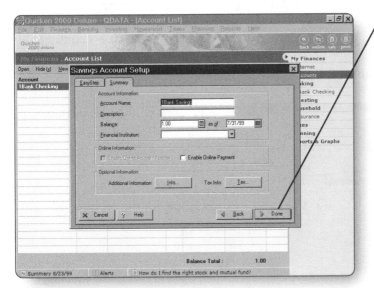

13. **Click** on **Done** if the information you entered is correct. The Create New Account wizard will disappear and you will return to the Account List.

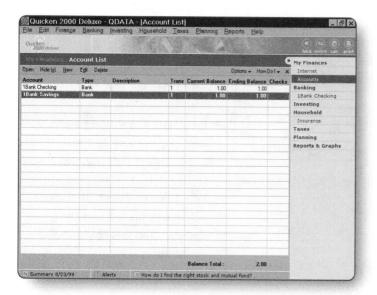

The Account List window shows the new account added to the list.

Updating Account Information

You can add some additional information to an account. For example, you may want to add a contact name and phone number for your bank or record interest rates.

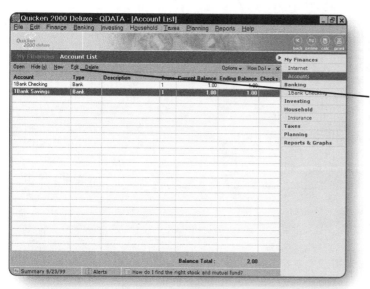

1. Click on the **account** that you want to update. The account will be selected.

2. Click on **Edit**. The Banking window for the account will appear.

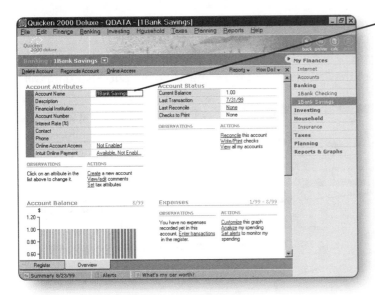

3. **Click** in the **Account Name field** located in the Account Attributes section of the window. The text in the field will be selected.

4. **Type** a **different name** for the account in the Account Name field.

5. **Click** in any other **Account Attributes field** to complete or change information. The field will be highlighted.

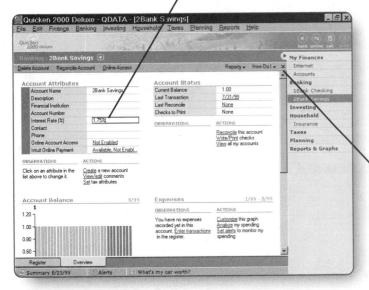

6. **Type information** about your account and/or the financial institution.

7. **Repeat steps 5 and 6** until you complete any or all fields to your satisfaction.

8. **Click** on the **Close button** when you are finished updating the account. The Banking window will close and you will return to the Account List window.

Hiding Accounts

If you're not using an account, you can make it disappear from the list. This is *not* the same as deleting it. Your data will still be retained by Quicken. You still have access to the account and can view it on the list even after the account has been hidden.

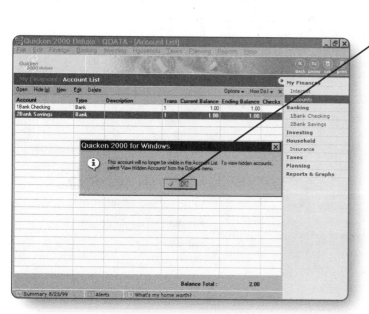

1. Click on the **account** that you want to hide from the account list. The account will be selected.

2. Click on the **Hide(x) button**. A confirmation dialog box will open.

3. Click on **OK**. You'll no longer see the account in the Account List.

NOTE

If you want to see the account, click on the Options button and select View Hidden Accounts from the menu that appears. A hand icon to the right of the account name will indicate the hidden account.

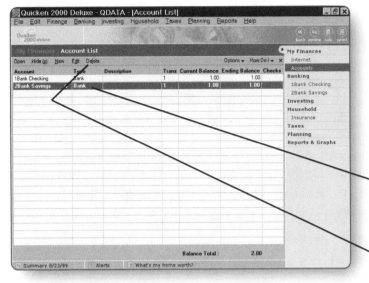

Deleting Accounts

When you delete an account, you also delete all the transactions that have been recorded in the account. There will be no trace of the account in the Quicken data file.

1. Click on the **account** that you want to delete. The account will be selected.

2. Click on the **Delete button**. A confirmation dialog box will open.

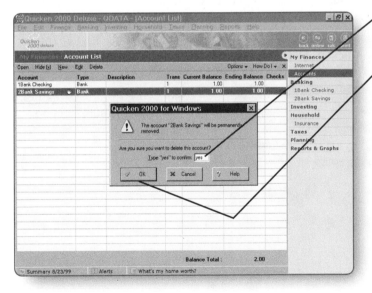

3. Type the word **yes** in the Type "yes" to confirm text box.

4. Click on **OK**. The account will be removed from the Account List.

Working with Multiple Quicken Files

Quicken stores every check you write, every paycheck you deposit, and every investment you make in a single data file. You can perform a number of tasks with this file, such as copying, renaming, and moving. Quicken also allows you to work with several data files. For example, you can have a separate file for your personal needs, a file for the kids to keep track of their allowance and spending, and perhaps a bookkeeping file for any organization to which you belong.

Creating a New File

You should keep separate records for the different activities in your life. You may want to keep your personal finances, a small business venture, and records for a club or charity in separate files.

1. Click on **File**. The File menu will appear.

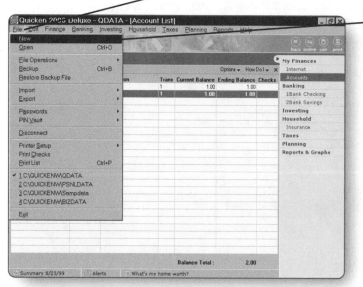

2. Click on **New**. The Creating new file: Are you sure? dialog box will open.

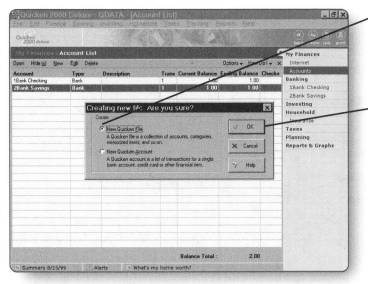

3. Click on the **New Quicken File option button**, if it is not already selected. The option will be selected.

4. Click on **OK**. The Create Quicken File dialog box will open.

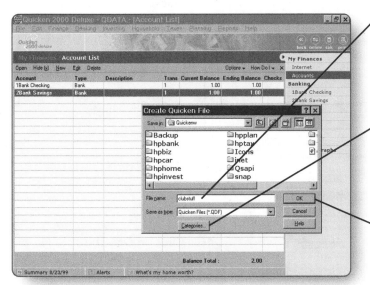

5. Type a **name** for the new file in the File name text box.

> ### TIP
> If you want to include categories other than the standard ones, click on the Categories button.

6. Click on **OK**. The new account will be created and the Create New Account wizard will appear so that you can set up your first account in the new file.

Switching Between Files

After you create several different Quicken files, you can work with each of them, but only one at a time. Here's how to switch between the different Quicken data files that you may have created.

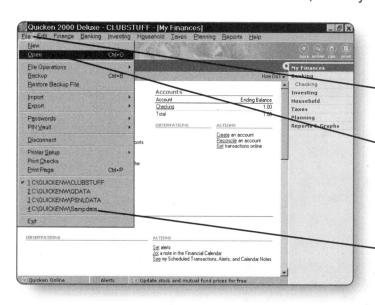

1. Click on **File**. The File menu will appear.

2. Click on **Open**. The Open Quicken File dialog box will open.

TIP

Quicken lists up to the last four files that you've opened. You'll find these at the bottom of the File menu. You can open one of these files by clicking on the file name.

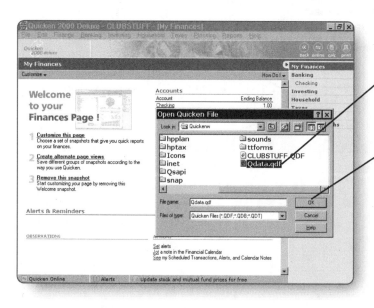

3. Click on the **file** with which you want to work. The file will be selected.

4. Click on **OK**. The data file will appear in the Quicken window.

Copying Quicken Files

If you need a quick start when creating a separate set of records, make a copy of a Quicken data file. This enables you to use certain types of records (such as memorized and scheduled transactions, or a customized category list) to start a new data file.

1. Open the **file** you want to copy. The file will appear in the Quicken window.

2. Click on **File**. The File menu will appear.

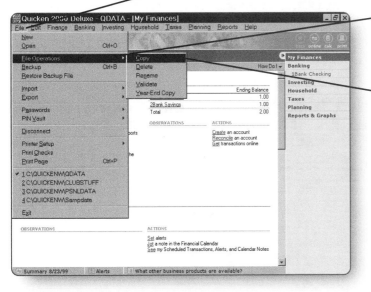

3. Move the **mouse pointer** to File Operations. A second menu will appear.

4. Click on **Copy**. The Copy File dialog box will open.

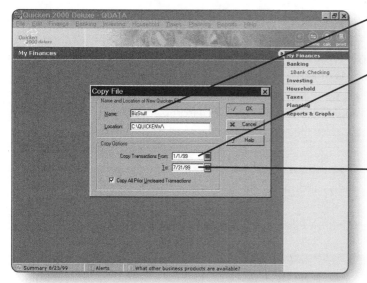

5. Type a **name** for the copy of the file in the Name text box.

6. Type the **beginning date** of the group of transactions that you want to copy in the Copy Transactions From text box.

7. Type the **ending date** of the group of transactions that you want to copy in the To text box.

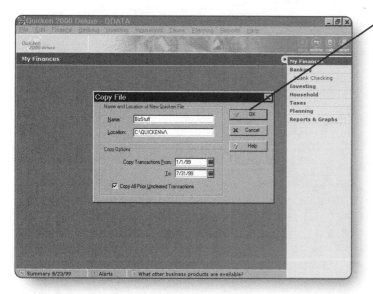

8. Click on **OK**. The File Copied Successfully dialog box will open.

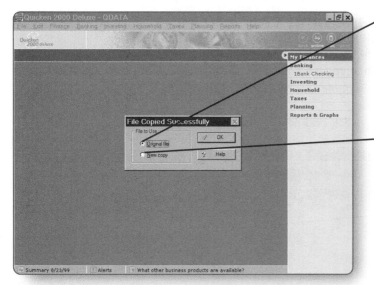

9a. **Click** on the **Original file option button** if you want to work with the original file. The option will be selected.

OR

9b. **Click** on the **New copy option button** if you want to work with the file you just created. The option will be selected.

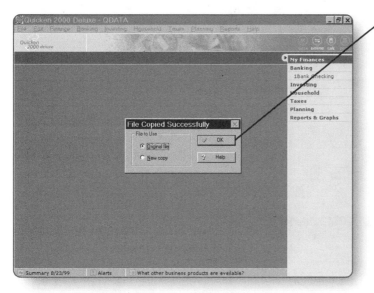

10. **Click** on **OK**. The file you selected will appear in the Quicken window so that you can work with it.

Renaming Quicken Files

You can also give Quicken data files a different file name. Once you begin adding files, you may find that you need to give older files more descriptive names.

1. Click on **File**. The File menu will appear.

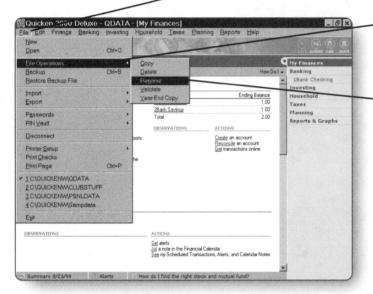

2. Move the **mouse pointer** to File Operations. A second menu will appear.

3. Click on **Rename**. The Rename Quicken File dialog box will open.

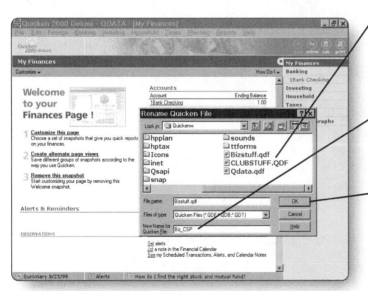

4. Click on the **file** that you want to rename. The file will appear in the File name text box.

5. Type a **different name** for the file in the New Name for Quicken File text box.

6. Click on **OK**. The file will be renamed.

5

Categorizing Your Spending Habits

In order to keep track of expenditures for different items (such as groceries and gasoline), you'll need a well-constructed chart of accounts. The *chart of accounts* lists sources of income and items of expenditure which you can use to determine whether you're saving money or falling into debt. Quicken provides a starting chart of accounts in the Category & Transfer List. You'll find it easy to customize this list to fit your lifestyle. In this chapter, you'll learn how to:

- Add and delete categories from the Category & Transfer List
- Divide categories into subcategories
- Print a category list
- Use classes to track particular expenses

Working with Categories

It is very important to keep track of expenditures. To do this, a chart of accounts, in the form of the Category & Transfer List, will contain items to which you'll assign each purchase and deposit you make to an account. By assigning each transaction to a category, it is easy to keep track of income deposits from a hobby or how much is spent on weekend entertainment.

Adding a Category

The Category & Transfer List contains a fairly complete list of categories to fit most of your needs. But, there may be an item that you want to track that isn't included in the list. You can modify the list to reflect your income sources and spending habits.

1. Click on **Finance**. The Finance menu will appear.

2. Click on **Category & Transfer List**. The Category & Transfer List window will appear.

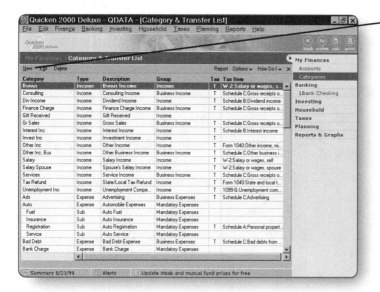

3. Click on **New**. The Set Up Category dialog box will open.

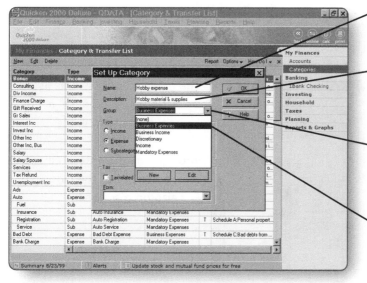

4. Type a **name** for the new category in the Name text box.

5. Type a brief **description** for the category in the Description text box.

6. Click on the **Group arrow**. A list of income and expense types will appear.

7. Click on the **group** to which you want to assign the category. The group will appear in the list box.

8a. **Click** on the **Income option button** if the category will be used to record money you receive. The option will be selected.

OR

8b. **Click** on the **Expense option button** if the category will be used to record money you spend. The option will be selected.

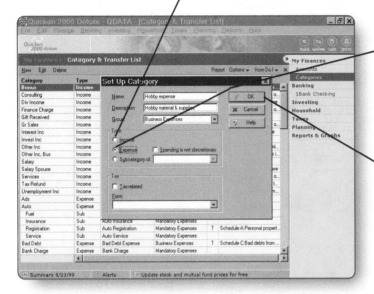

9. **Click** on **OK**. The category will be added to the Category & Transfer List.

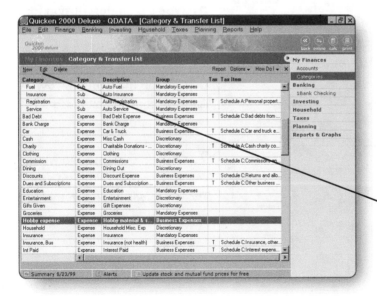

The new category will be listed by income and expense, in alphabetical order, in the Category & Transfer List. All the information you entered into the dialog box about the category will also be displayed.

TIP

You can make changes to a category. Just select the category and click on the Edit button. Make your changes in the Edit Category dialog box.

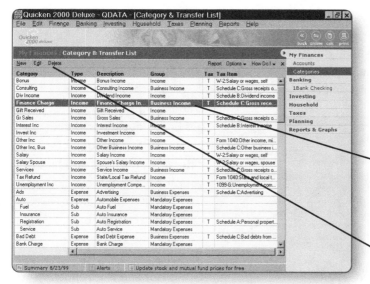

Deleting a Category

If you don't want to clutter the Category & Transfer List with categories that you'll never use, you can delete any unneeded categories.

1. Click on the **category** that you want to remove from the Category & Transfer List. The category will be selected.

2. Click on **Delete**. The Delete Category dialog box will open.

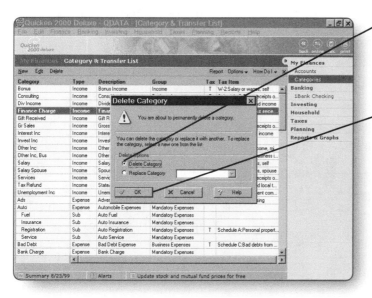

3. Click on the **Delete Category option button** if it is not already selected. The option will be selected.

4. Click on **OK**. The category will be removed from the Category & Transfer List.

Restoring Categories to the List

Even if you add and delete categories, Quicken still retains the original category items. If you find that you have a need for a deleted category, you can restore that category.

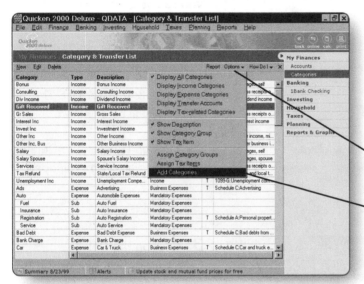

Depending on how you answered questions during the New User Setup, some categories may not appear in your list but you can still access them. You'll find them in Quicken's memory bank.

1. Click on **Options**. The Options menu will appear.

2. Click on **Add Categories**. The Add Categories dialog box will open.

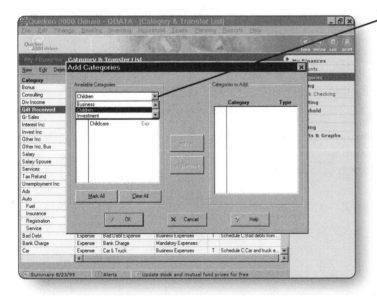

3. Click on the **Available Categories down arrow** and **click** on the **category type** from which you want to add a category. The classification will appear in the list box.

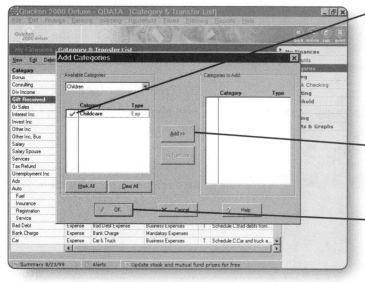

4. Click on the **category** that you want to add to the Category & Transfer List. The category will be selected and a check mark will appear to the left of the category.

5. Click on **Add**. The Category will appear in the Categories to Add list box.

6. Click on **OK**. The categories you added will appear in the Category & Transfer List and will be available to you when you begin recording transactions.

Creating Subcategories

After you've worked with Quicken for a while, you may find that too many transactions are going to a certain category. These transactions may all be related (such as utility bills), but could be broken into subcategories (such as phone, gas, and cable bills). You'll notice that subcategories are indented below the related category in the Category & Transfer List.

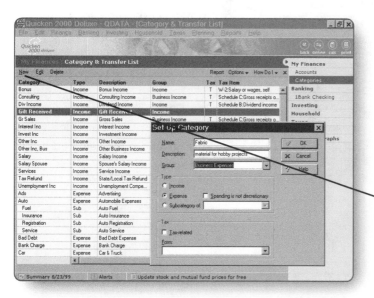

1. Click on **New**. The Set Up Category dialog box will open.

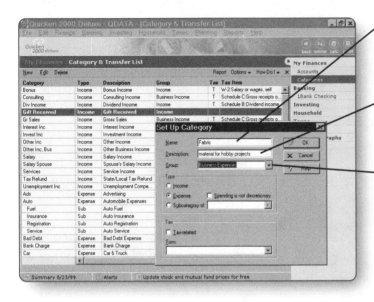

2. Type a **name** for the subcategory in the Name text box.

3. Type a **description** of the subcategory in the Description text box.

4. Click on the **Group down arrow** and **click** on a **group**. The group will be selected.

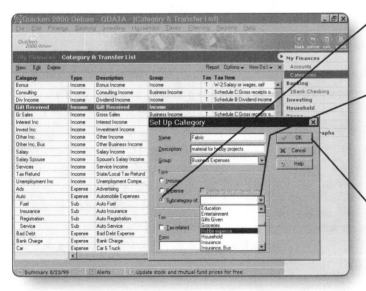

5. Click on the **Subcategory of option button**. The option will be selected.

6. Click on the **Subcategory of down arrow** and **click** on the **category** where the subcategory should be located. The category will be selected.

7. Click on **OK**. The subcategory will be added to the list under the selected category.

Printing a Category List

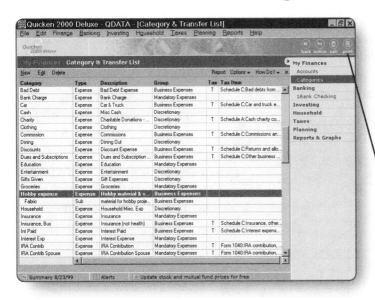

You may want to keep a printed copy of your chart of accounts. You can also save the chart of accounts as a file that you can import into a word processing program and make any changes there.

1. Click on the **Print icon**. The Print dialog box will open.

2. Click on the **option button** in the Print to area for the printer or file to which you want to print the Category & Transfer List. The option will be selected.

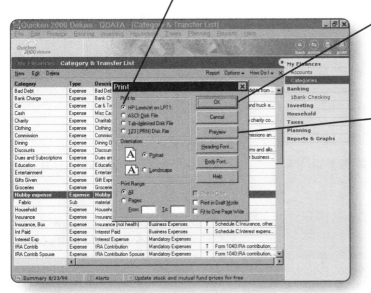

3. Click on **OK**. The list will be printed.

NOTE

Click on the Preview button to see what the list will look like on the printed page. You can also change the font style and size from the Heading Font and Body Font buttons.

Using Classes

Classes are an easy way to keep track of people, activities, or events that might incur expenses over several categories. If you have several hobbies, you might want to know how much gasoline, equipment rental, and meals are consumed for each hobby. Set up a separate class for each hobby. A business might set up a class for each of its projects. This makes it possible to determine what expenses are incurred for each project. You may also want to set up a class for each member of your family to keep track of individual expenses.

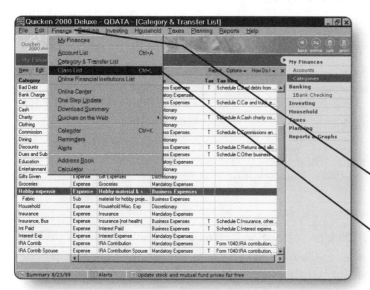

1. Click on **Finance**. The Finance menu will appear.

2. Click on **Class List**. The Class List window will appear.

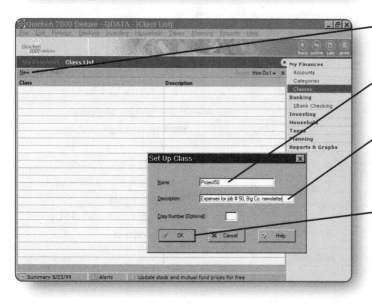

3. Click on **New**. The Set Up Class dialog box will open.

4. Type a **name** for the class in the Name text box.

5. Type a **description** of the class in the Description text box.

6. Click on **OK**. The new class will be added to the Class List.

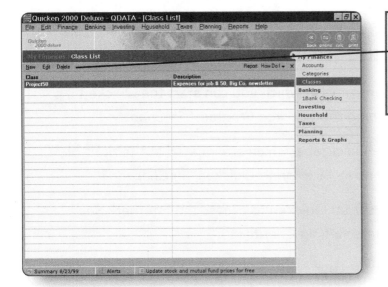

TIP

You can edit and delete classes by using the Edit and Delete buttons.

Part I Review Questions

1. What are two different ways in which you can start the Quicken program? *See "Opening the Quicken Program" in Chapter 1*

2. How do you hide the QuickTabs, which are located at the right of the Quicken window? *See "Exploring Quicken" in Chapter 1*

3. Where do you go to set up Quicken to access the Internet? *See "Connecting to the Internet" in Chapter 2*

4. Why should you register your copy of Quicken as soon as possible? *See "Taking Care of Business" in Chapter 2*

5. Which help feature allows you to search a topic list for answers to your questions? *See "Finding Program Help" in Chapter 3*

6. Where can you go to be entertained and learn about your finances at the same time? *See "Playing the Show Me Videos" in Chapter 3*

7. How do you create accounts for your checking, savings, and credit card accounts? *See "Working with Accounts and Files" in Chapter 4*

8. How would you keep personal records separate from records for a business venture? *See "Working with Multiple Quicken Files" in Chapter 4*

9. What is the purpose of the Category & Transfer List? *See "Working with Categories" in Chapter 5*

10. When would you want to assign classes to transactions? *See "Using Classes" in Chapter 5*

PART II

Tracking Financial Transactions

6

Recording Basic Transactions

In the first part of this book, you spent your time getting organized so that you could use Quicken to keep track of your finances. You learned program basics, how to go online, and where to find help. You then created banking accounts and customized a list of categories to keep track of your income and expenditures. Even though this chapter uses a checking account to show you how to record transactions, the process is the same in all registers. In this chapter, you'll learn how to:

- Enter checks and deposits into an account register
- Charge a transaction to several categories
- Look for and edit transactions
- View a check register

Entering a Few Transactions

Before you begin to enter payment and deposit transactions, gather up your checkbook and receipts and open a Quicken account register.

Displaying the Account Register

There are several ways to open any account register. If you want to find a complete list of your accounts, go to the Account List.

1. **Click** on **Banking**. The Banking menu will appear.

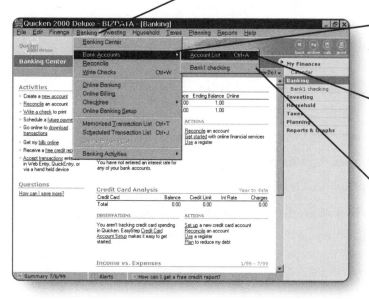

2. **Move** the **mouse pointer** to Bank Accounts. A submenu will appear.

3. **Click** on **Account List**. The Account List window will appear.

TIP

You can click on the account if it is listed under the Account List command.

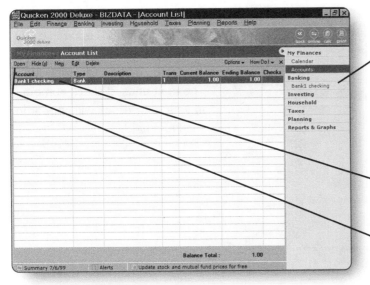

NOTE

If the account has a QuickTab, click on it to open the register. You'll also find accounts listed on the Banking QuickTab.

4. Click on an **account**. The account will be selected.

5. Click on **Open**. The register for the account will appear and a blank transaction line will be selected. This is where to enter your first check.

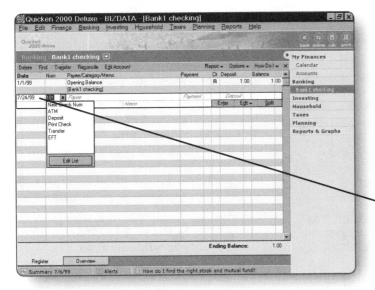

Recording a Check

Quicken keeps track of many things for you. For example, it can automatically type in the number for the checks that you write. Of course this only works if you write and record checks in numerical order.

1. Click in the **Date field** and **type** the **date** that you wrote the check.

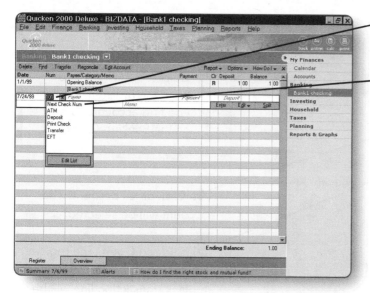

2. Click in the **Num field**. A drop-down list will appear.

3. Click on **Next Check Num**. The next unused check number in your checkbook will appear in the Num field.

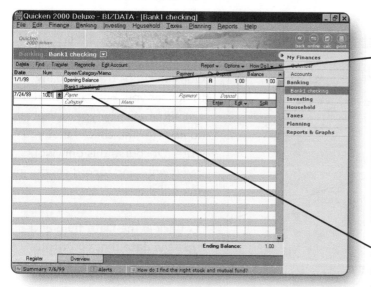

NOTE

If this is the first check you are recording for this account, you will need to specify the beginning check number. Just replace the default check number in the Num field with your actual check number.

4. Click in the **Payee/ Category/Memo field**. The insertion point will appear in the field.

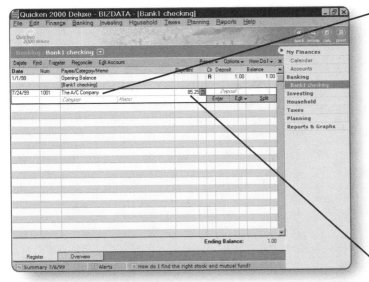

5. Type the **name** of the person or business to whom you wrote the check.

NOTE

Quicken stores these payee names. If you write a check to this person or business in the future, you can select the name from the Payee drop-down list.

---

6. Click in the **Payment field** and **type** the **amount** of the check.

7. Click in the **Category field**. A drop-down list will appear.

8. Click on the **category** to which you want to assign the transaction. The category will be selected.

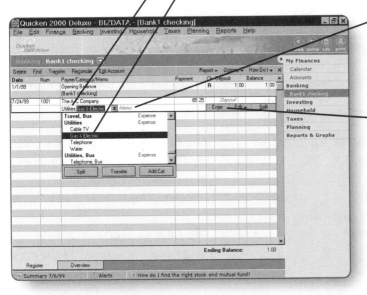

9. Click in the **Memo field** and type a **comment** or any notes that you want to remember about the transaction.

10. Click on **Enter**. The transaction will be recorded in the register.

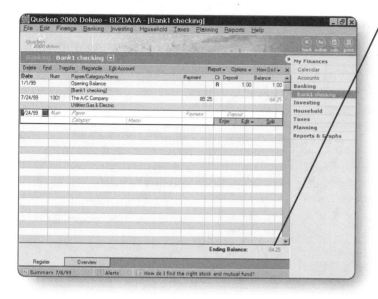

You'll notice that the balance of your account has been reduced. Also, the next transaction line in the register is selected and ready for you to record your next check.

Posting Deposits

Now let's do something a little more fun and put some money into your account.

1. Click in the **Date field** and **type** the **date** on which you made the deposit to the account.

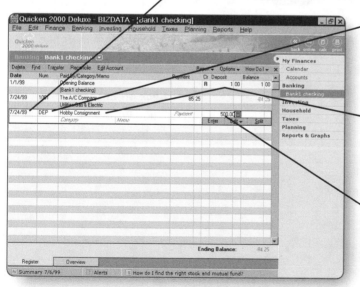

2. Click in the **Num field** and **click** on **Deposit** from the drop-down list. DEP will appear in the Num field.

3. Click in the **Payee field** and **type** the **name** of the person or business from whom you received the cash or check.

4. Click in the **Deposit field** and **type** the **amount** of the deposit.

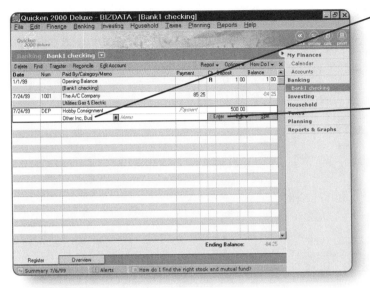

5. Click in the **Category field** and **select** an **income category** for the deposit. The category name will appear in the field.

6. Click on **Enter**. The deposit will be recorded in the register. You'll notice that the balance of the account has increased.

Transferring Funds Between Accounts

When you move money from one account to another (for example, from checking to savings.) you'll want to record this transaction as a transfer. This gives you a record of when the money was transferred and which accounts were involved.

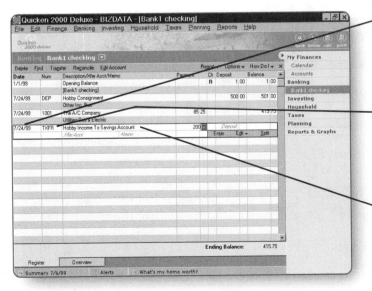

1. Click in the **Date field** and **type** the **date** on which you transferred money between accounts.

2. Click in the **Num field** and **click** on **Transfer** from the drop-down list. TXFR will appear in the Num field.

3. Click in the **Description field** and **type** a **note** that describes why the transfer was made.

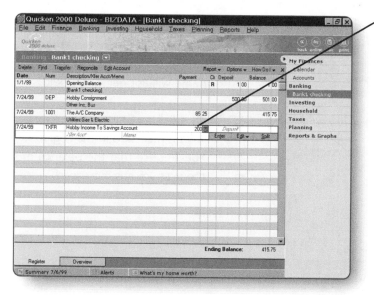

4. Click in the **Payment field** and **type** the **amount** of money you transferred between the accounts.

5. Click in the **Xfer account field.** A drop down list will appear.

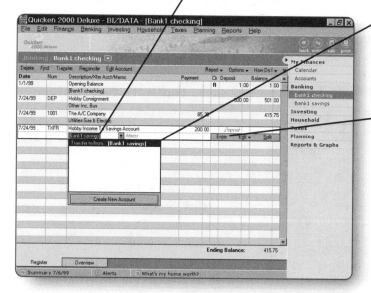

6. Click on the **account** to which the money is being transferred. The account will appear in the field.

7. Click on **Enter.** The transaction will be listed in the register. The balance of the selected account will be reduced by the amount of the transfer. If you open the register for the account to which the money was transferred, you'll see the transaction entered in the account register and the increase in the account balance.

Splitting a Transaction Between Categories

Entering a transaction and assigning it to a category is pretty simple. Most of the time when you go to the grocery store, you just buy groceries. But what if you also buy some stamps so you can send out a newsletter for your hobby or small business? You'll need to assign two categories to a single transaction. It takes a few more steps to enter a split transaction.

1. Click in the **Date field** and **type** the transaction **date**.

2. Click in the **Num field** and **click** on **Next Check Num** from the list. The next check number in sequence will appear.

3. Click in the **Payee field** and **type** the **name** of the person or business to whom you wrote the check.

4. Click in the **Payment field** and **type** the total **amount** of the check.

5. Click on **Split**. The Split Transaction Window will appear.

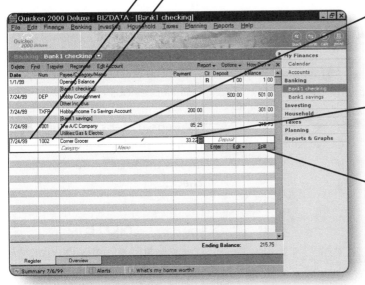

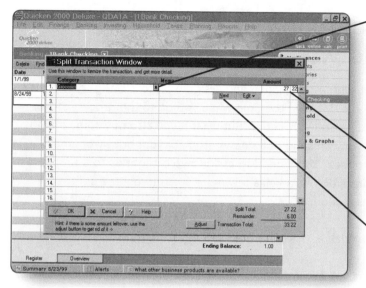

6. **Click** on the **Category down arrow** and **click** on the first **category** to which you want to assign part of the transaction. The category will appear in the list box.

7. **Click** in the **Amount field** and **type** the **amount** associated with the category.

8. **Click** on **Next**. The first category will be recorded and the next line will be selected.

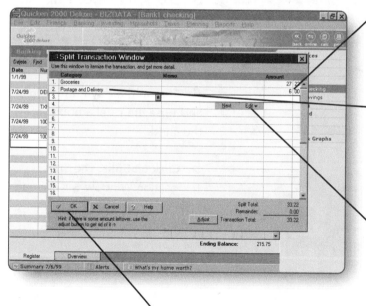

The amount listed in the Amount field for the selected line is the amount of the check less all previous entries.

9. **Repeat steps 6 through 8** until the total of the categories equals the total amount of the check.

NOTE

If you add an entry in error, delete it. Select the entry, click on the Edit button, and select Delete from the menu that appears.

10. **Click** on **OK**. The Split Transaction Window will close and the transaction will appear in the account register.

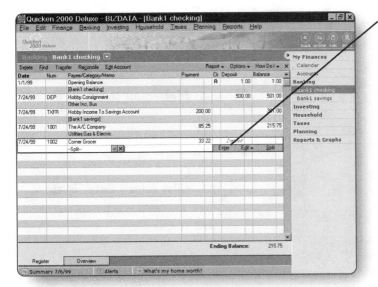

11. Click on **Enter**. The next line in the register will be ready for your next transaction.

Making Changes to a Transaction

After you have entered check and deposit transactions, take a minute to review the information. If you've misspelled any names, you can fix them and make sure that transactions are assigned to the proper categories. If you find that you've written a check in error, you can void the transaction.

Editing a Transaction

Making changes to any field in the account register is similar to working with text in a word processing program. If you want to change text, just click and drag over it and make your changes.

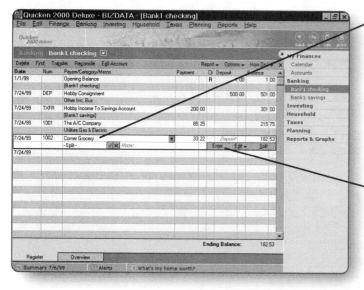

1. **Click** in the **field** in which you want to make the change. The field will be selected.

2. **Make** your **changes**. You can correct misspellings and amounts or change the assigned category.

3. **Click** on the **Enter button**. The changes will be applied to the transaction.

Voiding Checks

When you write a check in error, you'll want to keep a record of the destroyed check but not of the transaction. By voiding a check, any information stored about the transaction will be deleted.

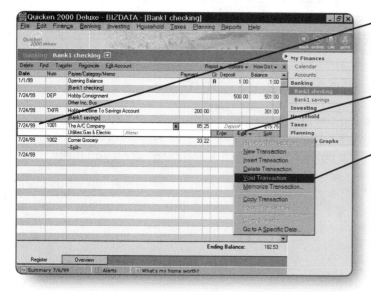

1. **Click** on the **transaction** that you want to void. The transaction will be selected.

2. **Click** on **Edit**. A menu will appear.

3. **Click** on **Void Transaction**. The word ****VOID**** will appear before the text in the Payee field and the amount field will be cleared.

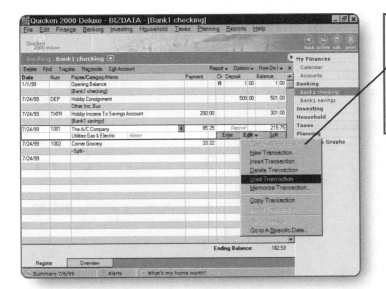

NOTE

You can restore a voided transaction. Select Restore Transaction from the Edit button menu.

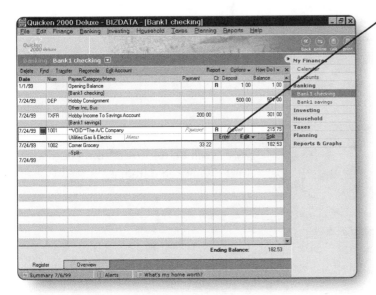

4. Click on **Enter**. The change will be saved. You'll notice that the register balance will be adjusted and that the transaction amount is no longer assigned to a category.

NOTE

The R in the Clr field indicates that the transaction will not be recognized when the account is reconciled.

Deleting a Transaction

Before you delete a transaction, make sure that you no longer need the information. Once the transaction is deleted, it is gone for good.

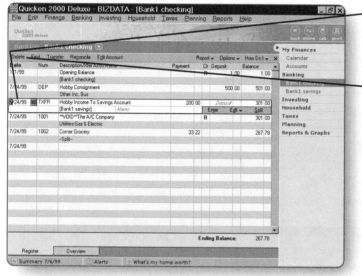

1. Click on the **transaction** that you want to delete. The transaction will be selected.

2. Click on the **Delete button**. A confirmation dialog box will open.

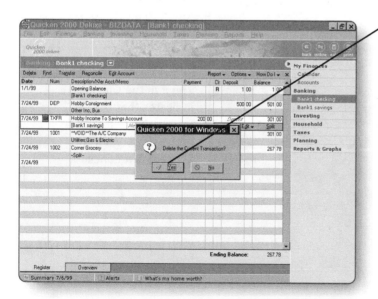

3. Click on **Yes**. The transaction will be removed from your Quicken data file.

Finding a Transaction

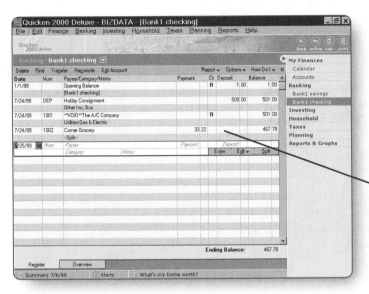

After you have entered a few transactions in a register, you may need to go back and look at a particular transaction. If your register is long, it may take some time to browse through the list. Quicken can help you find a specific transaction.

1. Open the **account register** that contains the transaction you want to find. The Banking window for the account will appear.

2. Click on **Edit**. The Edit menu will appear.

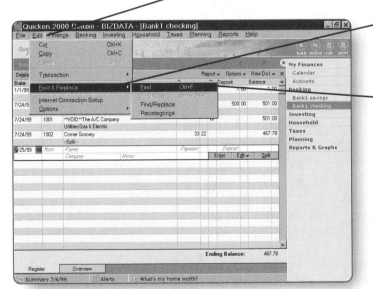

3. Move the **mouse pointer** to **Find & Replace**. A second menu will appear.

4. Click on **Find**. The Quicken Find dialog box will open.

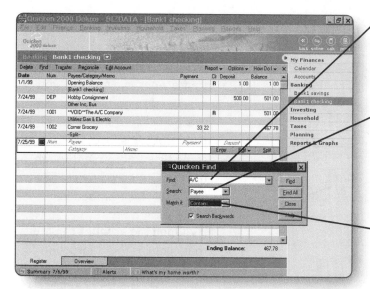

5. **Click** in the **Find text box** and **type** either **letters or numbers** that are contained in the transaction you want to find.

6. **Click** on the **Search down arrow** and **Click** on the **field** in the register that you want to search. The search field will appear in the list box.

7. **Click** on the **Match if down arrow** and **Click** on the **search parameters** that you want to add to the search. The search parameters will appear in the list box.

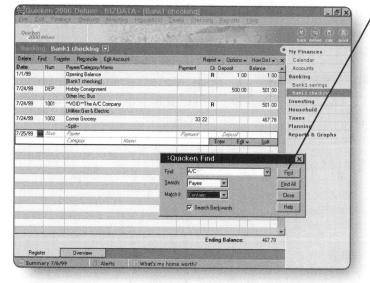

8. **Click** on **Find**. Quicken will look through the transactions in the register until it finds a match.

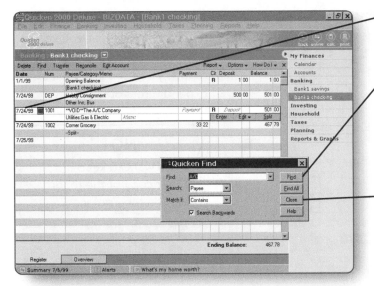

The first transaction that matches your search requirements will be selected in the register.

9. **Click** on **Find** if you want to search for another transaction that matches your search criteria. The match will be selected in the register.

10. **Click** on **Close** when you are finished searching for transactions in the register. The Quicken Find dialog box will close.

Viewing the Register Report

It's easy to keep a printed copy of the check register.

1. **Open** the **register** for which you want to print a Register Report. The account will appear in the Banking window.

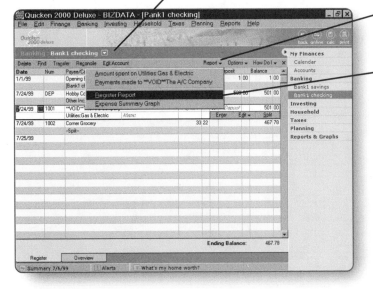

2. **Click** on the **Report button**. A menu will appear.

3. **Click** on **Register Report**. The Register Report will be created.

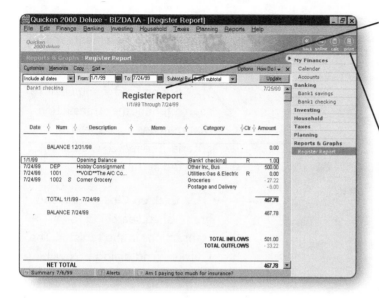

The Register Report shows all the transactions that you've entered. At the bottom of the report, you'll see income and expenditures totals.

NOTE

If you want to keep a paper copy of the report, click on the Print icon.

7

Recording Special Transactions

Some transactions aren't as easy to record as the examples shown in the last chapter. It's easy to track your paycheck as a deposit and just categorize the income. But, if you want to track the paycheck as well as the deductions, use the Paycheck Setup wizard to guide you through the process. You can then automatically record the deposit each payday. You might even want to keep track of unemployment compensation for tax purposes should that unfortunate event occur. If you have vacation, comp time, or sick leave that you want to track, you can set up a nonmonetary account. In this chapter, you'll learn how to:

- Keep track of payroll information automatically
- Record unemployment compensation
- Create and use nonmonetary accounts

Entering Your Paycheck

There's lots of information to record when you deposit your paycheck. Not only do you need to categorize the income, but there are also tax deductions and retirement deductions to consider. The Paycheck Setup wizard will walk you through the process.

Setting Up Your Paycheck

When you're ready to deposit your next paycheck, take a few minutes to give Quicken the information it needs to easily track your payroll tax information. This section will show you how to get started with the Paycheck Setup wizard.

1. **Click** on **Banking**. The Banking menu will appear.

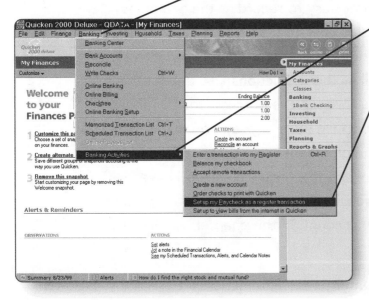

2. **Move** the **mouse pointer** to Banking Activities. A submenu will appear.

3. **Click** on **Set up my Paycheck as a register transaction**. The Paycheck Setup wizard will begin and the Welcome to PayCheck Setup screen will appear.

NOTE

You can also find the Paycheck Setup wizard in the Scheduled Transactions section of the My Finances QuickTab.

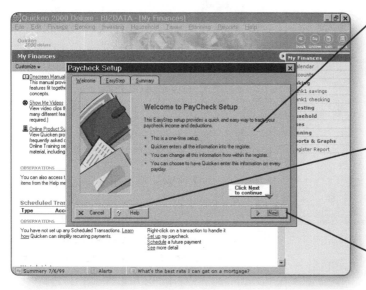

4. Read the **instructions** on each page. You will be prompted to enter information in text boxes and select options from option buttons and check boxes.

5. Click on **Help** if you need further instructions on how to complete the information asked in a screen. A Help window will appear.

6. Click on **Next**. The next screen in the wizard will appear.

7. Continue to **answer** the questions needed by the wizard and **click** on **Next** until you get to the Summary tab.

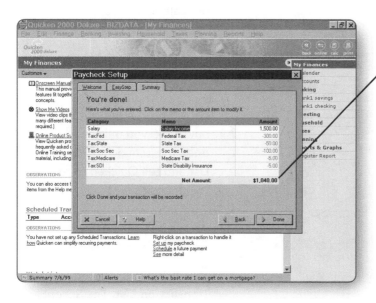

8. Compare the **Net Amount** listed at the bottom of the screen to the amount of your paycheck. These two amounts should match.

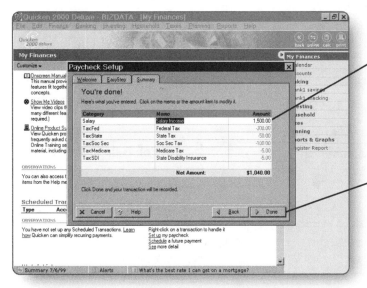

9. Click on **Done** when you finish. The transaction will be recorded in the selected account register. Also, the deposit will be remembered as a scheduled transaction. You can use this scheduled transaction the next time you need to deposit your paycheck.

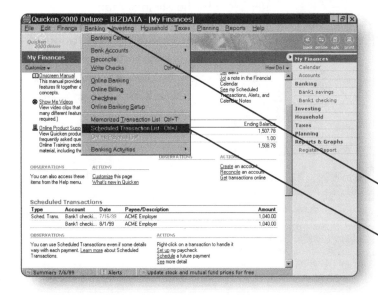

Depositing Your Paycheck

Each time you deposit your paycheck, you only need to open the Scheduled Transaction List and tell Quicken to record the deposit.

1. Click on **Banking**. The Banking menu will appear.

2. Click on **Scheduled Transaction List**. The Scheduled Transaction List window will appear.

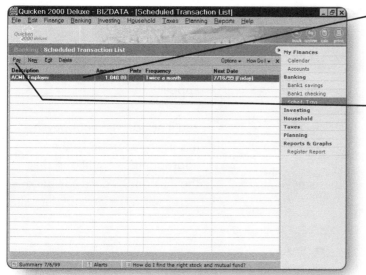

3. Click on the **paycheck** that you want to deposit. The scheduled transaction will be selected.

4. Click on **Pay**. The Record Scheduled Transaction dialog box will open.

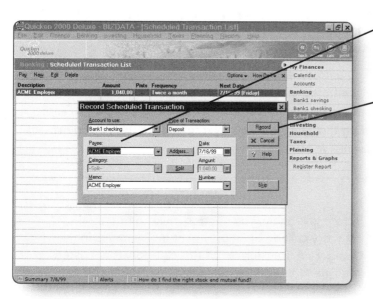

5. Verify that all the **information** in the dialog box matches your paycheck.

6. Click on **Record**. The deposit will be recorded and you will return to the Scheduled Transaction List window.

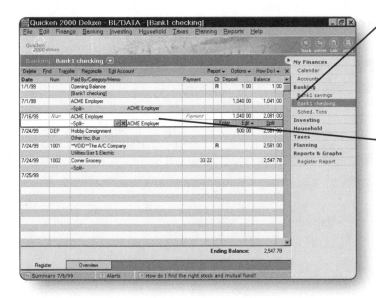

7. **Click** on the **QuickTab** for the account to which you deposited your paycheck. The register for the account will appear.

You'll notice that your paycheck has been recorded to the appropriate account and that the account balance has been increased to reflect the deposit.

Recording Unemployment Checks

If you unfortunately find yourself unemployed, Quicken can help with some of the burden by recording unemployment benefits. Depending on how much other income you earn during the year, you may have to declare the unemployment earnings at tax time.

NOTE

Before you begin, you need to make sure that a category called "Unemployment Inc" appears in the Category & Transfer List. If this category is not listed, you'll need to add the category. See "Restoring Categories to the List" in Chapter 5, "Categorizing Your Spending Habits."

---

1. Display the **register window** for the account into which you deposited the unemployment check. The register will appear.

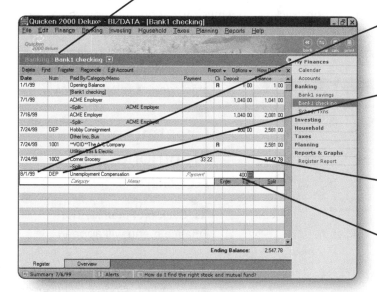

2. Type the **date** that you deposited the unemployment check.

3. Click in the **Num field** to display a drop-down list and **click** on **Deposit**. DEP will appear in the Num field.

4. Click in the **Payee field** and **type** a **description**.

5. Click in the **Deposit field** and **type** the **amount** of the unemployment check.

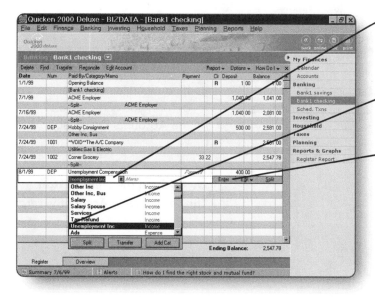

6. Click in the **Category field**. The list of categories will appear.

7. Click on **Unemployment Inc**. The category will be selected.

8. Click on the **Enter button**. The deposit will be recorded in your account and the unemployment income will be recorded in the appropriate category.

Keeping Track of Nonmonetary Items

You can keep track of how much vacation time you've earned and how much vacation time you've used. You can also keep track of accumulated sick leave. You don't have to limit these nonmonetary accounts to just employment related items.

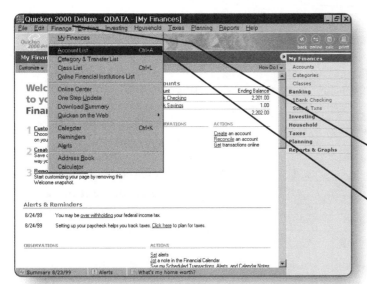

Creating a Nonmonetary Account

1. Click on **Finance**. The Finance menu will appear.

2. Click on **Account List**. The Account List window will appear.

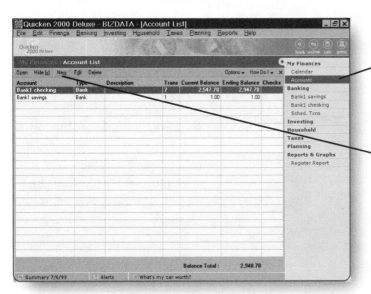

NOTE

If you've used this list before, you can click on the Accounts QuickTab.

3. Click on the **New button**. The Create New Account wizard will start.

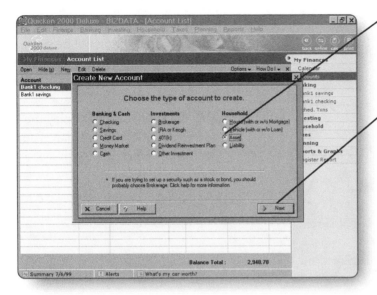

4. **Click** on the **Asset option button** in the Household category. The option will be selected.

5. **Click** on **Next**. The Asset Account Setup wizard will start and the Enter a name and optional description for this account screen will appear.

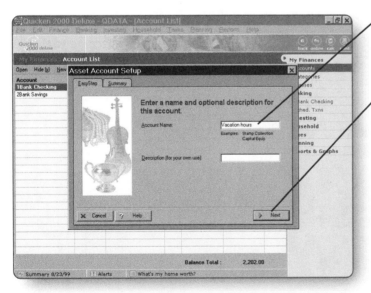

6. **Type** a **name** for the nonmonetary account in the Account Name text box.

7. **Click** on **Next**. The Quicken needs a starting point for this account screen will appear.

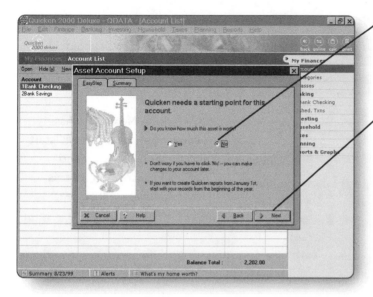

8. Click on the **No option button**. The option will be selected and the account will start with a zero balance.

9. Click on **Next** to display the screen entitled: That's okay, you can enter a balance for this account later.

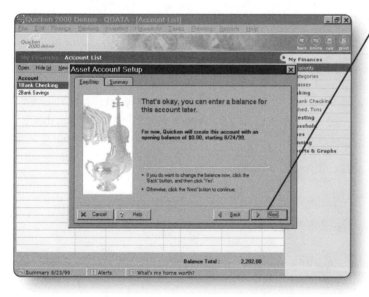

10. Click on **Next**. The Summary tab will come to the top of the stack.

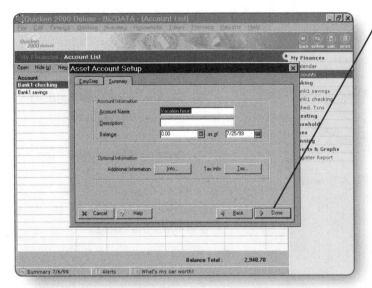

11. **Click** on **Done** after you have verified that the information is correct. The nonmonetary account will be added to the Account List.

Recording Nonmonetary Transactions

Once the nonmonetary account is created, you can begin keeping track of those items.

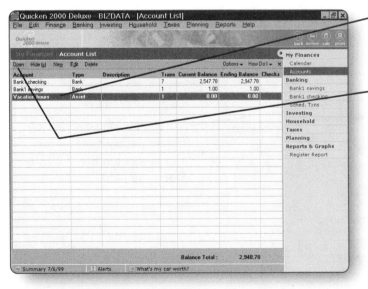

1. **Click** on the nonmonetary **account** that you want to use. The account will be selected.

2. **Click** on the **Open button**. The register window for the nonmonetary account will appear.

3. **Click** in the **Date field** and **type** the **date** on which the nonmonetary transaction was made. The date will appear in the Date field.

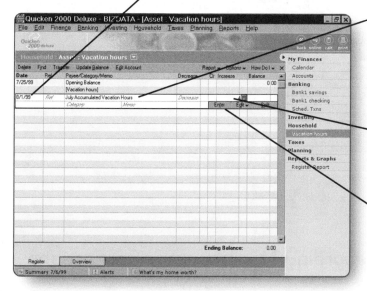

4. **Click** in the **Payee field**. The field will be highlighted.

5. **Type** a **description** of the transaction.

6. **Click** in the **Increase field** and **type** the **number** of units for the nonmonetary items.

7. **Click** on the **Enter button**. The nonmonetary transaction will be recorded.

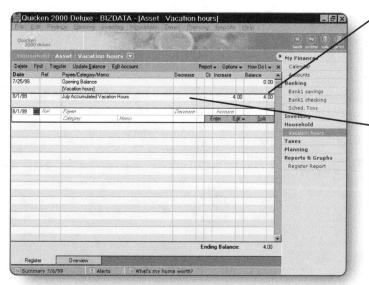

The balance of the nonmonetary item will appear in the last row of the Balance field.

NOTE

When you use your nonmonetary items, enter this amount in the Decrease field.

8

Making Mortgage Payments

One of the biggest purchases you may make during your lifetime is a home. Quicken includes features that help you keep track of the mortgage payments and the value of your home. Because there's a lot involved in a mortgage payment, such as principal reduction, interest payments, and deposits and payments to an escrow account, it's worth the time to set up a special way to handle this type of loan. In this chapter, you'll learn how to:

- Set up a mortgage loan account
- Make payments on your mortgage
- Produce mortgage and home equity reports

Setting Up a Mortgage Account

After you get moved into your new house and the furniture in place, you'll need to find an easy way to keep track of your mortgage and interest payments. Use the Quicken Loan Setup wizard to create an account for the mortgage. You can also set up an asset account to help keep track of the value of your home. If you have a variable interest rate loan, Quicken can automatically adjust the mortgage information.

Creating a Mortgage Loan Account

1. Click on **Household**. The Household menu will appear.

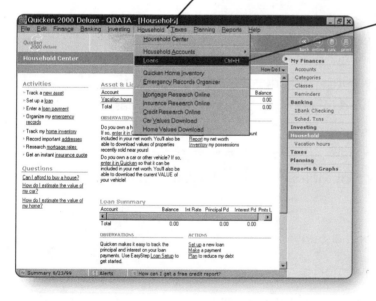

2. Click on **Loans**. The View Loans window will appear.

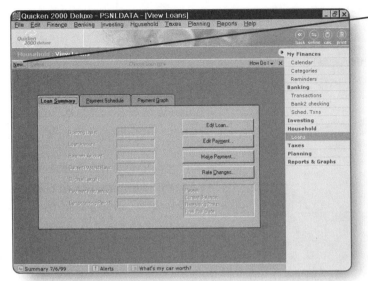

3. Click on the **New button**. The Loan Setup wizard will begin.

4. Click on the **Summary tab**. The Summary tab will come to the top of the stack.

5. Click on the **Borrow Money option button**, if it is not already selected. The option will be selected.

6. Click in the **New Account text box** and **type** a **name** for the asset account for your house.

7. Click on an **option button** in the Have Any Payments Been Made? section. The option will be selected.

8. Click on **Next**. The next screen of the Summary tab will appear.

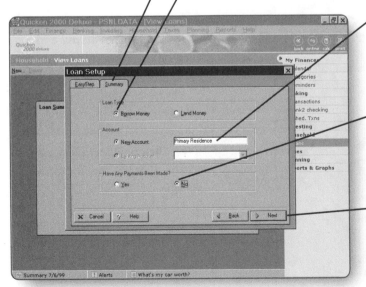

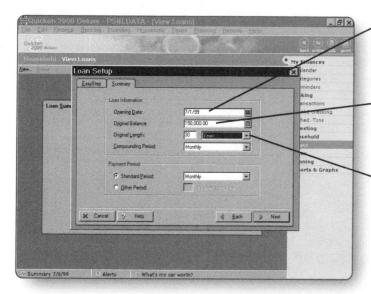

9. **Click** in the **Opening Date text box** and **type** the **date** on which you took out the loan.

10. **Click** in the **Original Balance text box** and **type** the original **amount** of the loan.

11. **Click** on the **Original Length down arrow** and **click** on the **time period** used to determine the length of the loan. The time period will be selected.

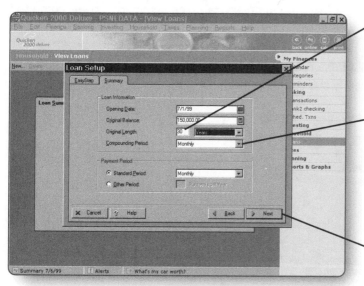

12. **Click** in the **Original Length text box** and **type** the **number** of time periods needed to pay off the loan.

13. **Click** on the **Compounding Period down arrow** and **click** on the **time period** used to calculate compound interest. The compounding period will be selected.

14. **Click** on **Next**. The last screen of the Summary tab will appear.

15. Click in the **Payment Amount (P+I) text box** and **type** the **amount** of your principal and interest payment as determined by your mortgage lender.

16. Click in the **due on text box** and **type** the **date** that your next mortgage payment is due.

17. Click in the **Interest Rate text box** and **type** the interest **rate** that you pay on your mortgage loan.

18. Click on **Done**. The Set Up Loan Payment dialog box will appear.

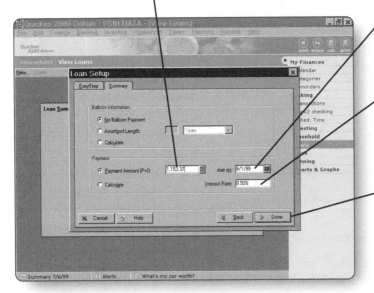

19. Click on **Edit**, if there are other amounts that will be added to your mortgage payment. The Split Transaction Window will appear.

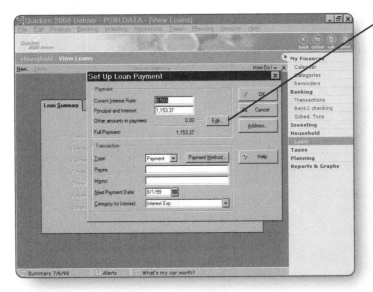

NOTE

There may be homeowner's insurance and property tax payments that your mortgage lender pays for you out of an escrow account.

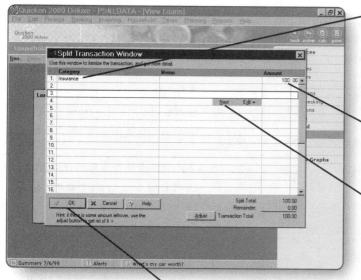

20. **Click** in the **Category field** and **select** the **category** that applies to the additional payment amount. The category will appear in the field.

21. **Click** in the **Amount field** and **type** the **amount** of the additional payment.

22. **Click** on the **Next button**. The second transaction line will be selected. You can add any additional payments in this transaction line.

23. **Click** on **OK**. The Set Up Loan Payment dialog box will appear. Notice that the amount in the Full Payment field will change to show the total mortgage payment.

24. **Click** in the **Payee field** and **type** the **name** of the mortgage lender to whom you will make your mortgage payments.

25. **Click** on **OK**. A confirmation dialog box will open.

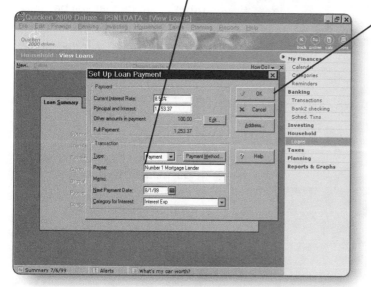

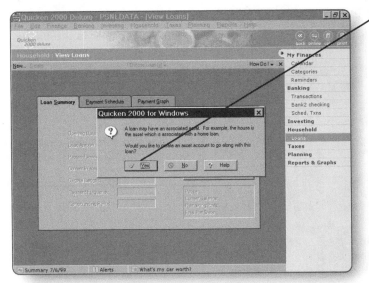

26. Click on **Yes**. The Asset Account Setup wizard will begin.

27. Click on the **Summary tab**. The Summary tab will come to the top of the stack.

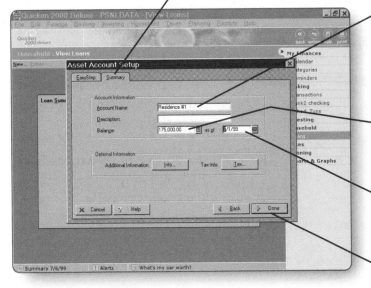

28. Click in the **Account Name text box** and **type** a **name** to describe the home for which you are tracking the mortgage payments.

29. Click in the **Balance text box** and **type** the **market value** of the house.

30. Click in the **as of text box** and **type** the **date** of the market valuation of the house.

31. Click on **Done**. You will return to the View Loans window.

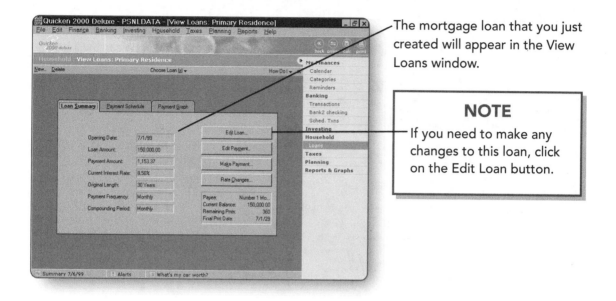

The mortgage loan that you just created will appear in the View Loans window.

NOTE

If you need to make any changes to this loan, click on the Edit Loan button.

Dealing with Adjustable Rate Loans

Most loans are for a fixed interest rate. If you have an adjustable rate mortgage, you'll need to enter the various interest rate changes and the date those changes go into effect.

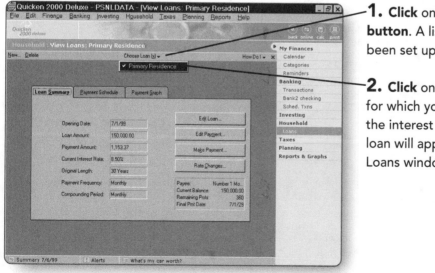

1. Click on the **Choose Loan button**. A list of loans that have been set up will appear.

2. Click on the **mortgage loan** for which you want to change the interest rate. The mortgage loan will appear in the View Loans window.

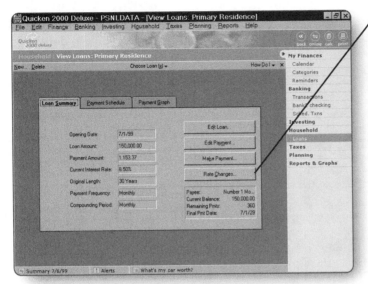

3. Click on **Rate Changes**. The Loan Rate Changes dialog box will open.

4. Click on the **New button**. The Insert an Interest Rate Change dialog box will open.

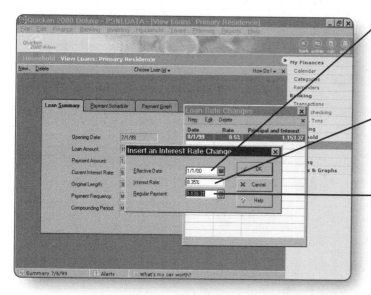

5. Click in the **Effective Date text box** and **type** the **date** on which the new interest rate will start.

6. Click in the **Interest Rate text box** and **type** the interest **rate**.

7. Click in the **Regular Payment text box**. The amount of the new payment will appear.

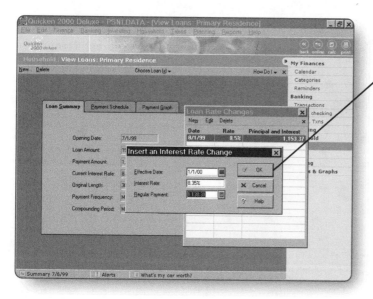

8. Verify that the new payment **amount** is correct.

9. Click on **OK**. You will return to the Loan Rate Changes dialog box.

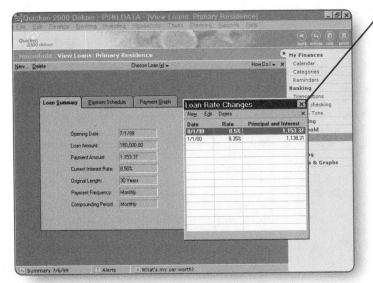

10. Click on the **Close button**. The new interest rate and payment will be set up and can be used when the rate changes go into effect.

Recording Mortgage Payments

When it's time to make a mortgage payment, use the payment function in the View Loans window to enter the payment in the proper account register. You can also record extra amounts that you might add to a mortgage payment if you are trying to pay off the loan faster.

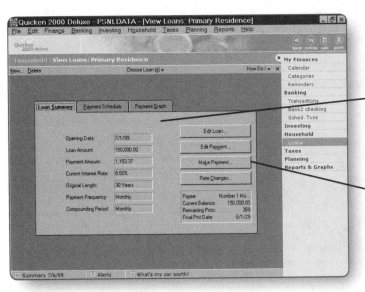

1. Display the **loan** on which you want to make the payment in the View Loans window. The loan will appear.

2. Click on **Make Payment**. The Loan Payment dialog box will open.

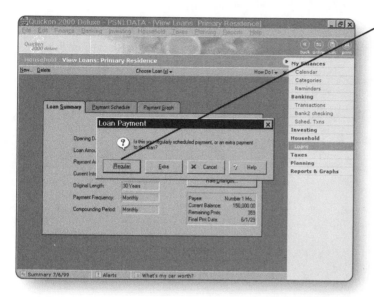

3. Click on **Regular**. The Make Regular Payment dialog box will open.

4. Click on the **Account to use down arrow** and **click** on the **account** from which you will be making the mortgage payment. The account will be selected.

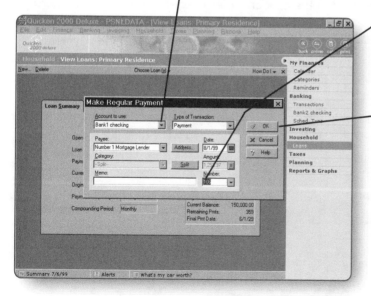

5. Click in the **Number text box** and **type** the **number** of the check you will use to make the payment.

6. Click on **OK**. The payment will be recorded in the selected account register.

Producing Mortgage Reports

When you want to find out the balance of your mortgage loan and your home equity, you can produce a couple of reports. The Payment Schedule will show you how much you have paid in principal and interest and how much is remaining on the mortgage loan. The second report shows you how much equity you have in your home.

Viewing the Payment Schedule

1. **Display** the **loan** for which you want to produce a payment schedule. The loan will appear in the View Loans window.

2. **Click** on the **Payment Schedule tab**. The Payment Schedule tab will come to the top of the stack.

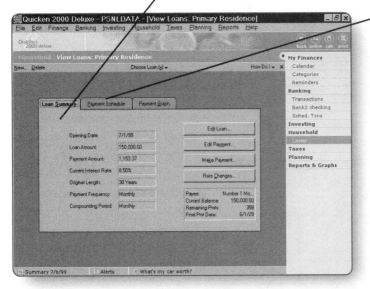

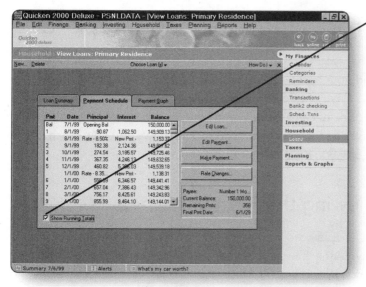

3. Click in the **Show Running Totals check box**. A check mark will appear in the box and the total amount of principal and interest payments you've made to date will display.

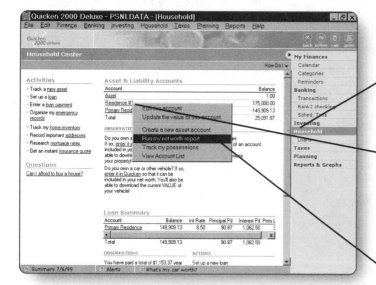

Creating a Home Equity Report

1. Click on the **Household QuickTab**. The HouseHold Center screen will appear.

2. Right-click on the **asset account** that you created for your house when you set up the mortgage loan. A menu will appear.

3. Click on **Run my net worth report**. The Net Worth Report will appear in the Reports & Graphs window. You'll need to customize this report to show only your mortgage loan and house asset accounts.

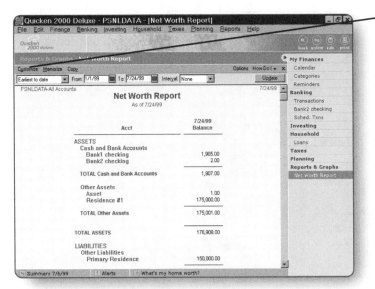

4. Click on the **Customize button**. The Customize Net Worth Report dialog box will open and the Display tab should be at the top of the stack. If it is not, click on the Display tab to bring it forward.

5. Click in the **Title text box** and **type** a **title** for the report.

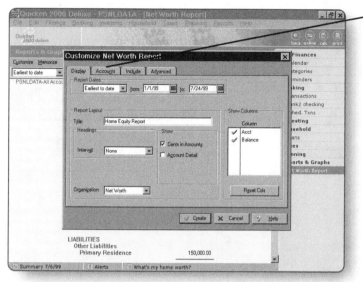

6. Click on the **Accounts tab**. The Accounts tab will come to the top of the stack.

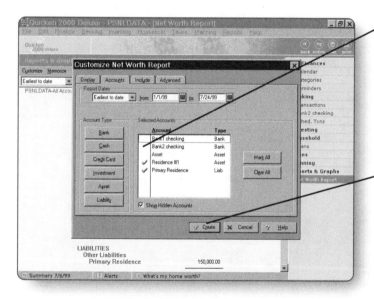

7. Click on the **check mark** next to those accounts that do not apply to your home or mortgage. The check mark will disappear and those accounts will not be included in the report.

8. Click on **Create**. The net worth report for your home will be updated and displayed in the Reports & Graphs window.

9

Automating Transactions

There are probably a number of bills that you pay each month to the same people and for about the same amounts. These bills fall in the categories of rent, cable service, and gasoline for your car. It would be too time consuming to enter these transactions each month. Quicken remembers your recently entered transactions and can recall the information so that it can be reused. Quicken also contains a scheduling feature that reminds you when to pay your bills. Then, when you pay the bill, the transaction is recorded automatically. In this chapter, you'll learn how to:

- Use QuickFill to make entering transactions easier
- Work with memorized transactions
- Schedule transactions to be dealt with in the future

Using QuickFill to Enter Transactions

Quicken remembers every transaction you enter and can use that information for similar transactions. This works well for payments that you make regularly, such as rent, phone bills, and trips to the coffee shop.

Using QuickFill

QuickFill allows you to recall a previously recorded transaction by typing a few letters in the Payee field. Before you begin, display the account register in which you want to work.

1. Click in the **Date field** and **type** the **date** of the transaction.

2. Click in the **Num field** and **click** on the **type** of transaction you want to record from drop-down the list. The transaction type will appear in the Num field.

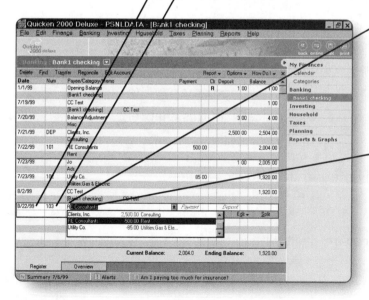

3. Click in the **Payee field** and **type** the **first letters** of the name of the person or business with whom the transaction was made. Quicken will attempt to complete the payee field.

4. Continue typing until the correct name appears in the Payee field.

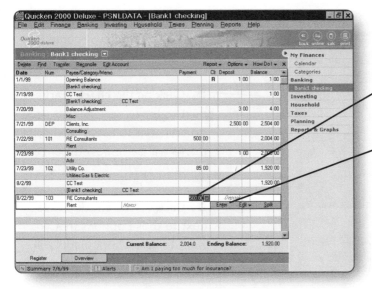

5. Press the **Tab key**. The rest of the transaction will be completed.

6. Make any necessary **changes**.

7. Click on the **Enter button**. The transaction will be recorded.

Changing QuickFill Options

If you're not entirely satisfied with how QuickFill performs, you can change a few options. By default, you move between fields in the register by pressing the Tab key but you could use the Enter key. If you don't want to use the drop-down lists that appear when you click in a field, turn them off. Look at the different options and see how QuickFill could work differently for you.

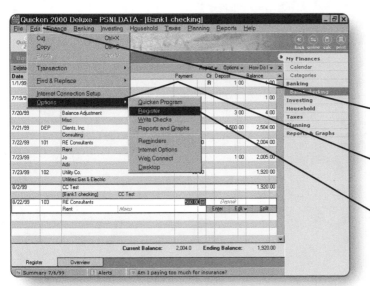

1. Click on **Edit**. The Edit menu will appear.

2. Move the **mouse pointer** to Options. A submenu will appear.

3. Click on **Register**. The Register Options dialog box will open.

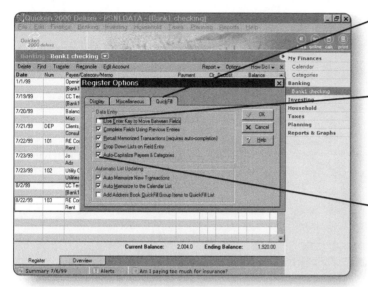

4. Click on the **QuickFill tab**. The QuickFill tab will come to the top of the stack.

5. Click on the **check marks** next to those options that you do not want to use. The check marks will be removed from the check boxes.

6. Click on the **check boxes** next to those options that you want to use. Check marks will appear in the check boxes.

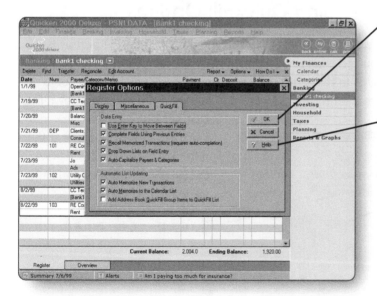

7. Click on **OK**. The settings you chose will be applied.

NOTE

Click on the Help button to find out what task an option performs.

Using the Memorized Transaction List

When you use the QuickFill feature, you are actually using transactions that appear in the Memorized Transaction List. This list can be customized so that it is easier to work with the QuickFill feature.

Adding a Memorized Transaction

A frequently occurring transaction can be added to the Memorized Transaction List. The next time you enter this transaction in the register, the process will be quick and easy.

1. Click on **Banking**. The Banking menu will appear.

2. Click on **Memorized Transaction List**. The Memorized Transaction List window will appear.

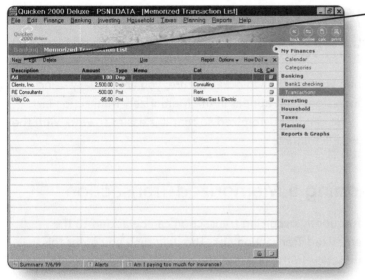

3. Click on the **New button**. The Create Memorized Transaction dialog box will open.

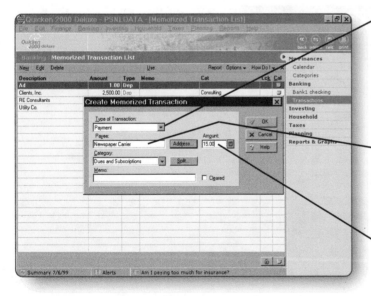

4. Click on the **Type of Transaction down arrow** and **click** on the **type of transaction** that you want to create. The transaction type will appear in the list box.

5. Click in the **Payee text box** and **type** the **name** of the person or business with whom you made the transaction.

6. Click in the **Amount text box** and **type** the **amount** of the transaction.

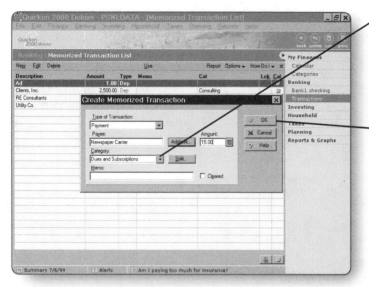

7. Click on the **Category down arrow** and **click** on the **category** that applies to the transaction. The category will appear in the list box.

8. Click on **OK**. The memorized transaction will appear in the list. You can now access this transaction when you are using the QuickFill feature.

NOTE

If you need to make changes to a memorized transaction, select the transaction from the list and click on the Edit button. You can make your changes in the Edit Memorized Transaction dialog box.

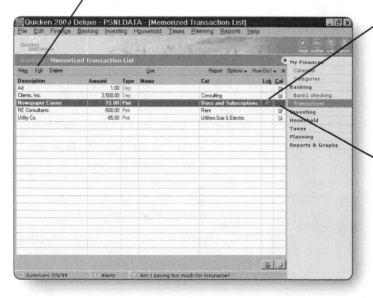

9. Click in the **Lck field** for those transactions that you want updated if you change the transaction when it is recorded in the register. The Lock icon will disappear from the field.

10. Click in the **Cal field** for those transactions that you do not want to appear in the Financial Calendar. The Calendar icon will be removed from the field.

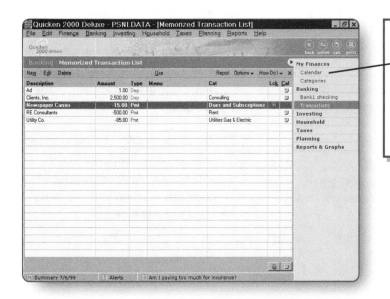

TIP

You'll find the Calendar by clicking on the Calendar QuickTab. You'll also find it in the Finance menu.

Recording a Memorized Transaction

Now that you've created a memorized transaction and made changes to the Memorized Transaction List and the QuickFill features to suite your needs, it's time to go to the register and enter the transaction.

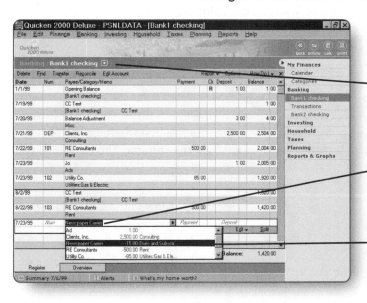

1. Display the **account register** in which you want to record the transaction. The register window will appear.

2. Click in the **Payee field** in a blank transaction line. A drop-down list will appear.

3. Click on the **memorized transaction** that you want to use.

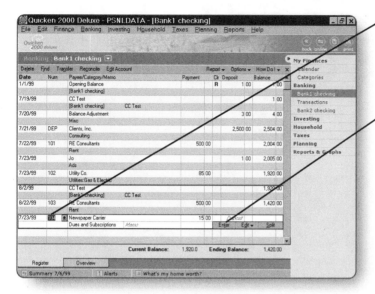

4. **Make** any **changes** to the transaction, if needed. You may need to add a check number or make a memo to yourself.

5. **Click** on the **Enter button**. The memorized transaction will be recorded in the register.

Scheduling Transactions

Quicken can help you remember when to pay your bills. When the bills start showing up in the mailbox, tell Quicken when they need to be paid. Quicken will set up the transaction so that all you need to do is tell Quicken a check number. The rest is done for you.

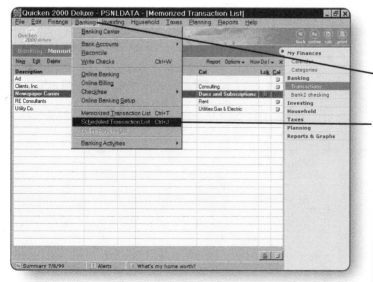

Creating a Scheduled Transaction

1. **Click** on **Banking**. The Banking menu will appear.

2. **Click** on **Scheduled Transaction List**. The Scheduled Transaction List window will appear.

NOTE

You can also click on the Sched. Txns QuickTab, if it is displayed.

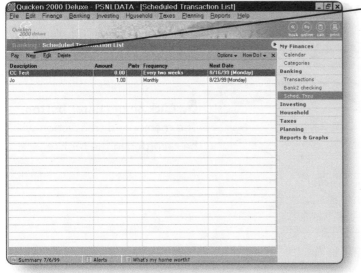

3. Click on the **New button**. The Create Scheduled Transaction dialog box will open.

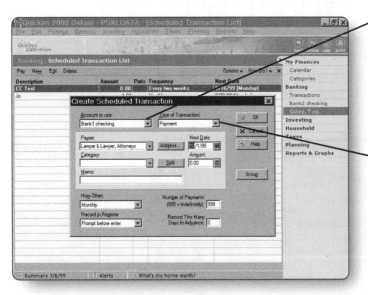

4. Click on the **Account to use down arrow** and **click** on the **account** to which the transaction should be recorded. The account will appear in the list box.

5. Click on the **Type of Transaction down arrow** and **click** on the **type of transaction**. The transaction type will appear in the list box.

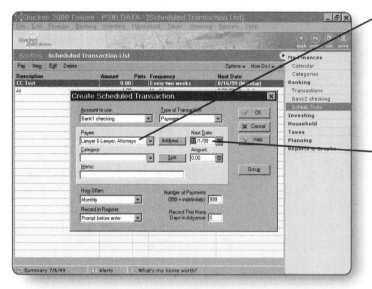

6. **Click** in the **Payee text box** and **type** the **name** of the person or business to which the transaction applies. You can also use the drop-down list box, if needed.

7. **Click** in the **Next Date text box** and **type** the **date** on which you want the first occurrence of the transaction to occur.

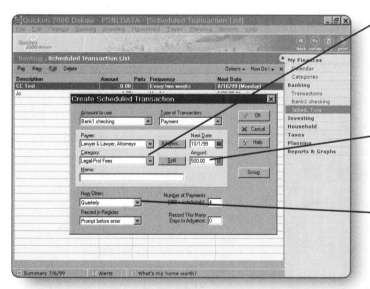

8. **Click** on the **Category down arrow** and **click** on the **category** to which the transaction should be applied. The category will appear in the list box.

9. **Click** in the **Amount text box** and **type** the dollar **amount** of the transaction.

10. **Click** on the **How Often down arrow** and **click** on the **frequency** that this transaction will occur. The frequency will appear in the list box.

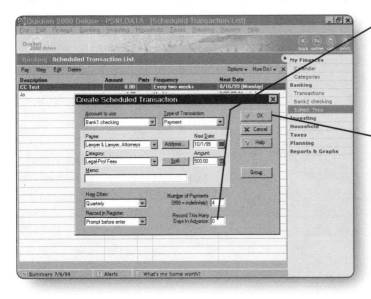

11. Select the **text** in the Number of Payments text box and **type** the **number** of payments that will need to be scheduled.

12. Click on **OK**. The new scheduled transaction will appear in the Scheduled Transaction List. If you need to make any changes to this transaction, select it and click on the Edit button.

Paying and Recording a Scheduled Transaction

Once you've scheduled a transaction, it's easy to make the payment. Here's how you can pay your bills from the Scheduled Transaction List.

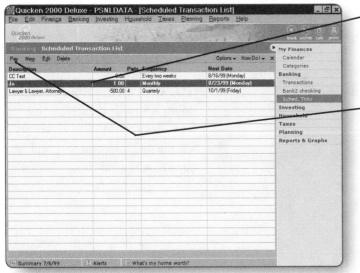

1. Click on the **scheduled transaction** that you want to pay. The transaction will be selected.

2. Click on the **Pay button**. The Record Scheduled Transaction dialog box will open.

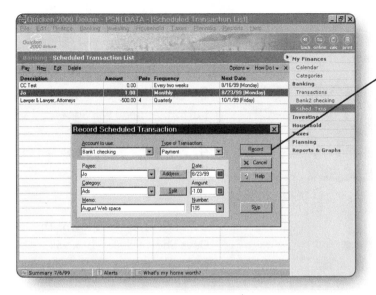

3. Make any **changes** to the transaction, if needed.

4. Click on **Record**. The transaction will be recorded in the register for the selected account. You'll notice that the Next Date column for the transaction will change to show the next due date for the scheduled transaction.

Using Billminder

Billminder is a quick way to manage your scheduled transactions. The Billminder displays all the bills that are coming due during a set time period. Here's how to find the Billminder and change its settings.

1. Click on **Finance**. The Finance menu will appear.

2. Click on **Reminders**. The Quicken Reminders window will appear.

The Quicken Reminders window shows you all those bills that are due to be paid within the next seven days—you can also change this length of time.

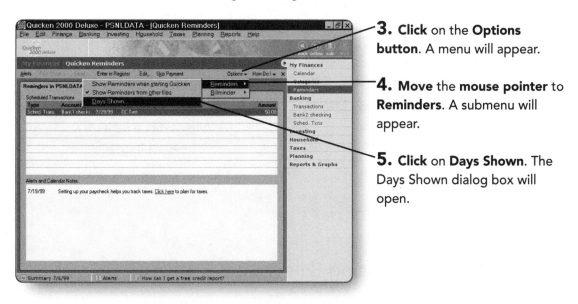

3. **Click** on the **Options button**. A menu will appear.

4. **Move** the **mouse pointer** to **Reminders**. A submenu will appear.

5. **Click** on **Days Shown**. The Days Shown dialog box will open.

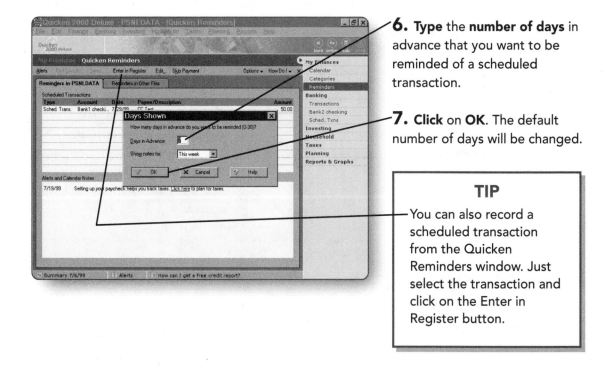

6. **Type** the **number of days** in advance that you want to be reminded of a scheduled transaction.

7. **Click** on **OK**. The default number of days will be changed.

TIP

You can also record a scheduled transaction from the Quicken Reminders window. Just select the transaction and click on the Enter in Register button.

10

Balancing Your Accounts

Each month you receive a statement for all of your bank, credit card, and investment accounts. Each statement reflects the status and value of your account with a particular financial institution. You'll need to make sure that your records match these statements. Quicken helps you keep track of your accounts and tells you when your records don't match the statements. Your first step is to reconcile the account. After you've compared your Quicken records to the statement, you can run a number of reports to help you locate reconciliation problems. In this chapter, you'll learn how to:

- Reconcile accounts to bank statements
- Create reports to help find reconciliation problems

Balancing Checking and Savings Accounts

The purpose of reconciling your accounts is to make sure that each transaction in the register has a match on the bank statement. You'll also want to verify that any cancelled checks that are mailed with the statement are recorded correctly on the statement.

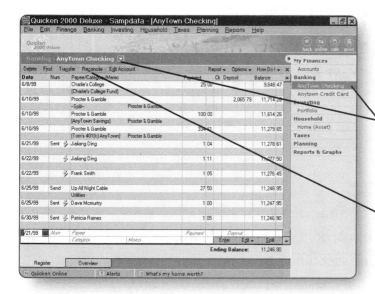

1. Display the **account** that you want to reconcile. The account register window will appear.

2. Click on the **Reconcile button**. The Reconcile Bank statement dialog box will open.

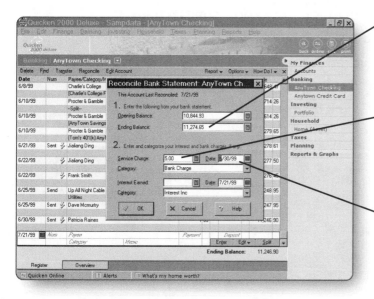

3. Click in the **Ending Balance text box** and **type** the **ending balance** as shown on the bank statement.

4. Click in the **Service Charge text box** and **type** the **amount** of any fees charged by the bank.

5. Click in the **Date text box** and **type** the **date** the bank charged the fee to your account.

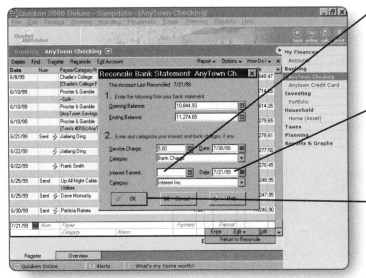

6. Click in the **Interest Earned text box** and **type** the **amount** of any interest income that the bank deposited to your account.

7. Click in the **Date text box** and **type** the **date** the bank deposited the interest to your account.

8. Click on **OK**. The Reconcile Bank Statement window will appear.

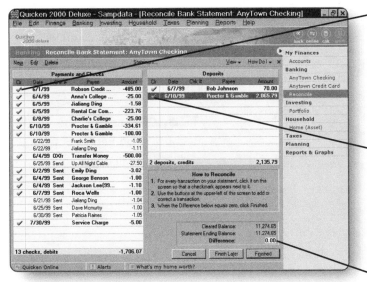

9. Click in the **Clr field** for the checks, cash machine withdrawals, and other payments that appear on the bank statement. A check mark will appear in the field.

10. Click in the **Clr field** for those deposits that appear on the bank statement. A check mark will appear in the field.

NOTE

As you check off each withdrawal and deposit, the amount in the Difference field will change. When this amount is zero, the account is balanced.

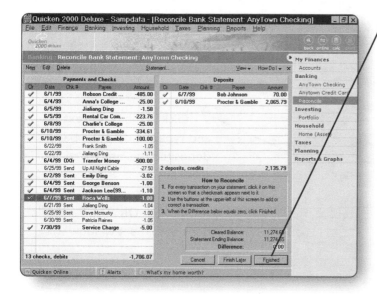

11. Click on **Finished**. The Reconciliation Complete dialog box will open. This dialog box gives you the opportunity to print a reconciliation report. This report shows the balance of the account if only reconciled transactions are considered. It then lists uncleared transactions to give you the current balance of your account.

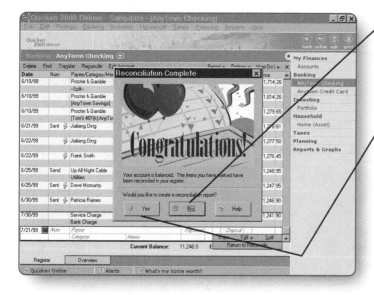

12a. Click on **No**. The register window for the account will appear.

OR

12b. Click on **Yes**. The Reconciliation Report Setup dialog box will open.

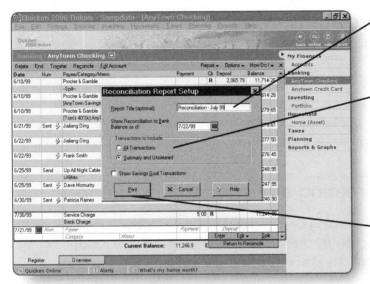

13. Click in the **Report Title (optional) text box** and **type** a **title** for the report.

14. Click on an **option button** in the Transactions to Include section to indicate what transactions you want to display in the report. The option will be selected.

15. Click on **Print**. The Print dialog box will open.

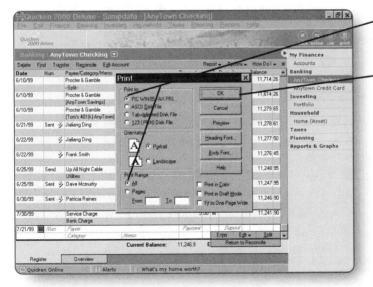

16. Select print **options**. The options will be selected.

17. Click on **OK**. The report will print on the selected printer.

Dealing with Reconciliation Problems

If your account register doesn't balance your bank statement, you can run several reports in Quicken to help you spot reconciliation problems such as missing checks and duplicate transaction entries.

Creating a Missing Checks Report

The Missing Checks report lists transactions in the account register by check number. You can easily spot a missing or duplicate check by checking the sequence of the check numbers.

1. Display the account **register** for the account on which you want to create the report. The register window will appear.

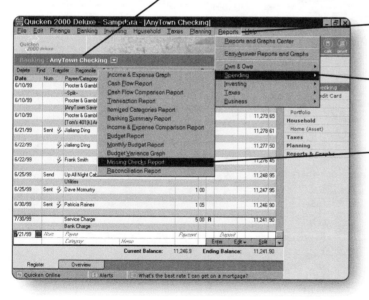

2. Click on **Reports**. The Reports menu will appear.

3. Move the **mouse pointer** to Spending. A submenu will appear.

4. Click on **Missing Checks Report**. The Missing Checks Report window will appear.

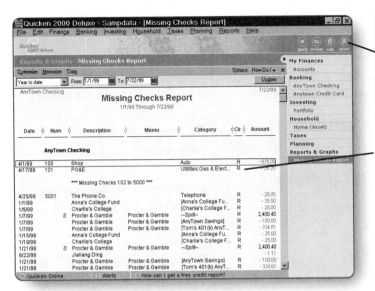

NOTE

You can print the report by clicking on the Print icon.

If the Clr field for a transaction contains an R, that transaction has been reconciled.

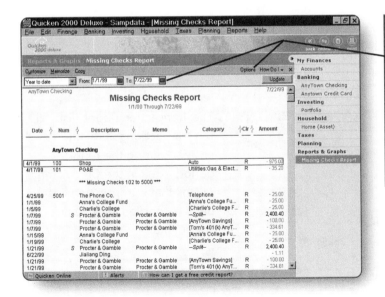

TIP

You can customize this report by selecting different report parameters from the drop-down lists in the report window, or by clicking on the Options button.

Creating a Transaction Report

The Transaction report lists all the transactions in a register. By default, this list is sorted by date, but you can sort transactions by payee, transaction date, or assigned category.

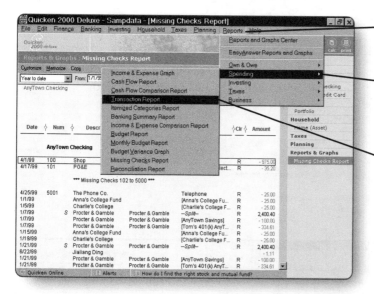

1. Click on **Reports**. The Reports menu will appear.

2. Move the **mouse pointer** to **Spending**. A submenu will appear.

3. Click on **Transaction Report**. The Transaction Report window will appear.

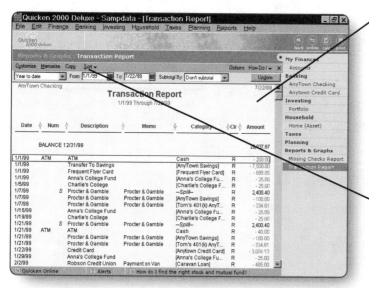

The Transaction Report lists all the transactions that you entered during the report period. An R in the Clr column means that a transaction has been reconciled with a bank statement.

TIP

You can sort the report by clicking on the Sort button. You can sort by date, check number, amount, payee, and category.

Creating a Register Report

The Register report lists all the transactions in an account register. This report comes in handy if you need to keep a paper copy of your checkbook.

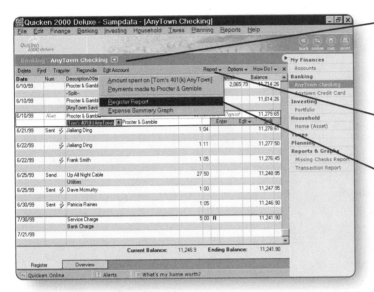

1. Display the **account** for which you want to create a Register Report. The account register window will appear.

2. Click on the **Report button**. A menu will appear.

3. Click on **Register Report**. The Register Report window will appear.

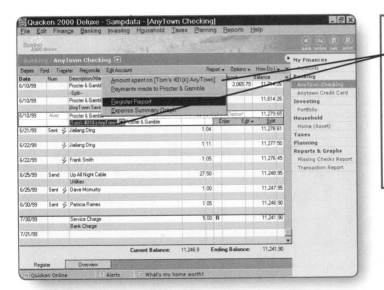

TIP

You can create a report that only lists certain transactions. You can click on a payee or category field in a register to display only that information when the Report button is clicked.

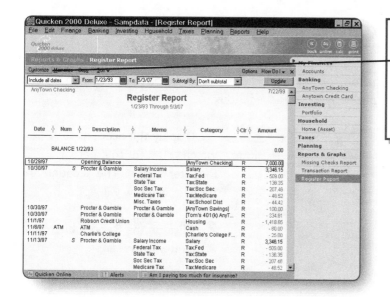

TIP

Click on the Customize button to limit the information that appears in the report.

11

Protecting Your Financial Records

The importance of protecting your financial records cannot be stressed enough. You can apply passwords to data files to keep your financial data out of the view of prying eyes and prevent the unauthorized changing of financial transactions. Be sure to keep backups of data files—it only takes a few seconds. It could take months to recreate the data from scratch. In this chapter, you'll learn how to:

- Password protect data files and transaction records
- Back up and restore data files

Assigning Passwords

Passwords are a great way to keep your financial records private. You can also prevent anyone from making changes to transactions without your authorization.

Password Protecting Transactions

When you assign a transaction password, you're only preventing others from making changes to any existing transactions or from adding new transactions. Other people will still be able to view the account registers and other Quicken features. Once you have password protected the transactions, you can change the password by following the same steps.

1. Click on **File**. The File menu will appear.

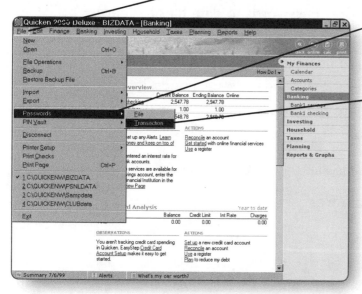

2. Move the **mouse pointer** to Passwords. A second menu will appear.

3. Click on **Transaction**. The Password to Modify Existing Transactions dialog box will open.

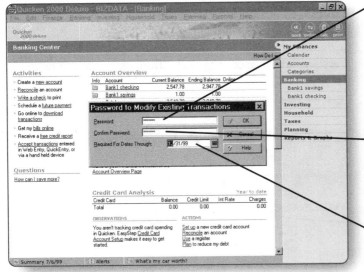

4. **Type** a **password** in the Password text box. Asterisks will appear in place of the characters you typed. Make sure you keep your password stored in a safe place.

5. **Type** the **same password** in the Confirm Password text box. Asterisks will appear in the text box.

6. **Type** the **date** of the last transaction that you want password protected in the Required For Dates Through text box.

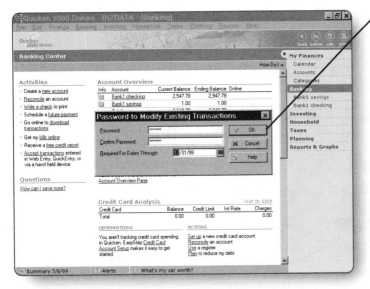

7. **Click** on **OK**. The transactions from the date you opened the data file until the last transaction date you specified will be password protected. Any attempt to edit these transactions will open a password dialog box. A password is needed to continue.

Password Protecting a Data File

If you want to prevent others from seeing your account registers and other account information, use a file password.

1. Click on **File**. The File menu will appear.

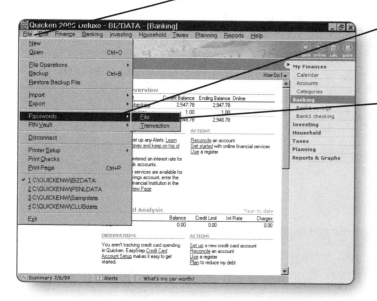

2. Move the **mouse pointer** to Passwords. A submenu will appear.

3. Click on **File**. The Set up Password dialog box will open.

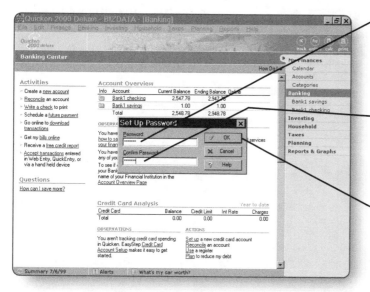

4. Type a **password** in the Password text box. Asterisks will appear in place of the characters you typed.

5. Type the **same password** in the Confirm Password text box. Asterisks will appear in the text box.

6. Click on **OK**. The file will be password protected. Whenever this data file is opened, a password will be required.

TIP

You can change your password later. Open the File menu, select Passwords, and then File. Make the changes in the dialog box that opens.

Backing Up Your Records

It's always a good idea to back up your Quicken data file after you enter any transactions or perform any other actions in Quicken. This way you'll always have a safe copy of your most recent financial records. The process of backing up and restoring a Quicken data file are the same, whether you are restoring the data file to the same computer or to a different computer.

Creating a Backup File

1. Open the Quicken **data file** that you want to back up. The data file will appear in the Quicken window.

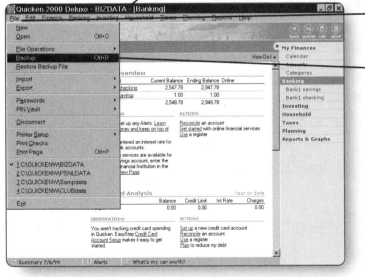

2. Click on **File**. The File menu will appear.

3. Click on **Backup**. A confirmation dialog box will open.

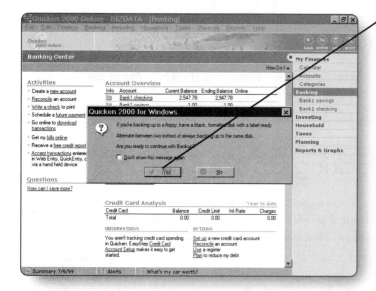

4. **Click** on **Yes**. The Select Backup Drive dialog box will open.

> **NOTE**
>
> Make sure that you have a blank, formatted backup media (such as a floppy disk, a tape backup, or a CD-ROM) in the drive to which you will copy the backup data file.

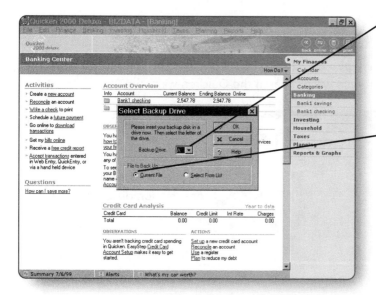

5. **Click** on the **Backup Drive down arrow** and **Click** on the **drive** to which you want to create the backup file. The drive letter will appear in the list box.

6. **Click** on the **Current File option button**, if it is not already selected. The option will be selected.

7. **Click** on **OK**. The information will be backed up to the drive you specified. When the backup is complete, a confirmation dialog box will appear.

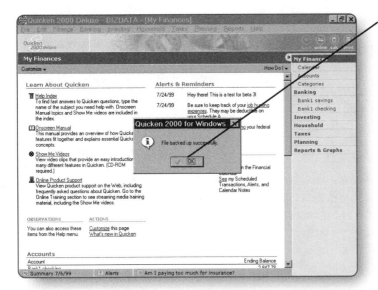

8. Click on **OK**. The data file will be backed up and you can remove the backup media from the drive.

Restoring Financial Data

1. Open Quicken on the computer to which you are going to copy the file. The Quicken window will appear.

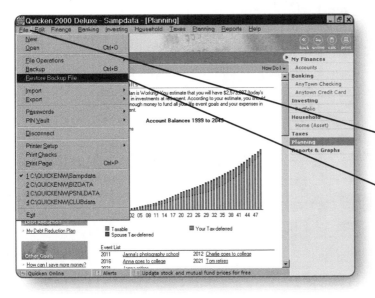

2. Place the **disk** that contains the backup file in the appropriate drive. This is the backup disk that you created in the last section.

3. Click on **File**. The File menu will appear.

4. Click on **Restore Backup File**. The Select Restore Drive dialog box will open.

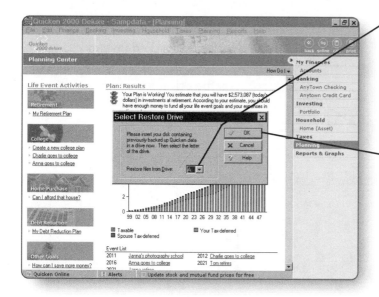

5. Click on the **Restore files from Drive down arrow** and **Click** on the **drive** where you placed the backup disk. The drive letter will appear in the list box.

6. Click on **OK**. The Restore Quicken File dialog box will open.

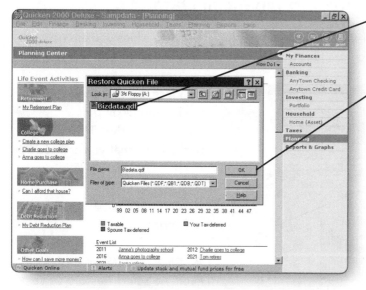

7. Click on the **data file** that you want to restore. The file will be selected.

8. Click on **OK**. A confirmation dialog box will open.

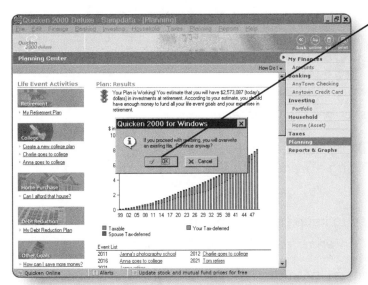

9. Click on **OK**. The data file will be restored on your computer and a confirmation dialog box will open.

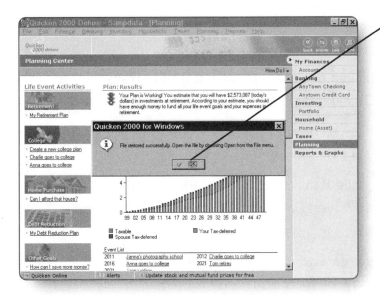

10. Click on **OK**. The restored data file will be loaded into the Quicken window.

Part II Review Questions

1. Name three ways in which you can open an account register. *See "Entering a Few Transactions" in Chapter 6*

2. How do you assign several categories of spending to one transaction? *See "Splitting a Transaction Between Categories" in Chapter 6*

3. What is the easiest way to keep track of your paycheck and related tax information? *See "Entering Your Paycheck" in Chapter 7*

4. Does Quicken have the ability to deal with adjustable rate mortgages? *See "Setting Up a Mortgage Account" in Chapter 8*

5. Which reports can help you keep track of your mortgage loan and mortgage payments? *See "Producing Mortgage Reports" in Chapter 8*

6. What feature does Quicken use to help make entering transactions quicker? *See "Using QuickFill to Enter Transactions" in Chapter 9*

7. How can you use Quicken to remind yourself when to pay your bills? *See "Scheduling Transactions" in Chapter 9*

8. What field in the Reconcile Bank Statement window tells you that an account is reconciled? *See "Balancing Checking and Savings Accounts" in Chapter 10*

9. Which reports can you create to help you find reconciliation problems? *See "Dealing with Reconciliation Problems" in Chapter 10*

10. Why is it important to backup your data files? *See "Backing Up Your Records" in Chapter 11*

PART III

Controlling Your Annual Finances

12

Planning for the Tax Man

No one likes to sit down at the end of the year and wade through endless mounds of receipts only to find out that money is owed. Make tax time a little less frustrating and let Quicken help you ease the burden of preparing your tax return. Quicken can keep track of income and deductions. In addition, Quicken contains some useful tools for estimating tax payments. You can print out a few reports to help you fill out your tax forms. In this chapter, you'll learn how to

- Prepare Quicken to track tax information
- Determine your allowable tax deductions
- Estimate your tax liability
- Prepare reports that you can use at tax time

Setting Up Quicken for Taxes

If you want Quicken to organize your transaction data, you'll need to spend some time making sure that each of your tax related categories is assigned to a tax form and line item.

Creating a Tax Profile

Before you dive into your taxes, take a minute to give Quicken a little information about yourself and your tax situation. Quicken will guide you through the information it needs.

1. **Click** on **Taxes**. The Taxes menu will appear.

2. **Click** on **Tax Profile**. The Review Your Tax Profile dialog box will open.

NOTE

You can also get to the Tax Profile from the Taxes Center. Just click on the Review my tax profile link in the Activities section.

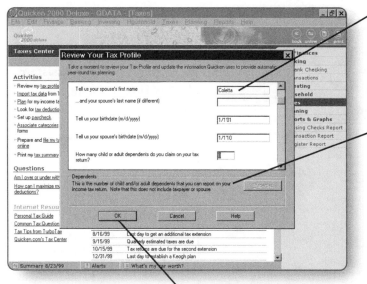

3. Click in the **text box** next to each question and **type** a **response**.

NOTE

Some questions will display additional information in the lower section of the dialog box. This can give you a hint as to the information that you should enter.

4. Click on **OK** when you have answered all the questions. The Review Your Tax Profile dialog box will close.

Assigning a Tax Form Line Item to a Category

A number of categories are already set up so that amounts recorded in a category are assigned to a tax form and to a line item on that tax form. If you have added new categories, or if a category is not assigned to a tax form, you can easily tell Quicken which tax form to use for a category. You can also obtain help deciding on an appropriate tax form. It's time to retain the services of the Tax Link Assistant.

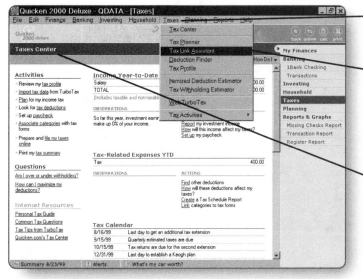

1. Click on **Taxes**. The Taxes menu will appear.

2. Click on **Tax Link Assistant**. The Tax Link Assistant will appear.

NOTE

The Taxes Center is a great place to see your tax situation at a glance, keep track of due dates on taxes, find tax related information on the Web, and find help with tax problems.

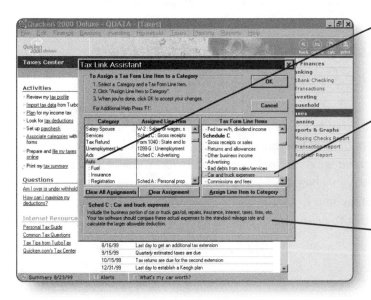

3. Click on a **category** in the Category list to which you want to assign a tax form. The category will be selected.

4. Click on the **tax form** and **line item** in the Tax Form Line Items list that you want to apply to the category. The tax form and line item will be selected.

5. Read the **description** of the type of income or expenditures that can be reported on the tax form to determine if the transactions you recorded in the category qualify.

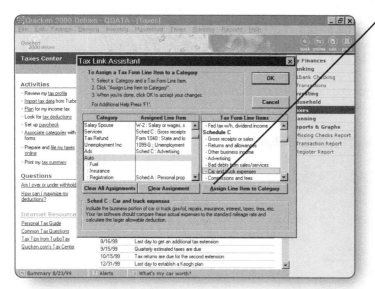

6. Click on the **Assign Line Item to Category button**. The tax form and line item will be assigned to the category.

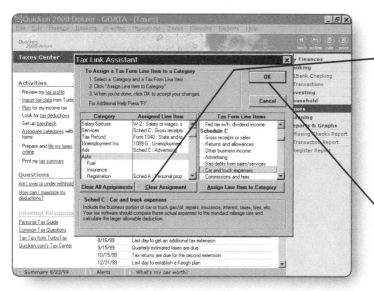

TIP

You can remove a tax form assignment from a category. Click on the category and then click on the Clear Assignment button.

7. Click on **OK**. The tax form changes will be applied to the category items.

Letting Quicken Help You Find Deductions

If you're not quite certain about all this tax deduction stuff, you can go to another place to get more information before

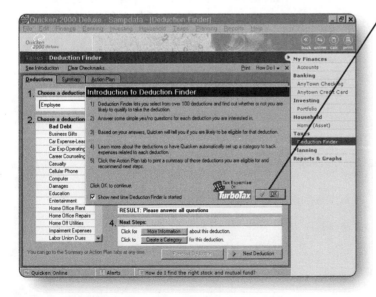

you begin assigning tax forms to categories. The Deduction Finder is a great tool for reviewing the available deductions and helping you determine if you qualify for the deduction.

1. Click on **Taxes**. The Taxes menu will appear.

2. Click on **Deduction Finder**. The Deduction Finder will open in the Taxes window and the Introduction to Deduction Finder dialog box will open.

3. Click on **OK**. You can begin working with the Deduction Finder.

4. Click on the **Choose a deduction type down arrow** and **click** on the **type of deduction** for which you are searching. The deduction type will appear in the list box and the list of available deductions for that type will appear in the Choose a deduction list box.

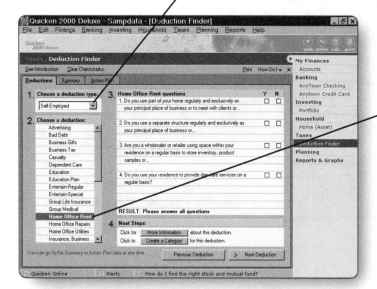

5. Click on the **deduction** for which you want to determine if you are eligible. The deduction will be selected and a list of questions will appear that can help you decide if you qualify for the deduction.

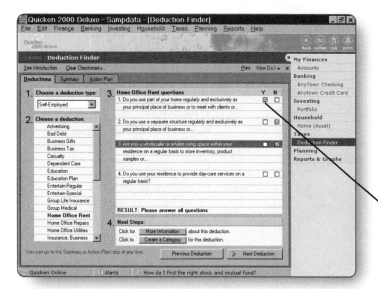

NOTE

You may also want to consult a tax specialist. A tax specialist can make sure that you have set up your categories and tax deductions properly.

6. Click in the **Y or N check box** to answer yes or no to each question. A check mark will appear in the check box.

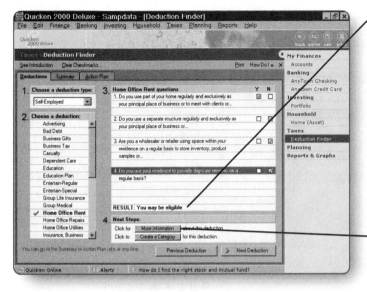

After you answer all the questions, the RESULT line will tell you whether or not you can take the deduction. If you qualify for a deduction, you'll want to know more about the deduction and how Quicken handles it. You'll also need to make sure that you have the appropriate categories set up for the tax deduction.

7. Click on the **More Information button**. A More Information dialog box will open.

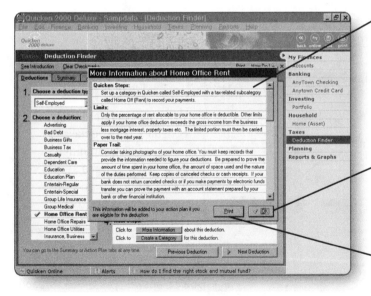

The More Information dialog box tells you how Quicken will handle the tax category, deduction limits, paperwork requirements, the tax form used, and other information that is pertinent to the deduction.

8. Click on **OK**. You will return to the Deduction Finder.

TIP

Keep a copy of this information by clicking on the Print button.

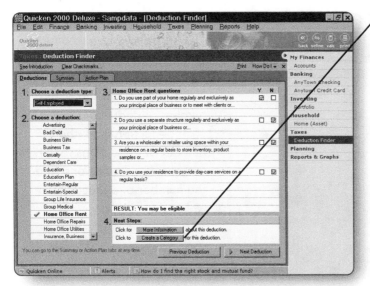

9. **Click** on the **Create a Category button**. The Create a category dialog box will open.

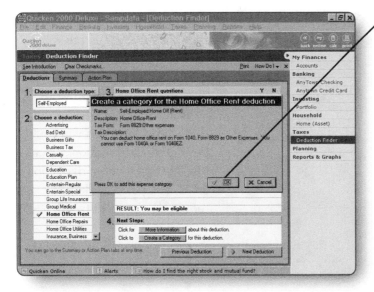

10. **Click** on **OK**. You will return to the Deduction Finder.

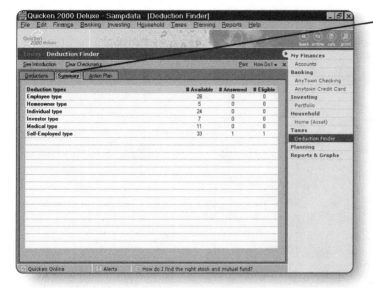

11. Click on the **Summary tab**. The Summary tab will come to the top of the stack.

The Summary tab shows the number of deductions listed for each deduction type, the number of deductions for which you answered questions, and the number of deductions for which you qualify.

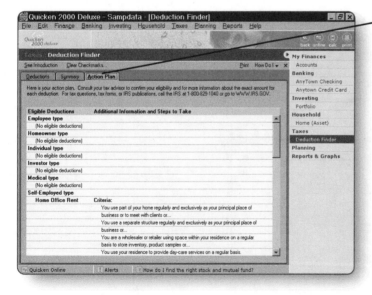

12. Click on the **Action Plan tab**. The Action Plan tab will move to the top of the stack.

The Action Plan tab provides information about each of the deductions for which you could be eligible. Information such as qualification criteria, deduction limits, and paperwork requirements are detailed.

Estimating Your Tax Burden

Quicken provides excellent aids for determining how much you owe in taxes for a given tax period. You'll need to know how much money to set aside for tax payments. Even though the information provided by Quicken is very good, you may want to take your tax information to a tax preparation specialist or use a tax preparation software program such as Intuit's TurboTax.

Finding the Tax Planner

An easy way to determine what you'll owe in taxes is to consult the Tax Planner. The Tax Planner takes the tax information from your Quicken data file and estimates the amount of taxes you owe or your tax refund. You can also use the Tax Planner to play some "What if?" scenarios and see how it affects your tax situation.

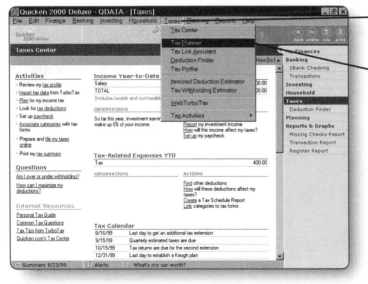

1. Click on **Taxes**. The Taxes menu will appear.

2. Click on **Tax Planner**. The Quicken Tax Planner will appear in the Taxes window.

NOTE

You can also find the Tax Planner by clicking on the Plan for my income tax activity in the Taxes Center.

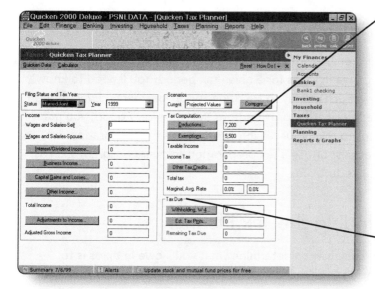

When the Tax Planner first opens, the totals from categories that are assigned to a tax form and line item will appear in the appropriate income and deduction fields. This Tax Planner takes into account the information you entered in the Tax Profile.

NOTE

Look in the Tax Due section to see if you may owe any taxes, or if you may be due a refund.

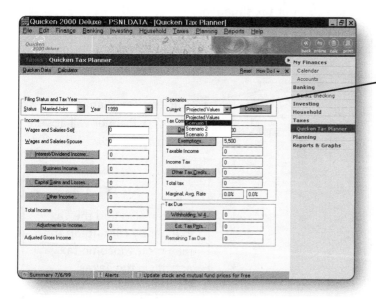

Making Forecasts with the Tax Planner

1. Click on the **Current down arrow** and **click** on a **selection**. The QTax dialog box will open.

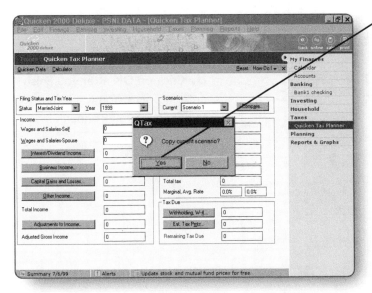

2. Click on **Yes**. A new scenario will be created, based on your actual tax figures, for you to try out different tax situations.

3. Click on the **Status down arrow** and **click** on the **tax filing status** that you want to use for the scenario from the drop-down list. The filing status will appear in the list box.

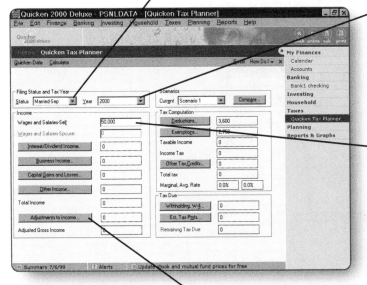

4. Click on the **Year down arrow** and **click** on the **year** for which you want to create the tax scenario from the drop-down list. The year will appear in the list box.

5. Click in the **text boxes** and **type** the **amounts** that you estimate will need to be declared on your tax return. As you move from field to field, notice that the amounts in the Tax Due section will change.

6. Click on any **button**. A dialog box will open in which you can enter amounts for the different types of income or deductions that are grouped together.

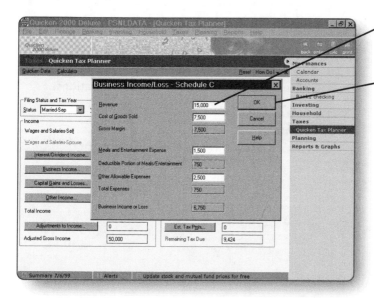

7. **Click** in any **text box** and **type** an **amount**.

8. **Click** on **OK** after you finish entering data. You will return to the Quicken Tax Planner.

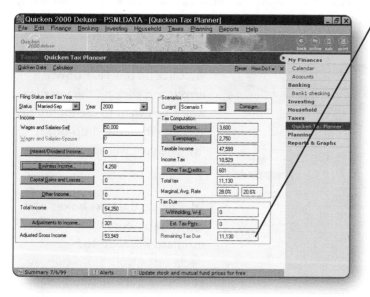

Notice that the amounts have been adjusted.

Comparing Different Tax Scenarios

If you want a closer look at the difference between your actual tax situation and any created scenarios, click on the Compare button.

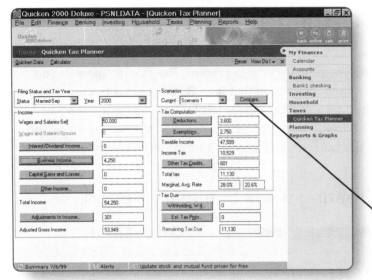

1. Click on the **Compare button**. The Tax Scenario Comparisons dialog box will open.

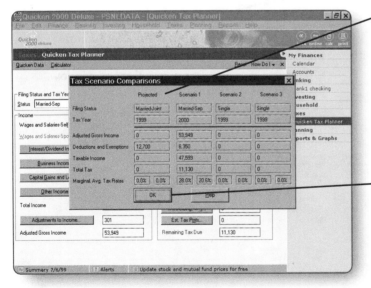

The Projected column shows your actual tax estimate based on the transactions you recorded in Quicken. The Scenario columns show the different scenarios that you created. Which scenario puts you at the best tax advantage?

2. Click on **OK**. The Tax Scenario Comparisons dialog box will close and you will return to the Quicken Tax Planner.

Creating Tax Reports

The Tax Summary Report and the Tax Schedule Report can help you prepare your tax return. The Tax Summary Report lists each transaction that is assigned to a tax related category and shows the totals for each category. The Tax Schedule Report lists each tax related transaction according to the tax form and the line item in which it belongs.

Creating a Tax Summary Report

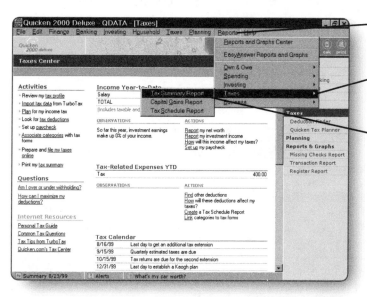

1. Click on **Reports**. The Reports menu will appear.

2. Move the **mouse pointer** to Taxes. A submenu will appear.

3. Click on **Tax Summary Report**. The Tax Summary Report will appear in the Reports & Graphs window.

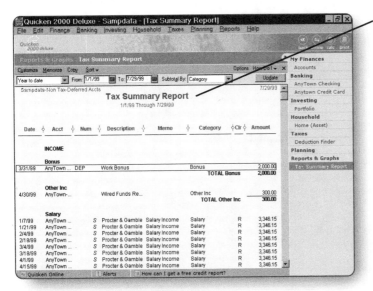

You'll find tax related information from all of your accounts in the report. Tax related transactions are grouped by category. There is a subtotal for each category.

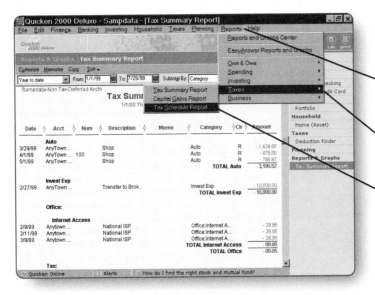

Displaying the Tax Schedule Report

1. Click on **Reports**. The Reports menu will appear.

2. Move the **mouse pointer** to Taxes. A submenu will appear.

3. Click on **Tax Schedule Report**. The Tax Schedule Report will appear in the Report & Graphs window.

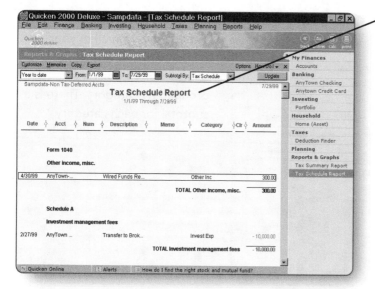

The Tax Schedule Report organizes your tax related transaction by tax form and line item. Each line item is subtotaled.

13

Preparing for a New Year

Before you close out your books for the old year, take some time and run a few reports. These reports can show you how well you managed your finances for the past year. Just as it is important to keep a backup of your Quicken data file, it's also a good idea to keep a paper copy of your financial picture. You'll then need to do some file maintenance to your data file so that Quicken can start the new year on the right foot. You'll want to create a separate archive of the past year's financial records. And, you'll want to store this in a safe place, away from fire and theft. In this chapter, you'll learn how to:

- Set up a printer to print reports
- Create year-end financial reports
- Archive a year-end data file and prepare a data file for the new year

Producing Year-End Reports

You can produce several reports to take a look at your financial picture for the past year. It's a good idea to print a copy of these reports so that you can file them away with your tax returns and other important financial information.

Setting Up Your Printer

Before you begin creating reports, take some time to set up your printer so that printed reports have the look that you like.

1. **Click** on **File**. The File menu will appear.

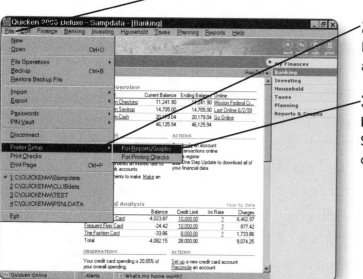

2. **Move** the **mouse pointer** to Printer Setup. A submenu will appear.

3. **Click** on **For Reports/Graphs**. The Printer Setup for Reports and Graphs dialog box will appear.

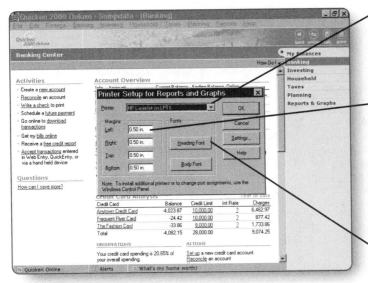

4. **Click** on the **Printer down arrow** and **click** on the **printer** that you want to use. The printer will appear in the list box.

5. **Click** in each of the **Margins text boxes.**

6. **Type** the **margin space** that you want to appear between the report edges and the paper edges.

7. **Click** on the **Heading Font button** and/or the **Body Font button** if you want to change the font style used to print the report. The Select Font dialog box will open.

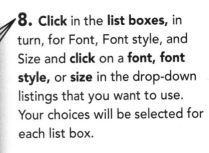

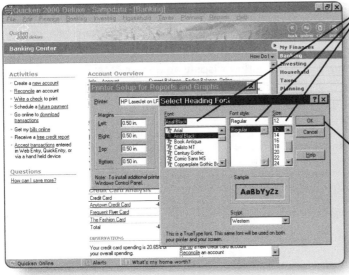

8. **Click** in the **list boxes,** in turn, for Font, Font style, and Size and **click** on a **font, font style,** or **size** in the drop-down listings that you want to use. Your choices will be selected for each list box.

9. **Click** on **OK**. You will return to the Printer Setup for Reports and Graphs dialog box.

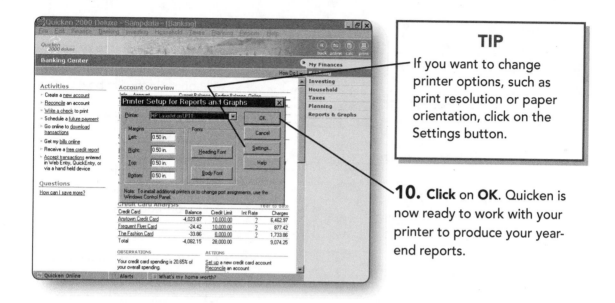

TIP

If you want to change printer options, such as print resolution or paper orientation, click on the Settings button.

10. Click on **OK**. Quicken is now ready to work with your printer to produce your year-end reports.

Creating a Summary Report

The Summary Report shows you the total of your income and the total of your expenses. Your income and expenses are broken into categories showing the total recorded in each category. It does not list the individual transactions in the category. You can either display an annual total for each category, or you can break up the categories into time periods, such as months or quarters.

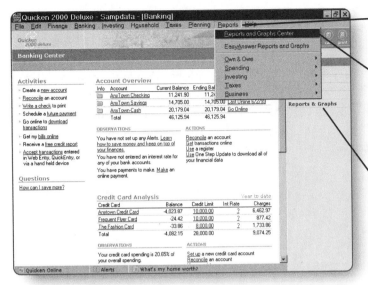

1. Click on **Reports**. The Reports menu will appear.

2. Click on **Reports and Graphs Center**. The Reports and Graphs Center window will appear.

NOTE

You can also click on the Reports & Graphs QuickTab, if it is available.

---

3. Click on the **How am I spending my money? tab**. The list of reports that will answer that question will appear.

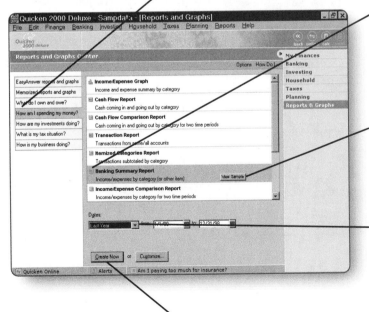

4. Click on **Banking Summary Report**. The report will be selected.

NOTE

Click on the View Sample button if you want to see a miniature example of the report.

---

5. Click on the **Dates down arrow** and **click** on **the desired date** from the drop-down list. The date you choose will appear in the list box.

6. Click on the **Create Now button**. The Summary Report will appear.

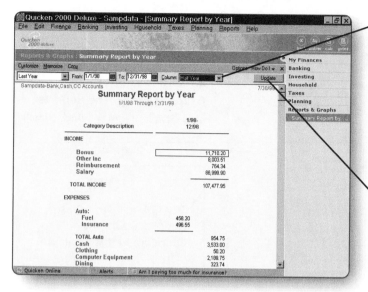

7. **Click** on the **Column down arrow** and **click** on a **time period** if you want the information in the report to be broken into time periods and then totaled for the entire year. The time period will appear in the list box.

8. **Click** on the **Update button**. The report will be updated.

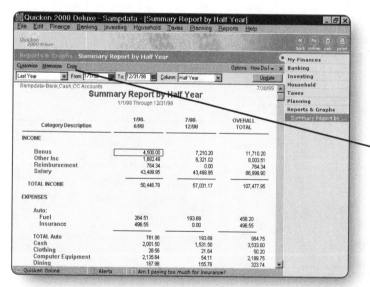

The reports, which are first organized by categories, are then displayed according to the time period that you selected.

TIP

Click on the Copy button to place a copy of the report on the Windows Clipboard.

Determining Your Cash Flow

The Cash Flow Report first shows your income for the year, broken down by category, and then your expenses for the year, which are also broken down by category.

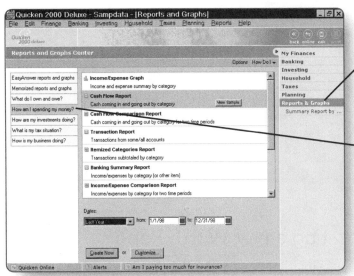
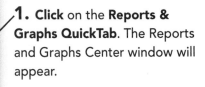

1. **Click** on the **Reports & Graphs QuickTab**. The Reports and Graphs Center window will appear.

2. **Click** on the **How am I spending my money? tab**. The list of questions that answer the question will appear.

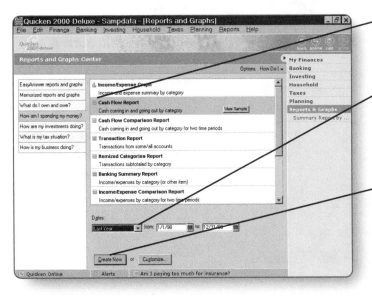

3. **Click** on **Cash Flow Report**. The Cash Flow Report will be selected.

4. **Click** on the **Dates down arrow** and **click** on **Last Year**. The Last Year option will appear in the list box.

5. **Click** on the **Create Now button**. The Cash Flow Report will appear.

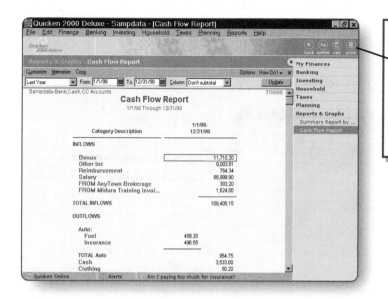

TIP

To print a copy of a report, display the report in the Reports & Graphs window and click on the Print button.

Creating a Net Worth Report

The Net Worth Report takes those items that you own and claim as assets and subtracts what you owe in loans and other bills, and computes your worth in dollars.

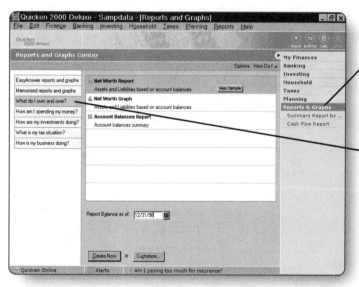

1. **Click** on the **Reports & Graphs QuickTab**. The Reports and Graphs Center window will appear.

2. **Click** on the **What do I own and owe? tab**. The list of questions that answer the question will appear.

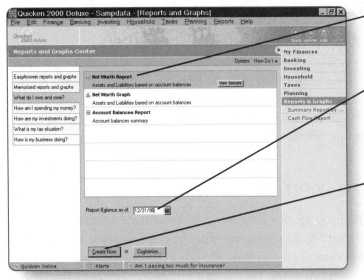

3. **Click** on **Net Worth Report**. The Net Worth Report will be selected.

4. **Click** in the **Report Balance as of text box** and **type** the **date** of the last day of the previous year.

5. **Click** on the **Create Now button**. The Net Worth Report will appear in the Reports & Graphs window.

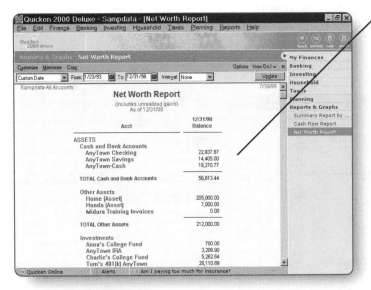

In bookkeeping terms, the Net Worth Report is the same as a balance sheet. You'll first see each of your assets listed with a total for the entire list of assets. You'll then see all your liabilities (or debts and loans) with their respective amounts. At the bottom of the report, you'll find your net worth.

Performing Year-End File Maintenance

Quicken offers two methods to close out your data file at the end of the year. It is recommended that you use the archival method unless your Quicken data file has become quite large. If it has, create a new file.

Archiving Your Files

When you archive data files, you copy the previous year's transactions to a separate file. You can then keep this file in a safe place. By doing this, you keep the previous year's transactions in the file you use for the current year. The advantage to this is that you can use the previous year's information when you run reports and create budgets and forecasts. The disadvantage is that your Quicken data file may become large and difficult to back up.

1. **Click** on **File**. The File menu will appear.

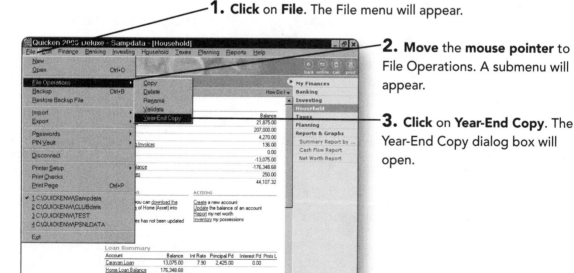

2. **Move** the **mouse pointer** to File Operations. A submenu will appear.

3. **Click** on **Year-End Copy**. The Year-End Copy dialog box will open.

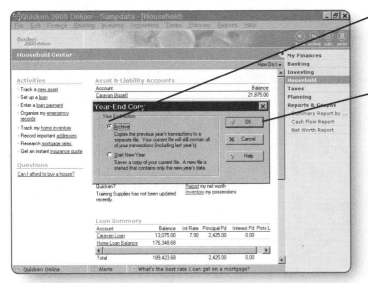

4. Click on the **Archive option button**, if it is not already selected.

5. Click on **OK**. The Archive File dialog box will open.

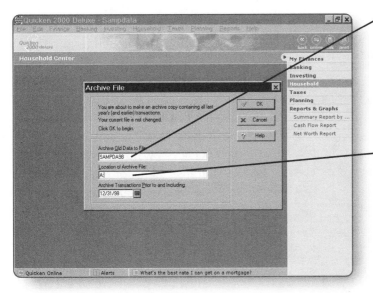

6. Click in the **text area** for the Archive Old Data to File text box and **type** a **file name** for the file that will contain the past year's transaction. You could also use the default file name.

7. Click in the **text area** for the Location of Archive File text box and **type** the **drive** and **directory** where you want to store the archived file, if you do not want to use the default directory location.

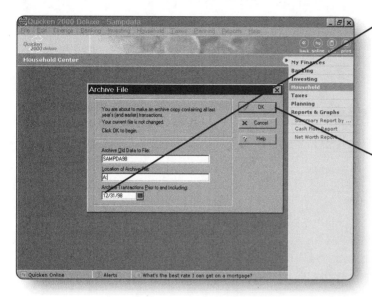

8. **Click** in the **text area** for the Archive Transactions Prior to and Including text box and **type** the **ending date** of the transactions that you want to archive.

9. **Click** on **OK**. The Archive process will start and the File Copied Successfully dialog box will open when the process has completed.

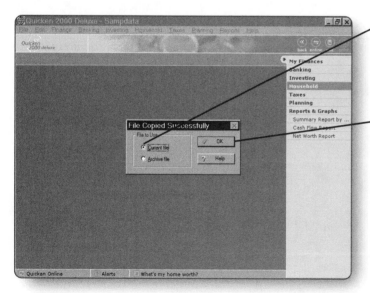

10. **Click** on the **Current file option button**, if it is not already selected. The option will be selected.

11. **Click** on **OK**. The original data file will appear in the Quicken window and all of your transactions for the prior year will still appear in the registers.

TIP

Protect the archived file with a password to ensure that no changes are made to it. See Chapter 11, "Protecting Your Financial Records," if you need help.

Setting Up a New File

By setting up a new file in which to keep your financial records for the new year, you only keep those transactions that are not reconciled in the previous year. The advantage is a smaller file size. The disadvantage is that you will not be able to compare your income and spending from previous years to the current year.

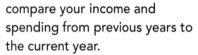

1. Click on **File**. The File menu will appear.

2. Move the **mouse pointer** to File Operations. A submenu will appear.

3. Click on **Year-End Copy**. The Year-End Copy dialog box will open.

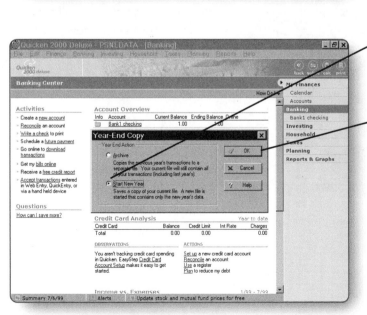

4. Click on the **Start New Year option button**. The option will be selected.

5. Click on **OK**. The Start New Year dialog box will open.

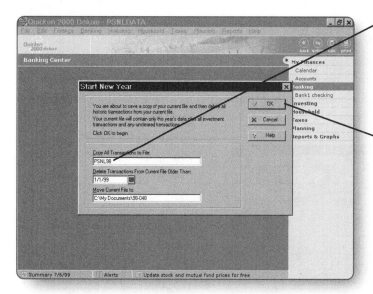

6. **Click** in the **Copy All Transactions to File text box** and **type** a **file name** for the file into which you want to place all the prior year's transactions.

7. **Click** on **OK**. The transactions for the prior year will be archived and the File Copied Successfully dialog box will open.

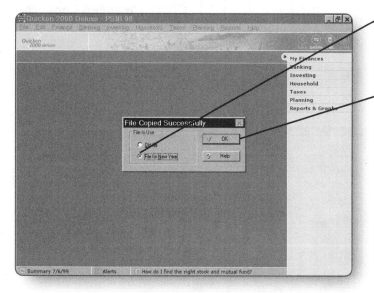

8. **Click** on the **File for New Year option button**, if it is not already selected.

9. **Click** on **OK**. You will return to the Quicken window.

14

Viewing Your Spending Habits

Quicken contains many reports that you can use to quickly calculate where your money is going. By looking at your spending habits, you can see places where you can reduce your spending or better manage your money. This is a first step toward saving money and planning for major purchases, such as a car or home. After you've created a few reports, you can customize the reports to display specific information. In this chapter, you'll learn how to:

- Create some quick and snappy spending reports
- View a few complex spending reports
- Customize reports and graphs

Creating Quick Reports

You can use two quick ways to find out where your money is going; however, they won't give you much detail.

Graphing Your Spending

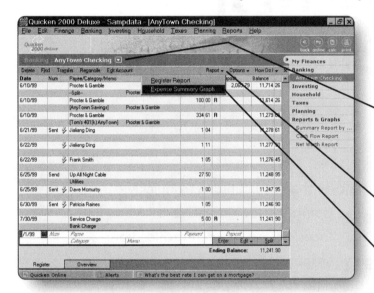

A simple pie chart is a quick way to graph your spending. You can create one that shows your top five spending categories.

1. Display the **account register** for which you want to view your spending. The register account window will appear.

2. Click on **Report**. A menu will appear.

3. Click on **Expense Summary Graph**. The Expense Summary window will appear.

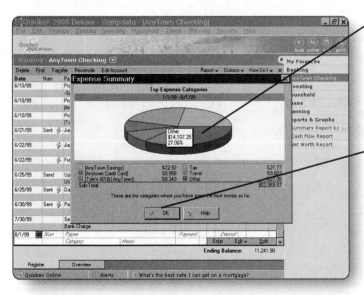

4. Hold the **mouse pointer** over an area of the pie chart. The name of the category, the dollar amount spent, and the percentage of total spending will appear in a ToolTip.

5. Click on **OK**. The Expense Summary window will close.

Using EasyAnswer Reports

If you'd like a little more information about your spending, but don't want to spend a lot of time looking for it, consult with the EasyAnswer Reports.

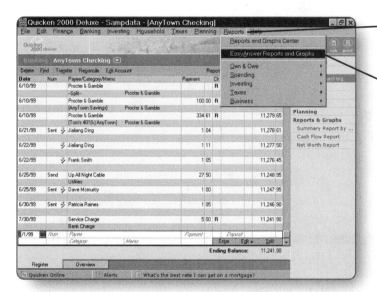

1. Click on **Reports**. The Reports menu will appear.

2. Click on **EasyAnswer Reports and Graphs**. The Reports and Graphs Center will appear.

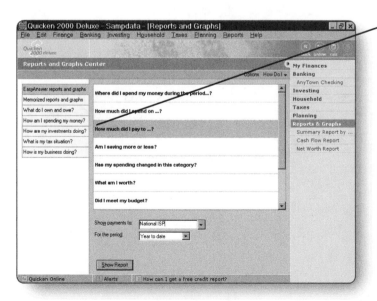

3. Click on a **question**. The question will be selected and the options shown below the list of questions will change depending on the question selected.

NOTE

The first five questions provide information about your spending habits.

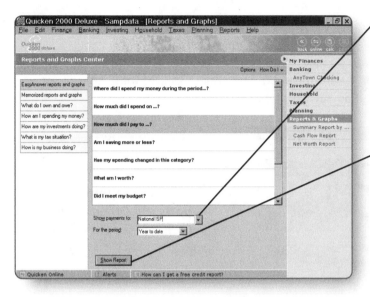

4. **Click** on the **down arrow** next to each list box and **click** on the **option** that will provide information to meet your needs. The option will appear in the list box.

5. **Click** on **Show Report**. The report will appear in the Reports & Graphs window.

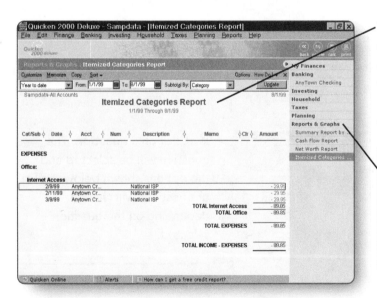

The report displays using the default options. You can further customize this and all other reports that you create. You'll learn how to do this later in the chapter.

NOTE

To get back to the EasyAnswer reports, click on the Reports & Graphs QuickTab.

Tracking Your Cash Flow

Quicken provides a number of reports and graphs that show the sources of your income and how you spend it. These reports and graphs can help you keep track of your spending and aid you in building a budget and savings plan.

Creating an Account Balances Report

Before you look at your income sources and where you spent your money, you should find out the values of the checking, savings, mortgage, and other accounts that you set up in Quicken.

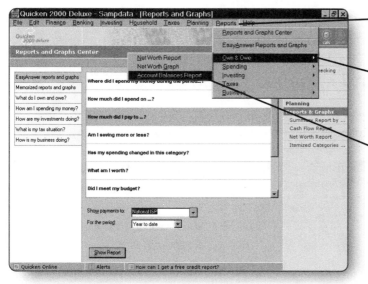

1. Click on **Reports**. The Reports menu will appear.

2. Move the **mouse pointer** to Own & Owe. A submenu will appear.

3. Click on **Account Balances Report**. The Account Balances Report will appear in the Reports & Graphs Window.

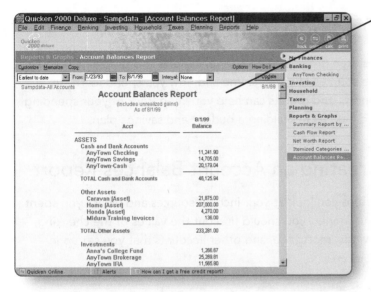

The Account Balances Report lists all accounts that you set up in the data file. The first accounts that are listed are your cash accounts, followed by personal assets, investments, and then your liabilities, such as credit cards and mortgages.

Producing an Income and Expense Graph

If you want a visual representation of your income and expenses, there's a quick graph that you can display.

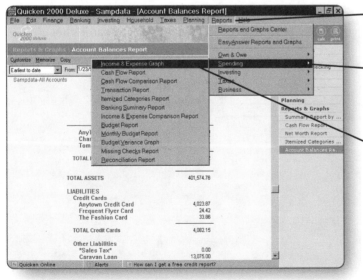

1. **Click** on **Reports**. The Reports menu will appear.

2. **Move** the **mouse pointer** to Spending. A submenu will appear.

3. **Click** on **Income & Expense Graph**. The Income and Expense Graph will appear in the Reports & Graphs window.

Bar chart. This chart compares your monthly income and monthly expenses over time. Hold the mouse pointer over an element in the chart to display a ToolTip that describes the category and the dollar amount.

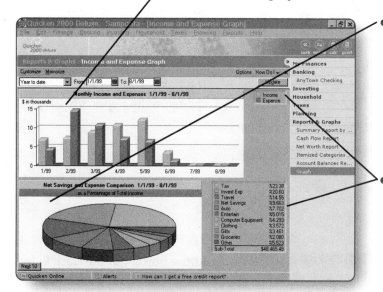

Pie chart. This chart shows your total income divided into the amounts spent for each of your expenses. This chart only shows 10 categories. Click on the Next 10 button to see the rest of your category items.

Legend. The legend at the right of each chart shows the colors that represent categories. You'll find other information about the category in the legend.

Creating a Cash Flow Report

Now that you've seen a few overview pictures of your spending, it's time to create a Cash Flow Report. A Cash Flow Report shows your money coming in and then shows it going out the door.

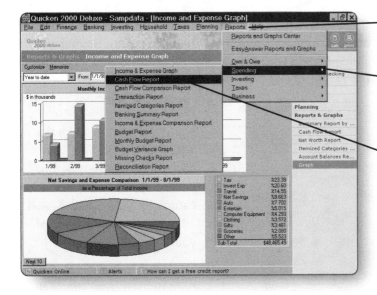

1. Click on **Reports**. The Reports menu will appear.

2. Move the **mouse pointer** to Spending. A submenu will appear.

3. Click on **Cash Flow Report**. The Cash Flow Report will appear in the Reports & Graphs window.

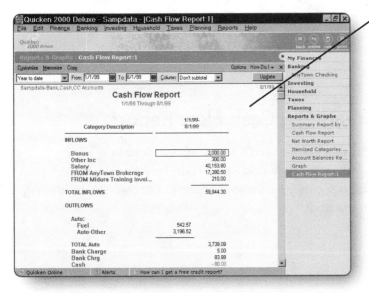

At the bottom of the Cash Flow Report, you'll see how much money you should have been able to save during the time period covered by the report.

Building a Cash Flow Comparison Report

Create a Comparison Report if you want to see how your spending compares for different time periods (for example, this year and last year, or this month and last month).

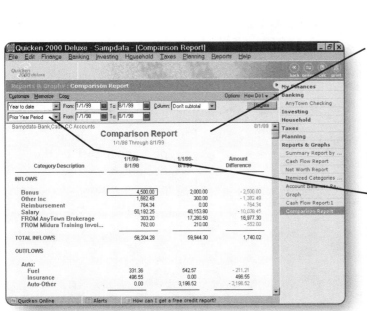

1. Click on **Reports**. The Report menu will appear.

2. Move the **mouse pointer** to Spending. A submenu will appear.

3. Click on **Cash Flow Comparison Report**. The Comparison Report will appear in the Reports & Graphs window.

By default, the Comparison Report lists the cash flow summary for each year that is contained in your Quicken data file.

TIP

You can change the periods that are used for comparison by selecting date options from the drop-down lists.

Itemizing Spending Categories

A Cash Flow Report can also provide details of each transaction in the income and expense categories.

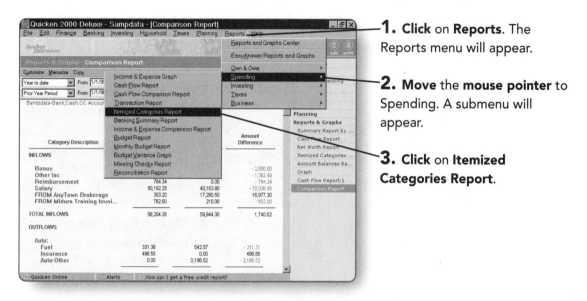

1. Click on **Reports**. The Reports menu will appear.

2. Move the **mouse pointer** to Spending. A submenu will appear.

3. Click on **Itemized Categories Report**.

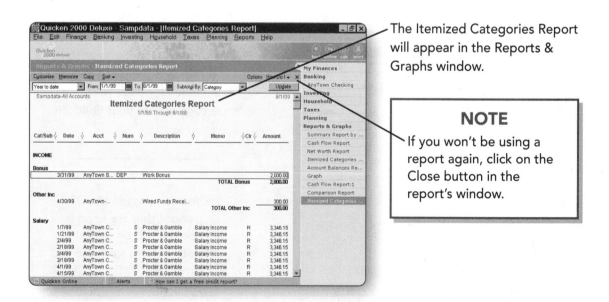

The Itemized Categories Report will appear in the Reports & Graphs window.

NOTE

If you won't be using a report again, click on the Close button in the report's window.

Getting More from Graphs

Earlier in the chapter, you learned how to create a couple of graphs that displayed the Quicken default options. You can easily change the information that displays in a graph.

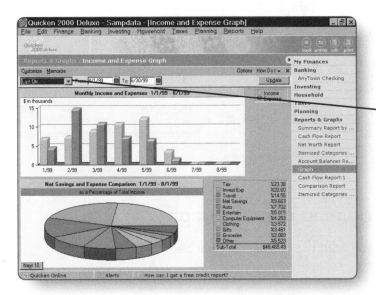

Changing the Time Period Used by the Graph

1. **Click** on the **Dates down arrow** and **click** on the **date range** that you want to show in the graph. The dates in the From and To text boxes will change. If you want to make changes to these dates, follow steps 2 and 3.

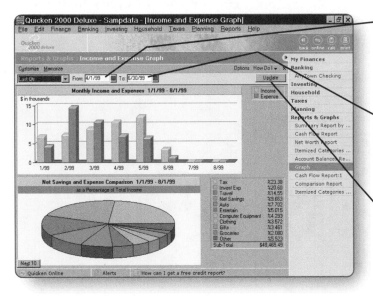

2. **Click** in the **From text box.** and **type** the **beginning date** of the transactions you want to include in the graph.

3. **Click** in the **To text box** and **type** the **ending date** of the transactions that you want in the graph.

4. **Click** on the **Update button**. The information in the charts will be updated.

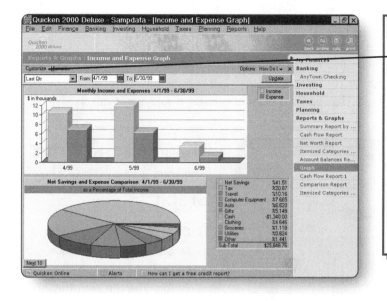

Zooming in on a Graph

If you want to see a section of a pie or bar chart in more detail, zoom in on that part of the graph.

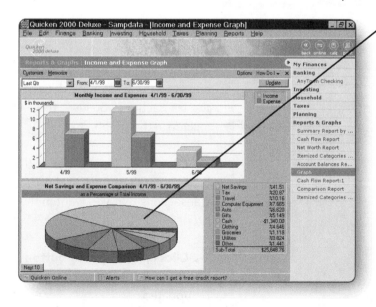

1. **Double-click** on an **area** of the chart that you want to see in more detail. A QuickZoom Graph will appear.

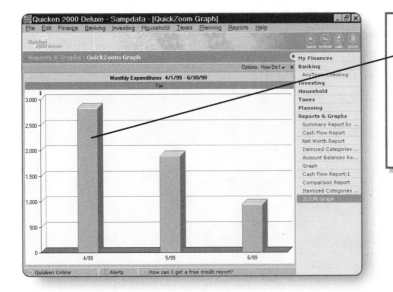

TIP

Double-click on an element in the chart to see a detailed list of the transactions included in the category for the selected time period.

Detailing Your Reports

After looking over a few of these reports, you may decide that they don't contain the information that you need. You may want to change the range of dates used by the report, or you may not want to include all the categories. You can change anything you want. And, you can change it for all reports that you create, or just for an individual report.

Changing the Default Report Options

To change the way information appears in all your future reports, you need to change the default report options.

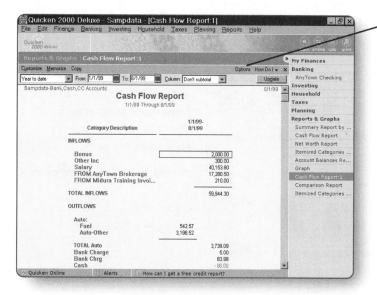

1. Click on **Options**. The Report and Graph Options dialog box will open.

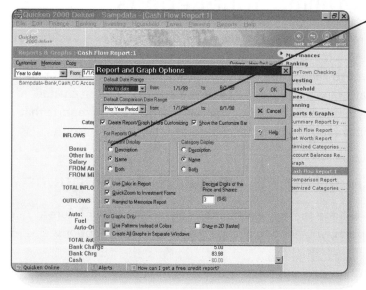

2. Click on those **options** that you want to change for future reports. The options will be selected.

3. Click on **OK**. The default options will be changed.

Customizing a Report

When you want to change the information in a single report, you'll need to customize that report. You can change the date range, the accounts used in the report, and the categories to be used. To begin, display the report that you want to change in the Reports & Graphs window.

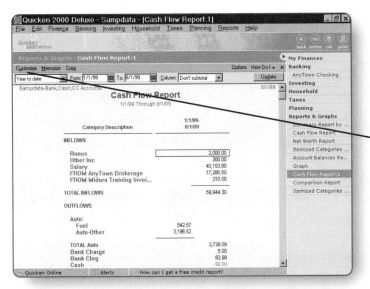

1. **Click** on **Customize**. The Customize Report dialog box will open and the Display tab should be on top.

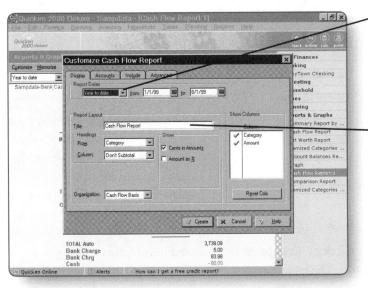

2. **Click** on the **Report Dates down arrow** and **click** on the **date range** that you want to use for the report. The date range will be selected.

3. **Click** in the **Title text box** and **type** a **different title** for the report.

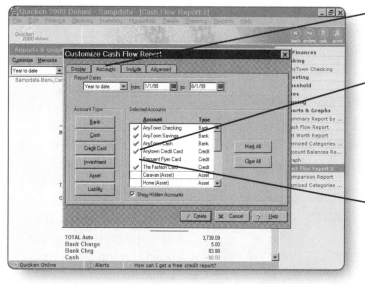

4. Click on the **Accounts tab**. The Accounts tab will come to the top of the stack.

- If an account is preceded by a check mark, the account is included in the report. To remove the account, click on the account and the check mark will disappear.

- If an account is preceded by a blank space, the account is not included in the report. To include the account in the report, click on the account and a check mark will appear.

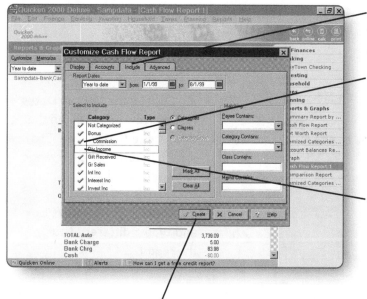

5. Click on the **Include tab**. The Include tab will come to the top of the stack.

- If a category is preceded by a check mark, the category is included in the report. To remove the category, click on the category and the check mark will disappear.

- If a category is preceded by a blank space, the category is not included in the report. To include the category in the report, click on the category and a check mark will appear.

6. Click on **Create** when you are finished customizing the graph. The new, customized report will appear in the Reports & Graphs window.

Saving Reports for Future Use

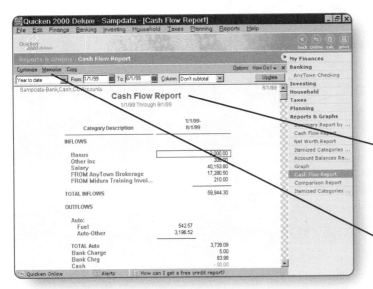

You may have created a custom report that you want to use over and over again. You'll want to memorize the report. There are several ways you can recall the report for future use.

1. Display the **report** that you want to save for future use. The report will appear in the Reports & Graphs window.

2. Click on **Memorize**. The Memorize Report dialog box will open.

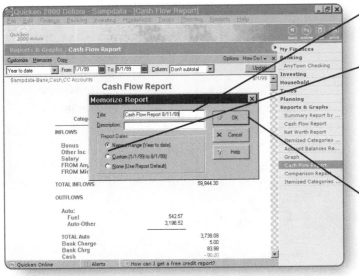

3. Click in the **Title text box** and **type** a **title** for the report.

4. Click on an **option button** in the Report Dates section to select the dates that will be contained in the memorized report. The option will be selected.

5. Click on **OK**. The report will be memorized.

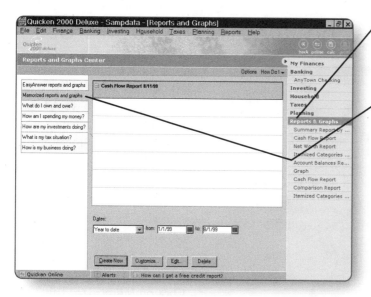

6. Click on the **Reports & Graphs QuickTab**. The Report and Graphs Center will appear.

7. Click on **Memorized reports and graphs**. You should see your memorized report in the list.

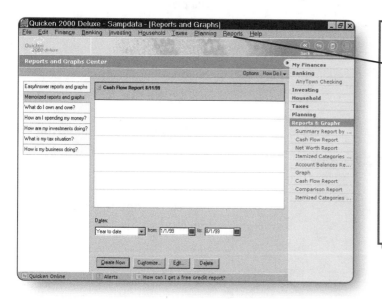

NOTE

You can also find the memorized report in the Reports menu. Open the Reports menu and move the mouse pointer to Memorized Reports and Graphs. A submenu will appear that contains all the reports that you've memorized.

15

Creating an Annual Budget

If you feel that you need to get a handle on your spending habits, your first step is to create a budget; a budget can help you limit what you spend on various items. Quicken makes it easy to create a budget—you can even use data that you've already entered in Quicken to get started. After you get some preliminary figures entered, you can adjust the numbers so that you are spending the desired amount. After you put together a budget, you'll need to monitor your progress; Quicken can help warn you when you're getting dangerously close to going over budget. In this chapter, you'll learn how to:

- Create a fast and easy budget to fit your needs
- Warn yourself before you exceed budget goals
- Watch your progress toward meeting budget goals

Getting Started

Quicken contains an easy-to-use feature that helps you create and maintain a budget. You can elect to start your budget from scratch, or you can use data from transactions you've already entered into Quicken.

Building a Basic Budget

Your first step in building a budget is to add some preliminary numbers to the budget and determine which categories you want to track.

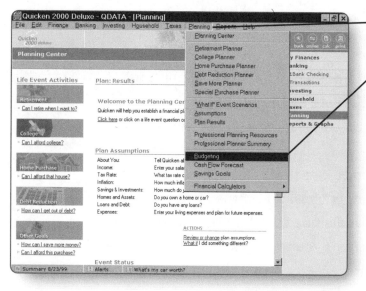

1. Click on **Planning**. The Planning menu will appear.

2. Click on **Budgeting**. The Budget will appear in the Planning window. The budget numbers that appear may or may not be the numbers with which you want to start.

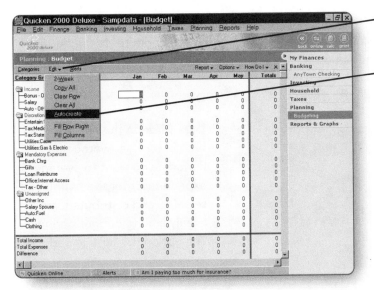

3. Click on **Edit**. A menu will appear.

4. Click on **Autocreate**. The Automatically Create Budget dialog box will appear.

5. Click in the **From text box** and **type** the **beginning date** of the transactions that you want to include in the budget.

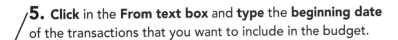

6. Click in the **To text box** and **type** the **ending date** of the transactions that you want to include in the budget.

7. Click on the **Round Values to Nearest down arrow** and **click** on the **value** to which you want numbers rounded. The value will appear in the list box.

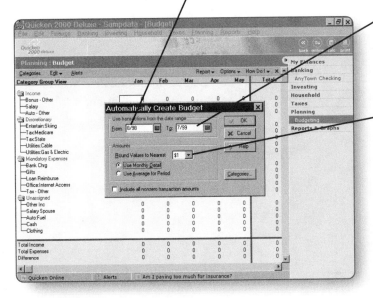

8a. **Click** on the **option button** for Use Monthly Detail if you want to use your actual monthly expenditures in the budget. The option will be selected.

OR

8b. **Click** on the **option button** for Use Average for Period if you want to average expenditures for the period you selected and distribute them evenly among budget periods. The option will be selected.

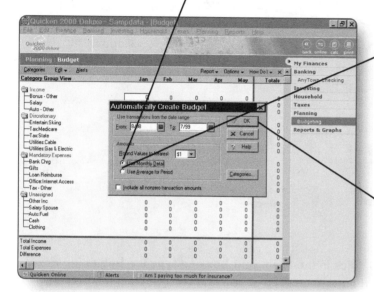

9. **Click** on **OK**. You will return to the budget.

You can change the categories that appear in the budget.

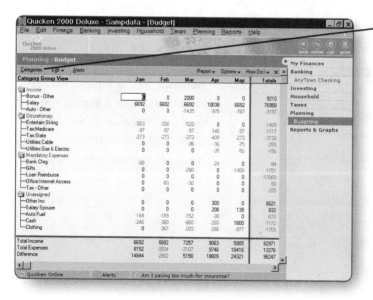

10. **Click** on **Categories**. The Select Categories to Include dialog box will open.

11. Click on a **category** that has a check mark to the left of the category name. The check mark will be cleared and the category will not be included in the budget.

12. Click on a **category** that has a blank space to the left of the category name. A check mark will appear in the space and the category will be included in the budget.

13. Click on **OK**. The budget will be updated and will show only those categories that you selected. You're ready to begin adjusting the budget numbers.

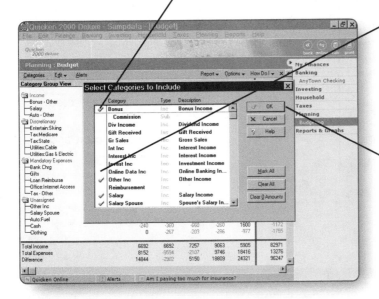

Editing Budget Amounts

Your budget now contains some starting budget numbers, which are based on a selected period of past transactions and contains only those categories that you selected. You can further adjust these numbers, if needed.

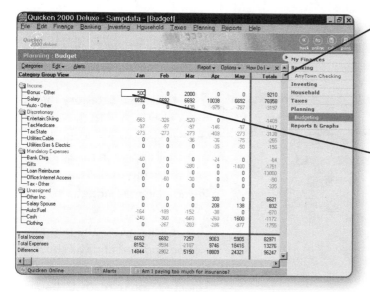

1. Click and **drag** the **scroll bars** to display the category and month for which you want to change a budget amount. A different area of the budget window will appear.

2. Click on an **amount field**. The amount will be selected.

3. Type a new **amount** and **press** the **Enter key**.

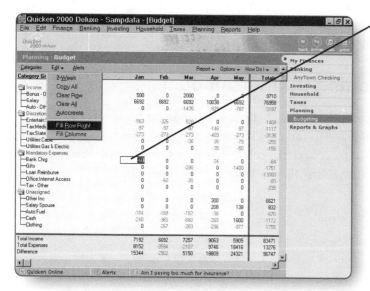

4. Click on the **amount field** that contains the value that you want to use to fill the amount fields located to the right (and on the same row). The field will be selected.

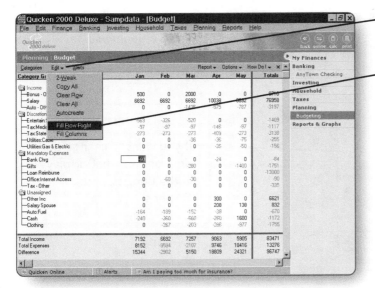

5. **Click** on **Edit**. A menu will appear.

6. **Click** on **Fill Row Right**. A confirmation dialog box will appear.

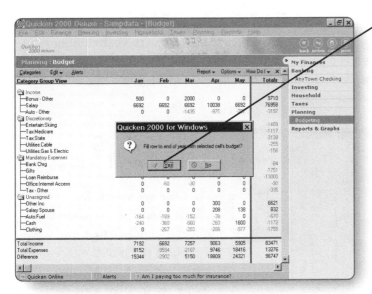

7. **Click** on **Yes**. The selected amount is copied to all of the fields to the right of the selected field.

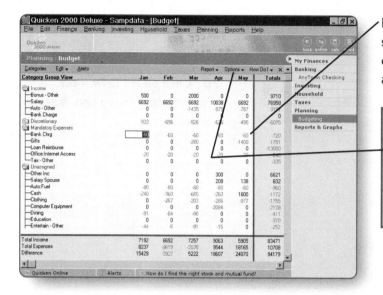

Each amount to the right of the selected amount will be changed to match the selected amount.

TIP

If you want to change the time periods that display in the Budget, click on Options.

Setting Budget Alerts

Quicken can tell you when you are close to your category spending limit. You need to set monthly limits for each category and decide how far in advance you'd like to be warned.

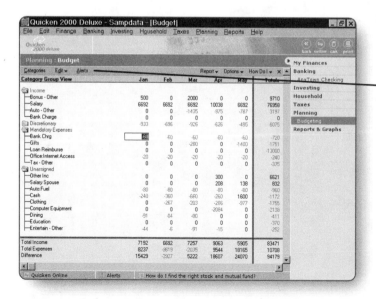

Determining Spending Limits

1. Click on **Alerts**. The Set Up Alerts dialog box will open. You'll also notice that the Accounts tab is at the top of the stack and that the Monthly Expenses account alert is selected. This is the alert for your budget items.

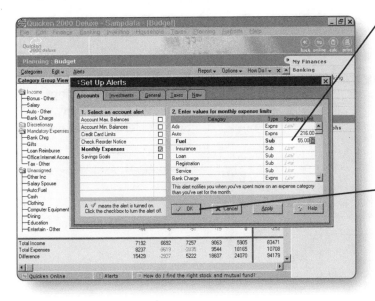

2. Click in the **Spending Limit field** for each category for which you want to set an alarm. The pointer will appear in the field.

3. Type the **amount** that you want to set as the spending limit for the month.

4. Click on **OK** when you finish setting spending limits for the categories. The Alert will be set.

Setting Alert Options

When your spending approaches the limit you set in the previous section, Quicken alerts you. You can change the advance time that Quicken will warn you.

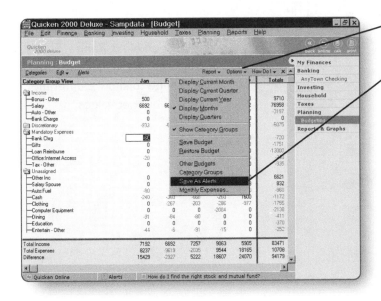

1. Click on **Options**. A menu will appear.

2. Click on **Save As Alerts**. The Save Budget Alerts Options dialog box will open.

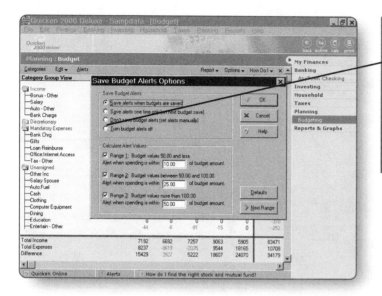

NOTE

If you do not want to be notified when you are approaching a spending limit, click on the Turn budget alerts off option button.

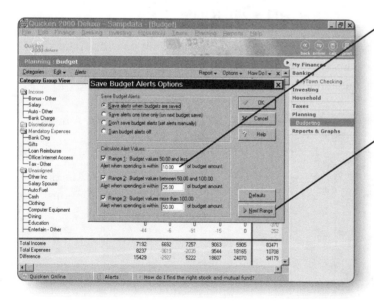

3. **Click** in a **Calculate Alert Values text box** and **type** the **dollar amount** at which you want to be warned that you are reaching a spending limit.

4. **Click** on **Next Range**. The Calculate Alert Values section will change to show a different range of budget values.

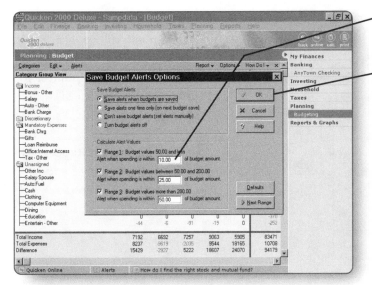

5. Repeat steps 3–5 until you finish setting spending limits.

6. Click on **OK**. You will return to the Budget window. When you approach a spending limit, Quicken will let you know.

Keeping Track of Your Budget

Once you have your budget in place, you can run a number of reports that will help you determine just how well you are keeping to your budget goals.

Creating a Budget Report

The Budget Report lists each category you are tracking in your budget. The report shows your actual spending to date compared to the amount you budgeted for the year for each category item.

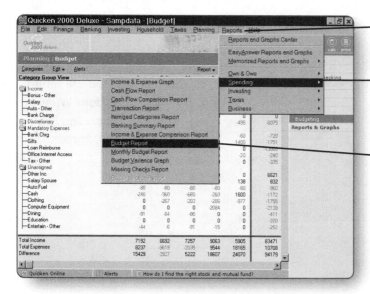

1. Click on **Reports**. The Reports menu will appear.

2. Move the **mouse pointer** to Spending. A submenu will appear.

3. Click on **Budget Report**. The Budget Report will appear in the Reports & Graphs window.

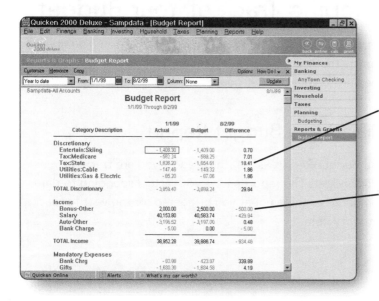

The last column in the Budget Report tells you how close you are to actually meeting your budget.

- **Positive number**. A positive number means that you are spending less than you budgeted.

- **Negative number**. A negative number means that you are spending over your budget limit.

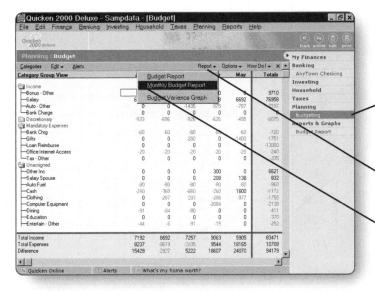

Displaying the Monthly Budget Report

1. Click on the **Budgeting QuickTab**. The Budget will appear in the Planning window.

2. Click on **Report**. A menu will appear.

3. Click on **Monthly Budget Report**. The Monthly Budget Report will appear in the Reports & Graphs window.

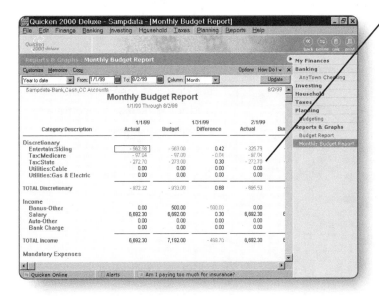

The Monthly Budget Report gives you the same information as the Budget Report, but the information is broken into months.

Producing a Budget Variance Graph

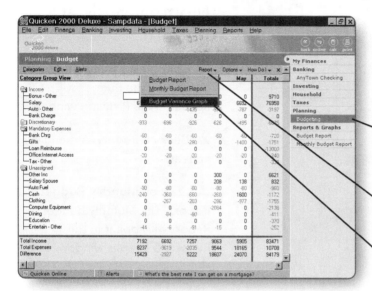

If you want a visual representation of how well you are doing at meeting your budget goals, try out the Budget Variance Graph.

1. Click on the **Budgeting QuickTab**. The Budget will appear in the Planning window.

2. Click on **Report**. A menu will appear.

3. Click on **Budget Variance Graph**. The Budget Variance Graph will appear in the Reports & Graphs window.

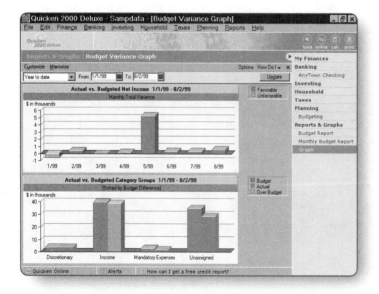

The graph shows how well you are doing at meeting your budget in terms of income and category groups.

16

Creating a Savings Plan

Having money stashed away in a savings account is always a good idea, no matter what the reason. You may want to keep a reserve in case your regular source of income disappears. You may also want to save money to buy a particular item, such as a computer or a musical instrument, instead of taking out a loan or using your credit card. In this instance, you need to know what the item will cost and then set up a schedule to make regular savings contributions. Quicken provides lots of savings ideas and can help you save for a rainy day. In this chapter, you'll learn how to:

- Find resources that can help you build a savings plan
- Set aside money for special purchases
- Create savings goals and contribute to them

Learning to Save

Quicken contains a handy tool that walks you through the process of determining where you can cut money from your expenses and begin saving. The Save More Planner can also show you other places where you can learn more about saving money and how to use Quicken to help you in this process.

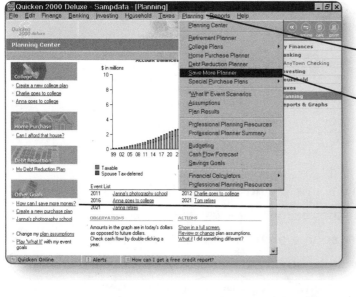

1. Click on **Planning**. The Planning menu will appear.

2. Click on **Save More Planner**. The Save More Planner will appear in the Planning window.

NOTE

You can also click on the How can I save more money? link in the Planning Center.

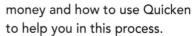

The Save More Planner will walk you through the process of finding ways to save more money. Make sure you read each screen carefully as you work with the planner.

3. Click on **Next**. The What's my monthly net income? screen will appear.

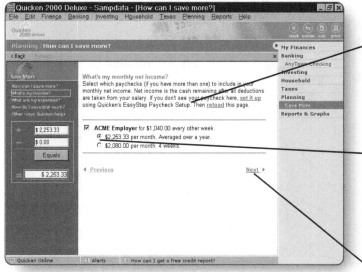

NOTE

The EasyStep Paycheck Setup is covered in Chapter 7, "Recording Special Transactions."

4. Click on the **option button** next to the paycheck that you want to include in your savings calculation. The option will be selected.

5. Click on **Next**. The What are my expenses? screen will appear.

This screen uses either the amounts you entered in a budget or your past year's transactions to fill in your average monthly spending.

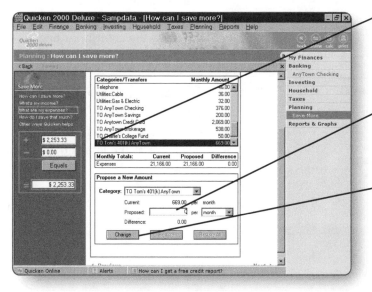

6. Click on a **category** for which you want to change the monthly amount. The category will be selected.

7. Click in the **Proposed text box** and **type** the **amount** you want to apply to the category.

8. Click on **Change**. The Monthly Amount field for the category will be updated.

You can also add categories to the Save More Planner.

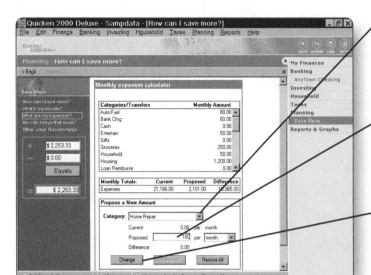

9. Click on the **Category down arrow** and **click** on the **category** that you want to add. The category will be selected.

10. Click in the **Proposed text box** and **type** the **amount** you will be spending on the category each month.

11. Click on **Change**. The category and monthly amount will be added to the list. You'll also notice that the Proposed amount will be changed.

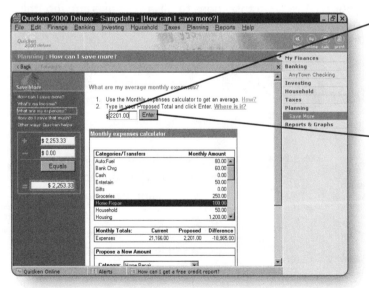

12. Type the **Proposed amount** in the number 2 text box when you are finished adjusting the categories and amounts.

13. Click on **Enter**. The amount of your monthly expenses will appear in the calculator at the left of the screen.

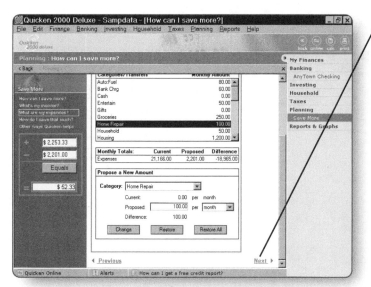

14. Click on **Next**. The How do I save that much? screen will appear.

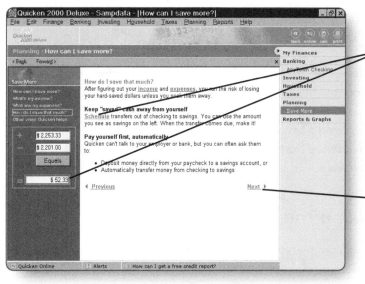

TIP

If you want to begin saving any residual money, you can have Quicken remind you to transfer the money to your savings account.

15. Click on **Next**. The Other ways Quicken can help you save screen will appear.

16. **Click** on any of the **topics** to learn more about them.

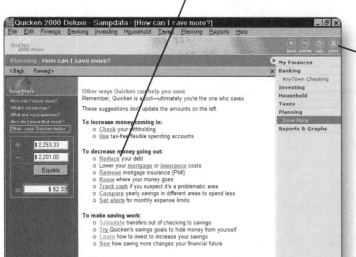

NOTE

You can click on Back to return to this page.

Establishing Savings Goals

Savings goals can help you set aside money for a particular purpose. Maybe you just need a few hundred dollars for a new scanner, digital camera, and a color printer. Or, maybe you need a few thousand dollars to buy a second car. You have two different options to help you plan for a special purchase.

Using the Special Purchase Planner

If you are planning a special purchase in the future, such as a car, a wedding, or a new business, you may want to consider the Special Purchase Planner. This planner can help you if you think the purchase price may change before you have enough money saved. It is also useful if you will be borrowing money to finance part of the purchase.

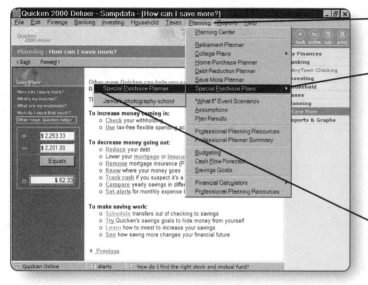

1. Click on **Planning**. The Planning menu will appear.

2. Move the **mouse pointer** to Special Purchase Plans. A submenu will appear. Skip this step if you have never created a purchase plan before. After purchase plans are created, they are listed here.

3. Click on **Special Purchase Planner**. The Special Purchase Planner will appear in the Planning window.

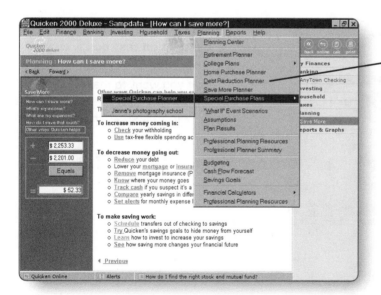

TIP

Another good way to save money is to reduce your debt. The Debt Reduction Planner has some good ideas and contains loads of information for doing so.

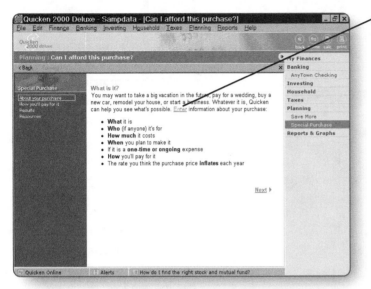

4. Click on the **Enter link**. The Add Special Expense dialog box will open.

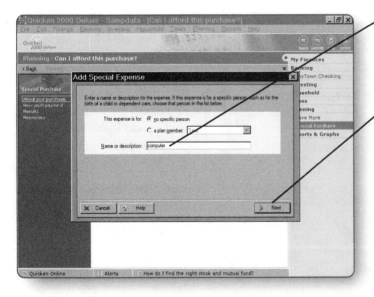

5. Click in the **Name or description text box** and **type** a **description** of the purchase that you want to make.

6. Click on **Next**. The next screen of the Add Special Expense dialog box will appear.

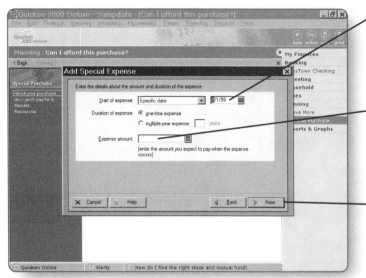

7. Click in the **Start of expense text box** and **type** the **date** on which you want to begin saving money for the purchase.

8. Click in the **Expense amount text box** and **type** the **amount** of the intended purchase.

9. Click on **Next**. The last screen of the Add Special Expense dialog box will appear.

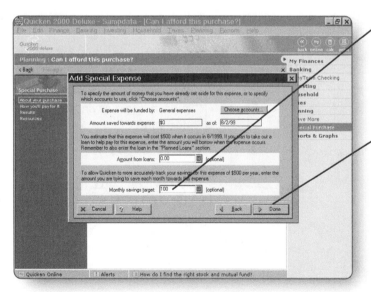

10. Click in the **Monthly savings target text box** and **type** the **amount** you want to set aside each month toward the purchase.

11. Click on **Done**. You will return to the Special Purchase Planner. You'll notice that the special expense has been added to the planner.

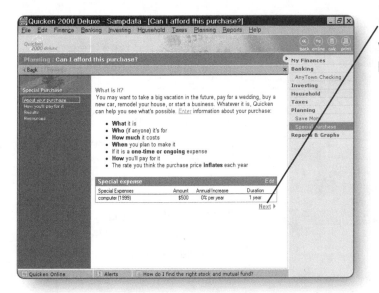

12. Click on **Next**. The How will you pay for it? screen of the planner will appear.

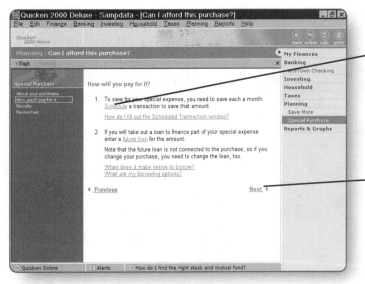

NOTE

You'll want to set up a scheduled transaction to transfer the amount each month into a savings account.

13. Click on **Next**. The Results screen of the planner will appear.

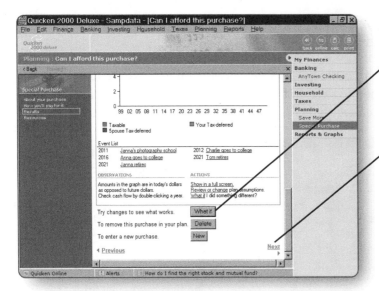

TIP

To make changes in the planner, click on the What if button.

14. **Click** on **Next**. The Resources for special purchases screen of the planner will appear.

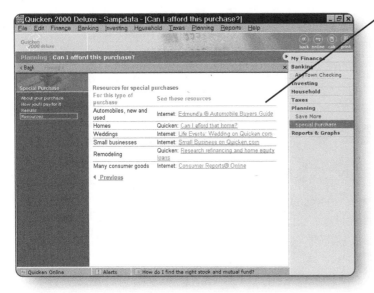

The resources page lists some places where you can find more information about saving for and making special purchases.

Working with Savings Goals

Another way to set money aside for a special purchase is to use savings goals. These goals help you decide how much you need to save and when you need to save it. You can then hide the savings amount away in your account register. When you've stashed away enough cash for the special purchase, it's time to go shopping!

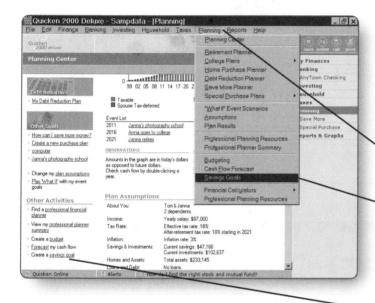

Creating a Savings Goal Account

1. Click on **Planning**. The Planning menu will appear.

2. Click on **Savings Goals**. The Savings Goals will appear in the Planning menu.

NOTE

You'll also find a link to the Savings Goals in the Other Activities area of the Planning Center.

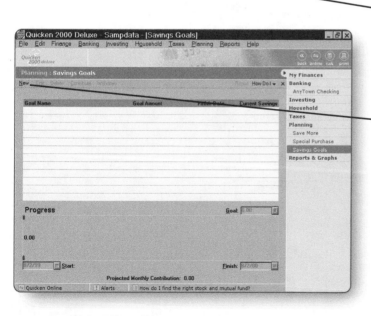

3. Click on **New**. The Create New Savings Goal dialog box will open

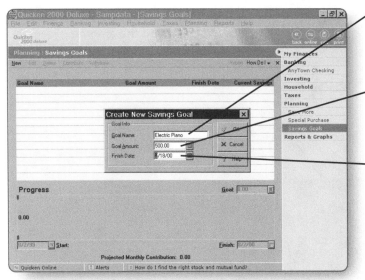

4. **Click** in the **Goal Name text box** and **type** a **name** to describe the goal.

5. **Click** in the **Goal Amount text box** and **type** the **amount** of money you want to save.

6. **Click** in the **Finish Date text box** and **type** the **date** on which you want to have accumulated the entire goal amount.

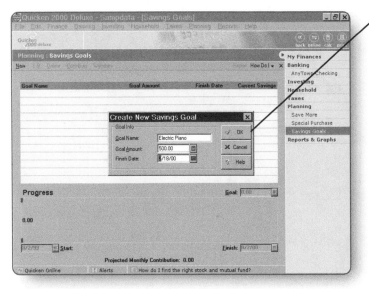

7. **Click** on **OK**. The new goal will appear in the Savings Goals list.

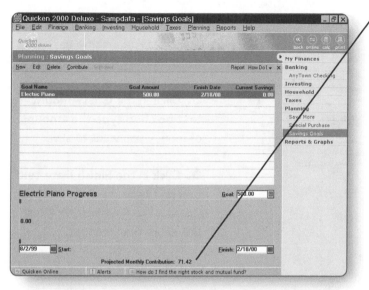

At the bottom of the window, you'll find the amount of money that you'll need to contribute to the goal each month.

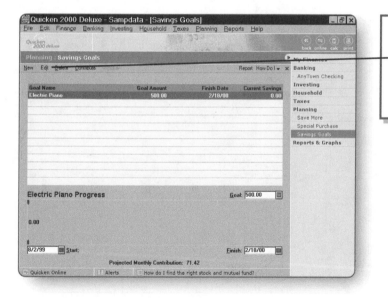

TIP

To make changes to the goal, select the goal and click on the Edit button.

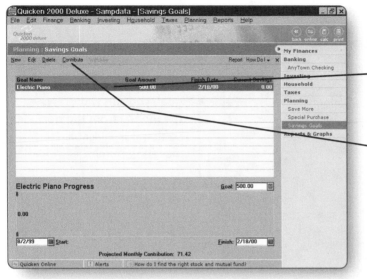

Contributing to Your Goal

1. Click on the **goal** for which you want to set aside money. The goal will be selected.

2. Click on **Contribute**. The Contribute To Goal dialog box will appear.

3. Click on the **From Account down arrow** and **click** on the **account** from which you want to make the contribution to the goal. The account will appear in the list box.

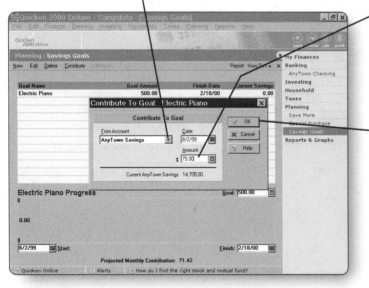

4. Click in the **Amount text box** and **type** the **amount** that you want to set aside for the goal, if this differs from the monthly average.

5. Click on **OK**. The contribution will be shown in the Savings Goals and will also display in the register for the selected account.

Notice the progress bar at the bottom on the window.

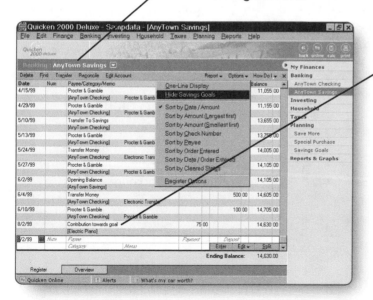

NOTE

When you have met the goal, you can withdraw the money from the goal so that it is available to make the purchase.

6. Display the **register** for the account from which you made the savings goal contribution. The register will appear in the Banking window.

NOTE

A transaction should appear in the register for the contribution with the adjusted account balance.

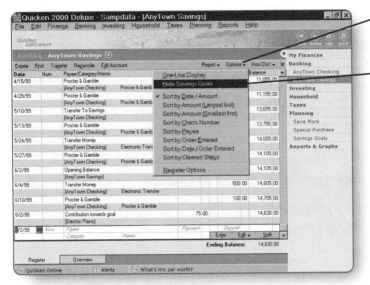

7. **Click** on **Options**. A menu will appear.

8. **Click** on **Hide Savings Goals**. The transaction line for the contribution will be hidden.

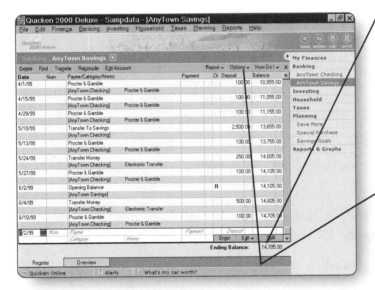

By hiding the contribution transactions, you show the actual balance of the account. The account no longer reflects any money set aside for the savings goals.

NOTE

To display the savings goal contributions in the register, click on Options and click on the Hide Savings Goals command from the menu that appears.

Part III Review Questions

1. Which Quicken feature can help you decide if a category should be declared on your taxes? *See "Letting Quicken Help You Find Deductions" in Chapter 12*

2. Where can you go to determine your estimated tax payment or refund? *See "Estimating Your Tax Burden" in Chapter 12*

3. What reports should you prepare at the end of each year to see your financial picture? *See "Producing Year-End Reports" in Chapter 13*

4. Why is it better to archive your data file at the end of the year instead of starting a new data file? *See "Performing Year-End File Maintenance" in Chapter 13*

5. Where can you find several easy-to-use reports that will show you how you spend your money? *See "Creating Quick Reports" in Chapter 14*

6. How do you change the information that appears in the reports you create? *See "Detailing Your Reports" in Chapter 14*

7. How do you warn yourself that you are about to spend more in a category than you budgeted? *See "Setting Budget Alerts" in Chapter 15*

8. What is the purpose of the Budget Report? *See "Keeping Track of Your Budget" in Chapter 15*

9. Where can you go if you want to learn about saving money and making planned purchases? *See "Learning to Save" in Chapter 16*

10. What's an easy way to hide money from yourself so that you can save a specified amount? *See "Working with Savings Goals" in Chapter 16*

PART IV

Preparing for an Emergency

17

Keeping a Home Inventory

No one wants to think about submitting a claim to an insurance company because of the theft or destruction of personal belongings. But, it's best to be prepared. The Quicken Home Inventory keeps track of your possessions. You must enter each belonging—such as computer equipment, artwork, jewelry, and cameras—into the Home Inventory, paying special attention to those items that are covered by an insurance policy. After you've created your home inventory, you can create a couple of reports that you can print and keep in a safe place. In this chapter, you'll learn how to:

- Start the Quicken Home Inventory
- Enter your household items into the inventory list
- Generate reports that list your belongings and their value

Starting the Home Inventory

The first time you start the Quicken Home Inventory a file will be automatically created in which you can save the information about your household belongings. You can also create separate files if you want to keep personal belongs separate from home office equipment.

Opening the Quicken Home Inventory

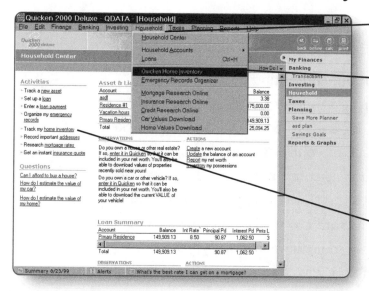

1. Click on **Household**. The Household menu will appear.

2. Click on **Quicken Home Inventory**. The Quicken Home Inventory program will open and the Welcome To dialog box will open.

NOTE

You'll also find the Home Inventory in the Activities section of the Household Center. Look for the Track my home inventory link.

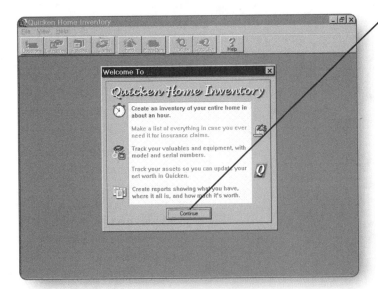

3. Click on **Continue**. The Quicken Home Inventory will start and the default file will be set up so that you can begin entering your information.

Creating Separate Inventory Files

1. Click on **File**. The File menu will appear.

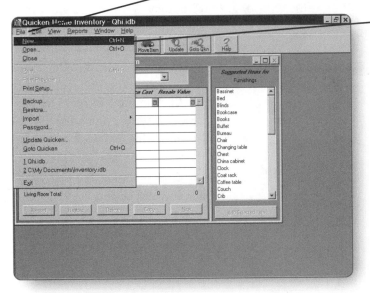

2. Click on **New**. The Automatic Backup dialog box will open.

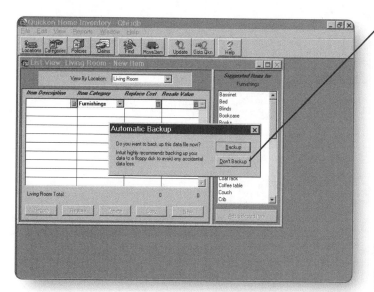

3. Click on the **Don't Backup button**. The New Home Inventory File dialog box will open.

TIP

Each time you close the Quicken Home Inventory, you'll be asked to back up the inventory file. It's a good idea to perform this backup each time you use the program.

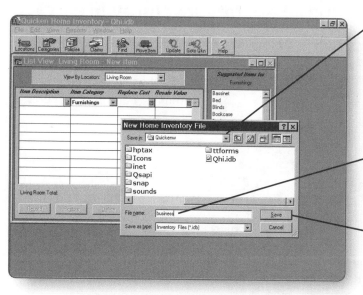

4. Click on the **Save in down arrow** and **click** on the **directory** in which you want to save the inventory file. The directory will appear in the list box.

5. Click in the **File name text box** and **type** a **name** for the inventory file.

6. Click on **Save**. The List View window will appear.

Adding Items to the Inventory

Before you begin entering items into your inventory list, you'll want to go through each room in your home and decide which items need to be inventoried. Begin with items which are insured or for which you need to keep serial numbers. As you get more time, you can inventory other, less important items.

1. **Click** on the **View By Location down arrow** and **click** on the **room** in which the item is located. The room will appear in the list box.

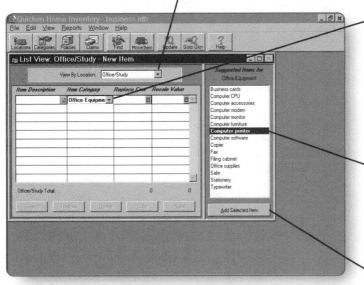

2. **Click** on the **Item Category down arrow** and **click** on the **category** that best describes the item. The category will appear in the list box and the list of Suggested Items will change.

3. **Click** on the **item** in the Suggested Items list that most closely matches the item you are inventorying. The item will be selected.

4. **Click** on **Add Selected Item**. A description, the default replacement cost, and the default resale value will appear in the list.

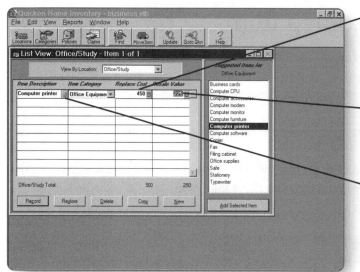

5. **Click** in the **Replace Cost field** and **type** the **actual cost** of the item. The amount will display in the field.

6. **Click** in the **Resale Value field** and **type** an estimated **resale price** for the item.

7. **Click** on the **Item Description icon**. The Detail View window for the item will appear.

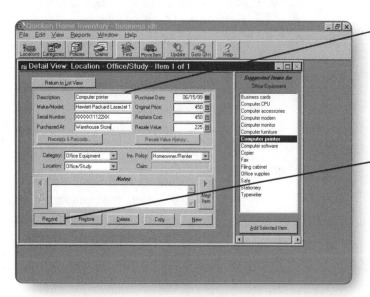

8. **Click** in each of the **fields** and **type** as much **information** about the item as you can. The more information that you can provide, the easier it will be to make an insurance claim

9. **Click** on the **Record button**. The information about the item will be recorded in the file.

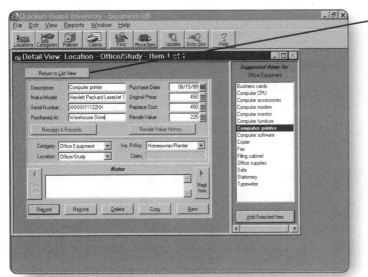

10. **Click** on the **Return to List View button**. The List View will reappear. The item will be recorded in the inventory and the next line in the inventory list will be selected.

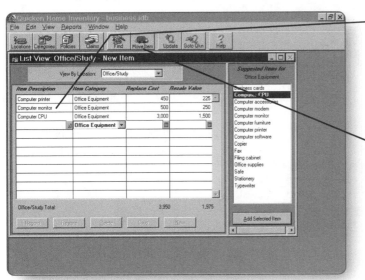

11. **Continue adding items** to the inventory until you have a record of all your important belongings.

TIP

If you later move an item from one room to another, select the item in the List View and click on the Move Item button.

Customizing the Home Inventory

After you've worked with the Home Inventory, you may find that it doesn't contain the same rooms that you have in your house. You may also find that you need a different category in which to group your household items. You can easily create rooms and categories.

Adding New Rooms to the Inventory

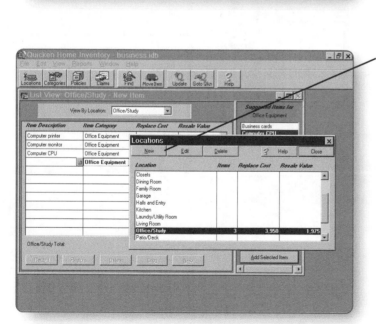

1. Click on the **Locations button**. The Locations dialog box will open.

2. Click on **New**. The New Location dialog box will open.

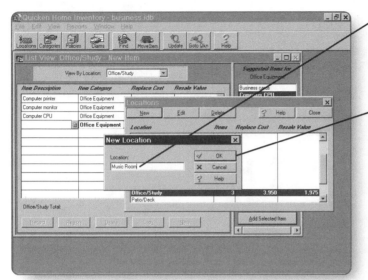

3. Click in the **Location text box** and **type** a **name** that describes the room you want to add to the location list.

4. Click on **OK**. The room will be added to the list of locations.

5. Click on **Close**. The Locations dialog box will close and the new location will be available from the View By Location drop-down list.

Creating New Categories

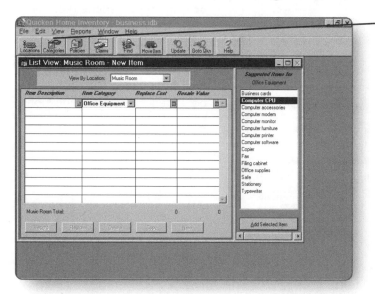

1. Click on the **Categories button**. The Categories dialog box will open.

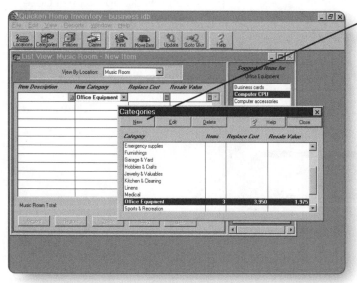

2. Click on the **New button**. The New Category dialog box will open.

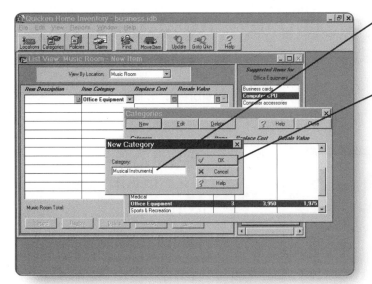

3. Click in the **Category text box** and **type** a **name** for the category.

4. Click on **OK**. You will return to the Categories dialog box.

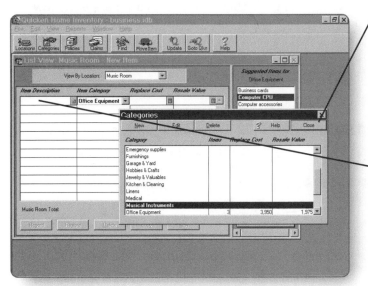

5. Click on **Close**. The category will be added to the category list and can be accessed from the Item Category drop-down list.

> **NOTE**
>
> You'll want to add a description of the individual item you are placing in the inventory in the Item Description field of the inventory list.

Creating Inventory Reports

Now that you've finished the monumental task of inventorying your personal belongings, it's time to create a few reports, print them, and store them in a safe place, like a safe deposit box.

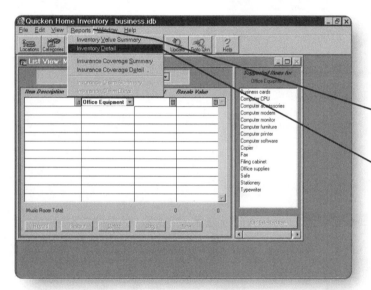

Viewing a List of Your Inventory Items

1. Click on **Reports**. The Reports menu will appear.

2. Click on **Inventory Detail**. The Inventory Detail Report will appear in a separate window.

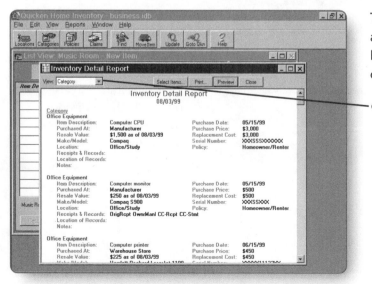

The Inventory Detail Report lists all the items you entered in the Home Inventory. You can customize this report.

- **View.** Click on the View down arrow and select a location. The list will be sorted so that you can see which items are contained in each location in your home.

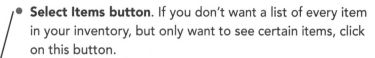

• **Select Items button**. If you don't want a list of every item in your inventory, but only want to see certain items, click on this button.

• **Print button**. Keep a paper record of your home inventory by clicking on the Print button.

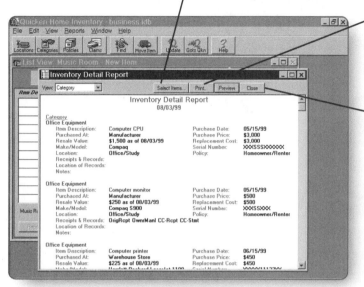

3. Click on the **Close button** when you are finished with the report. The report window will close.

Reporting the Value of Your Household Items

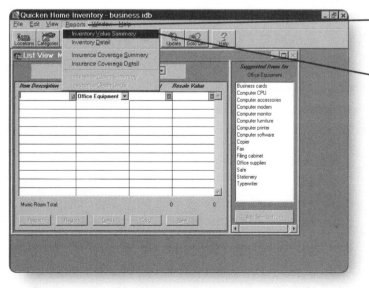

1. Click on **Reports**. The Reports menu will appear.

2. Click on **Inventory Value Summary**. The Inventory Value Summary Report will appear in a separate window.

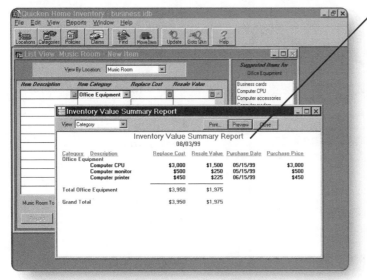

The Inventory Value Summary Report shows the actual cost of each inventory item and its resale value. The bottom of the report lists the total value of your inventoried items.

18

Organizing Important Records

Another important step in preparing for emergencies is to know details about and the location of your important records, such as birth certificates, insurance policies, and wills. This makes it easier to locate these documents, plus you'll have detailed information in case you need to replace a document. You'll also want to organize a contact list that provides information about who to contact in case of an emergency, what physician should be called, and other medical history. This information is useful in case of an accident and it makes it easy to leave a list for the babysitter. In this chapter, you'll learn how to:

- Add and update important information and records with the Emergency Records Organizer
- Print individual and groups of records
- Create detailed reports about your important records and information

Getting Started with the Emergency Records Organizer

The Emergency Records Organizer provides an easy way to keep track of all your personal information, emergency contacts, medical information, location of important documents, financial institutions with which you do business, and employment information. By keeping track of this information in one place, you can save yourself many hours of useless searching through closets, drawers, and filing cabinets.

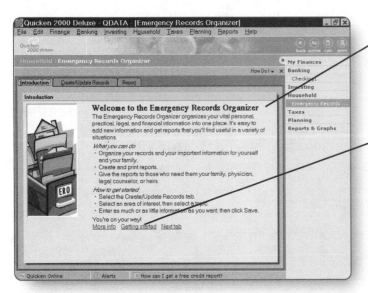

1. Click on **Household**. The Household menu will appear.

2. Click on **Emergency Records Organizer**. The Emergency Records Organizer will appear in the Household window.

3. Read the **information** on the Introduction tab.

NOTE

The More info and Getting started links open a Help window that contains information on how to use the Emergency Records Organizer.

Adding Records to the Organizer

Take some time to look at the different areas that the Organizer will track. Each area contains a number of topics, and each topic contains a form to fill in. Decide which type of information that you want to track and organize your records before you begin.

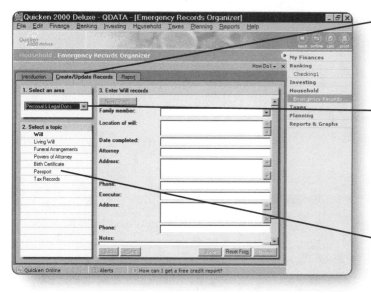

1. Click on the **Create/Update Records tab**. The Create/Update Records tab will come to the top of the stack.

2. Click on the **Select an area down arrow** and **click** on the **type of record** that you want to enter in the Emergency Records Organizer. The area will appear in the list box.

3. Click on the **topic** that most closely matches the type of information that you want to enter. The topic will be selected and a form will appear in the Enter records area.

4. Enter the **information** in the appropriate text boxes on the form by first clicking in the text box and then typing the information.

5. Click on the **Save button**. The information will be saved to your Quicken data file and a check mark will appear next to the topic showing that you've completed a form for the topic.

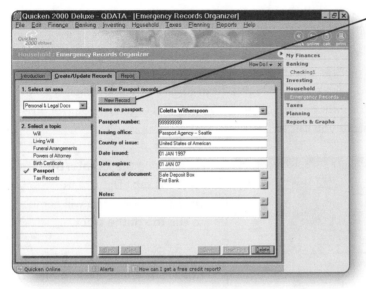

6. Click on the **New Record button** if you want to add another record for the same topic. The fields will be cleared and you can enter information for another record.

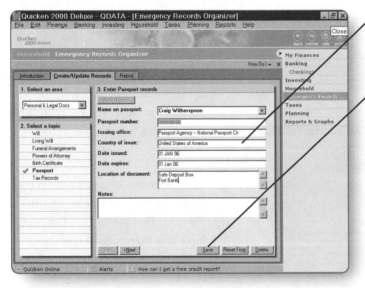

7. Enter the **information** in the appropriate text boxes on the form.

8. Click on the **Save button**. The information will be saved to your Quicken data file.

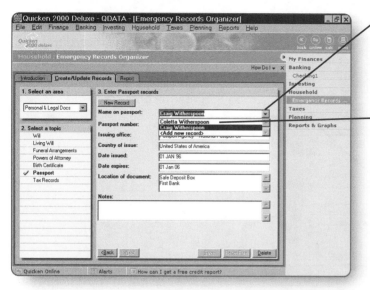

9. Click on the **down arrow** for the first field in the form. A drop-down list of all the records for the topic will appear.

10. Click on the **record** that you want to view. The information that you entered for the record will appear in the list box.

Updating Emergency Records

Information changes all the time. For example, contacts in your contact list may have changed their phone numbers, or you may have renewed your passport and need to record the new expiration date. It is easy to update your records in Quicken.

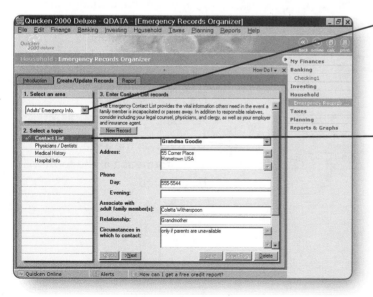

1. Click on the **Select an area down arrow** and **click** on the **area** where the record is located. The area will appear in the list box.

2. Click on the **topic** where the record is located. The topic will be selected and the last form that you filled out for that topic will appear in the Enter Contact List records area.

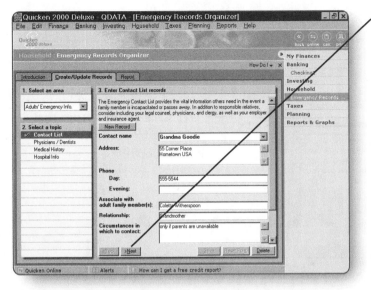

3. **Click** on the **Next button** until you see the record that you want to update. The next record in the topic list will appear in the Enter records area.

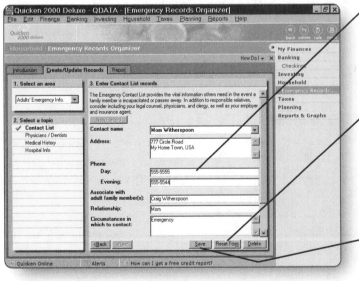

4. **Change** the **information** on the form as needed.

TIP

If you made a change in error, click on the Reset Form button. The information that was last saved will be used in the form text boxes.

5. **Click** on the **Save button**. The information in the form will be updated.

Printing Records

It's easy to print the records that you've entered into the Emergency Records Organizer. You can print a single record, or you can print a group of records.

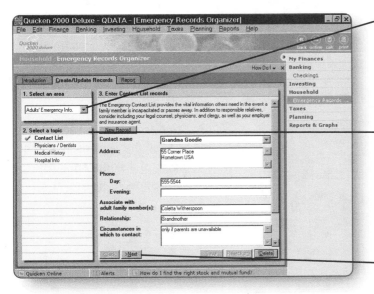

1. Click on the **Select an area down arrow** and **click** on the **area** where the record you want to print is located. The area will appear in the list box.

2. Click on the **topic** where the record is located. The topic will be selected and the last form that you filled out for that topic will appear in the Enter records area.

3. Click on the **Next button** until you see the record that you want to update. The next record in the topic list will appear in the Enter records area.

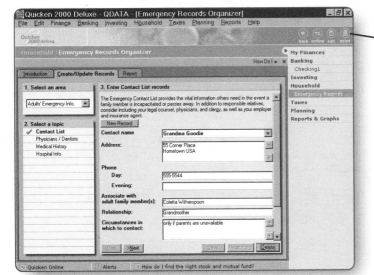

4. Click on the **Print button**. The Print area, topic or record dialog box will open.

5. Click on an **option button** in the Choose what to print area. The option will be selected.

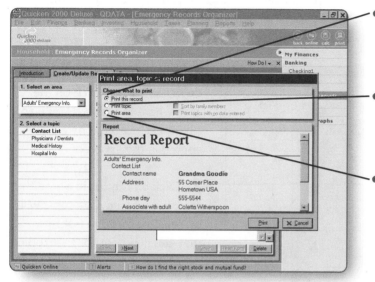

● **Print this record.** If you only want to print the record that is displayed, select this option button.

● **Print topic.** If you want to print all the records in a single topic, click on this option button.

● **Print area.** If you want to print all the records in all the topics of a single area, use this option.

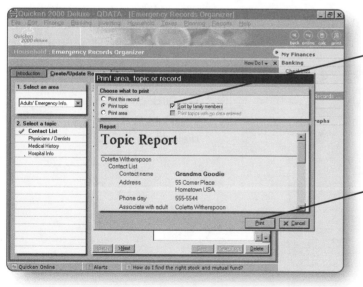

NOTE

If you want to display information for each family member separately, click to place a check mark in the Sort by family members check box.

6. Click on **Print**. The report will be sent to your printer. It will look much like the sample report in the dialog box.

Viewing Emergency Reports

The Emergency Records Organizer contains a number of reports that you can create using the information you entered. These reports can be printed so that you can either keep them in a safe place or give them to someone who may need the information, such as another family member or a babysitter.

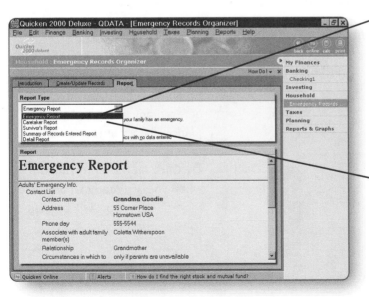

1. Click on the **Report tab**. The Report tab will come to the top of the stack.

2. Click on the **Report Type down arrow**. A list of available reports will appear.

3. Click on the **report** that you want to create. The report will appear in the list box.

- **Emergency Report.** This report lists whom to contact in case you or another member of your family requires emergency medical attention. It also includes physician information and medical history.

- **Caretaker Report.** This report should be given to any person who is responsible for watching your property while you are away. It contains information about the property and who to contact in an emergency.

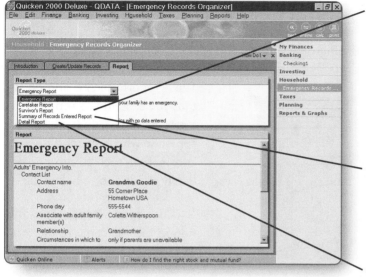

- **Survivor's Report.** This report is to be used in the unfortunate instance of a death in your immediate family. It includes people to contact, location of wills and birth certificates, and other information needed for the estate.

- **Summary of Records Entered Report.** When you want the complete list of all the records that you've entered, use this report.

- **Detail Report.** When you want to see the complete list of records and the detail for each one, choose this report.

4. Click in the **check box** for Sort by family members if you want the information to display according to each member in the family. A check mark will appear in the box.

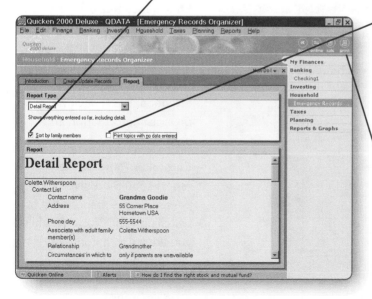

5. Click in the **check box** for Print topics with no data entered if you want to see the topics for which you haven't entered any records. A check mark will appear in the box.

6. Click on the **Print button** when you are ready to print the report. The report will be sent to your printer.

19

Determining Insurance Needs

Another way you can protect yourself is to make sure you carry adequate insurance coverage. Determining what types of insurance and how much coverage you'll need can be an overwhelming task. You may be used to dealing with purchasing car and homeowner's insurance. But what do you do when faced with all the alternatives available for life insurance policies? If you're connected to the Internet, you may want to check out the Quicken InsureMarket. InsureMarket is a comprehensive collection of insurance information, calculators, and quotes. Spend some time at InsureMarket and get answers to your insurance questions and concerns before you go shopping. You can then gather up a few quotes so that you can compare insurance policies before you make a decision. In this chapter, you'll learn how to:

- Find basic insurance information at the Quicken InsureMarket
- Research car insurance needs and obtain quotes
- Determine home insurance needs
- Obtain medical and life insurance

Connecting to the Quicken InsureMarket

If you need to purchase any type of insurance, or if you're just curious about your insurance options, check out the Quicken InsureMarket. This chapter will take you on a whirlwind tour of InsureMarket and show you some of the information and tools available to you. Before you begin, connect to your Internet service provider.

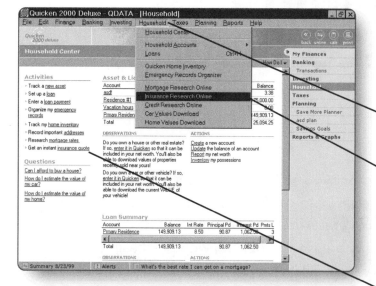

1. Click on **Household**. The Household menu will appear.

2. Click on **Insurance Research Online**. The InsureMarket home page will appear in the Household window.

NOTE

You can also click on the Get an instant insurance quote link in the Activities section of the Household Center.

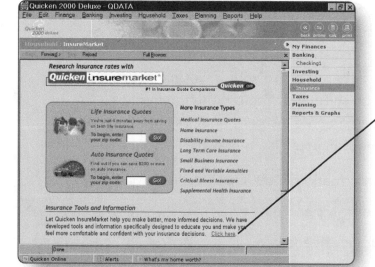

3. Click on the **Click here link** if you want to learn some easy ways to determine your insurance needs. The Insurance Tools and Information page will appear.

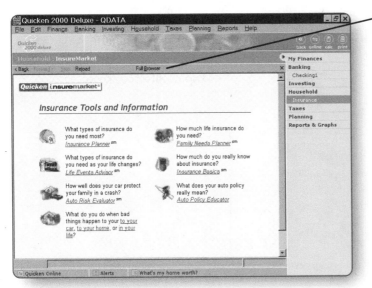

4. Click on **Full Browser**. The page will appear in your default Web browser and you'll be able to surf the InsureMarket Web site using your browser.

NOTE

If you find a page that you may want to come back to later, you can save it in your Favorites list.

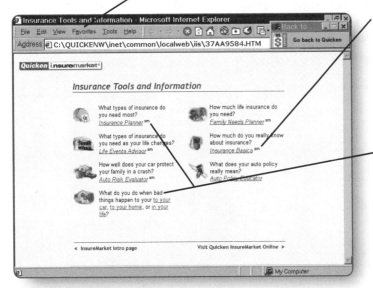

5. Click on the **Insurance Basics link**. A list of insurance terms will appear on the Insurance Basics page.

TIP

If you want help determining your insurance needs, take a look at the Insurance Planner. For tips on what to do in an emergency, check out the What do you do when bad things happen links.

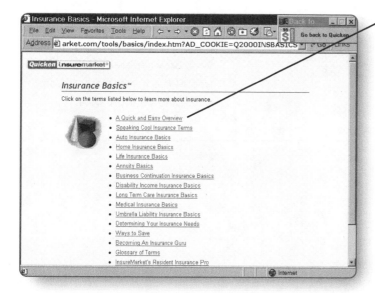

6. Click on a **topic** that you want to read about. A page that provides information about the topic will appear.

7. Read the **information**. Use the scroll bar to see the rest of the page.

8. Click on the **Back arrow** when you are finished reading the page.

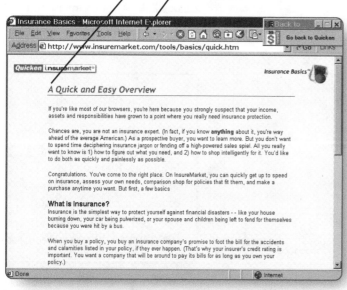

9. Select any **other topics** that are of interest to you.

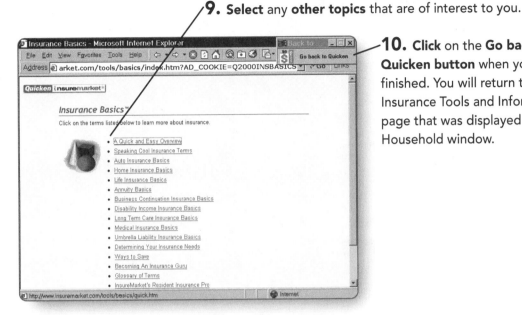

10. Click on the **Go back to Quicken button** when you are finished. You will return to the Insurance Tools and Information page that was displayed in the Household window.

Finding Affordable Automobile Insurance

Before you shop for automobile insurance, you may want to take a look at the Auto Policy Educator. The Auto Policy Educator explains, in easy-to-understand language, what each line on an auto policy means. It's a good idea to know exactly what your policy covers.

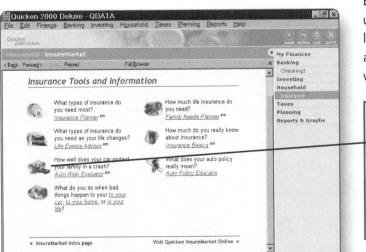

TIP

Are you curious as to how safe your car really is? Click on the Auto Risk Evaluator link and enter the information about your car.

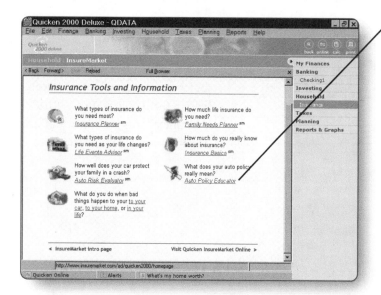

1. **Click** on the **Auto Policy Educator link**. The Auto Policy Educator page will appear.

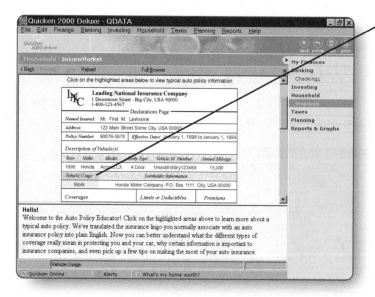

2. **Click** on a **field** in the form. The field will be highlighted.

An explanation of the field will appear. This information also includes explanations of all the variables that could be found in the field.

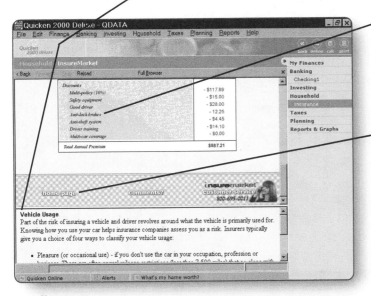

3. **Click** on any **other fields** about which you want to know more. The description will appear in the bottom pane of the browser window.

4. **Click** on the **home page link** at the bottom of the page. You'll return to the Quicken InsureMarket home page. This page may look different than the page you first opened.

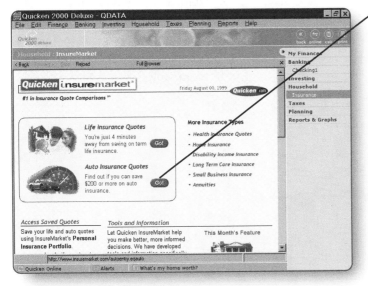

5. **Click** on the **Go! link** in the Auto Insurance Quotes section. The Welcome to Quicken InsureMarket's Auto Marketplace page will appear.

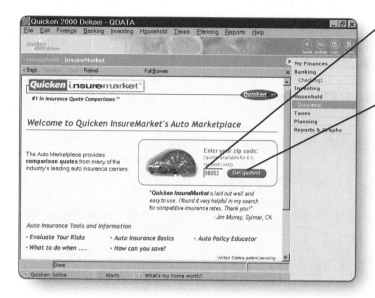

6. **Click** in the **Enter your zip code text box** and **type** the **zip code** in which you live.

7. **Click** on the **Get quotes! link**. The EasyQuote Auto page will appear.

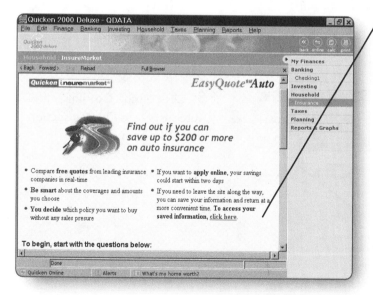

8. **Read** the **information** on the page and **answer** the **questions** as you are prompted. You will remain anonymous throughout the quote process. Your identity will only become known if you decide to contact an insurance company.

Determining Home Insurance Needs

If you own your home and pay a mortgage, you are required by your mortgage holder to carry insurance to insure against the loss of the physical structure. You'll also want to consider insuring your belongings—even if you rent.

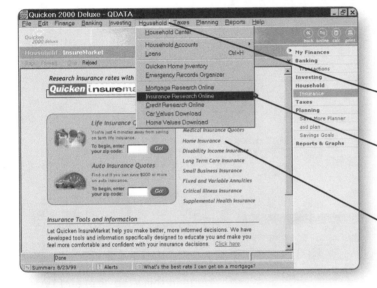

1. Click on **Household**. The Household menu will appear.

2. Click on **Insurance Research Online**. The Quicken InsureMarket page will appear.

3. Click on the **Home Insurance link**. The Home Insurance page will appear.

4. Click on a **link** in the navigation frame to learn more about home insurance.

- **What is it?** This link explains the fundamentals of home insurance such as the different types of home insurance, what items are covered, and tips on how to save money.

- **How can I save?** This link tells you some of the variables that can affect your insurance rates.

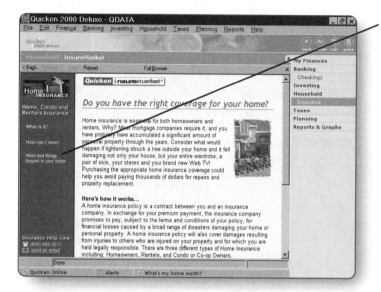

● **When bad things happen to your home.** This link is a great place to help you plan for an emergency or disaster. This is a must read for every member of your family.

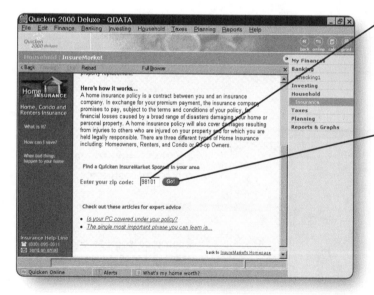

5. **Click** in the **Enter your zip code text box** (which can be found at the bottom of each page in this Web site) and **type** the **zip code** in which you live.

6. **Click** on the **Go! link**. The Companies Offering Home Insurance page will appear.

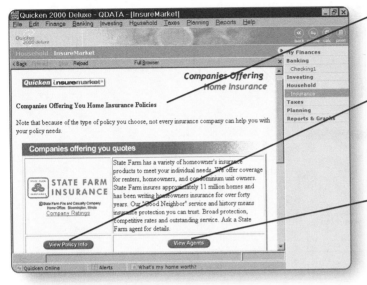

7. Read the **information** on the page and select from one of the participating insurance companies.

- **View Policy Info**. This link displays information about the home insurance policies that are available from that insurance company.

- **View Agents.** If you want to pursue the policy further, click on this link. You can find an agent that is located near you and send an e-mail to request more information.

Looking for Medical Insurance

Not everyone is covered by an employer-paid medical plan. Or, if you are, maybe there are some medical expenses that you'd like to cover that your employer doesn't. InsureMarket can also help you with your medical insurance needs by providing good information and easy access to quotes.

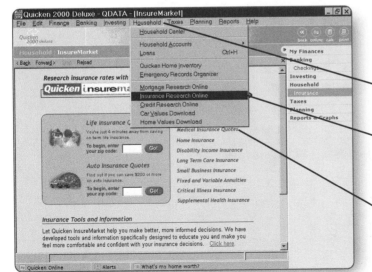

1. Click on **Household**. The Household menu will appear.

2. Click on **Insurance Research Online**. The Quicken InsureMarket page will appear.

3. Click on the **Medical Insurance Quotes link**. The Medical Insurance page will appear.

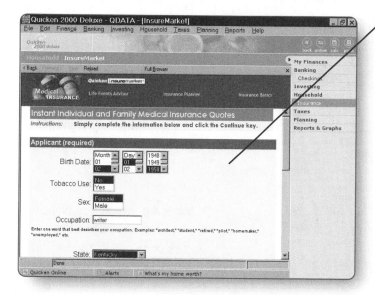

4. Supply an **answer** for each of the fields in the form. Your response will appear in a list box.

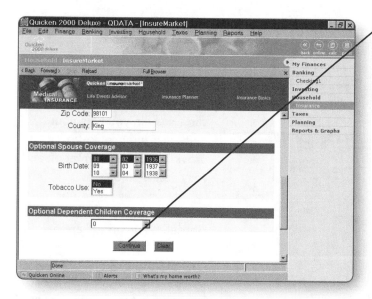

5. Click on the **Continue button** at the bottom of the page when you finish filling out the form. The Medical Insurance Coverage Selector page will appear.

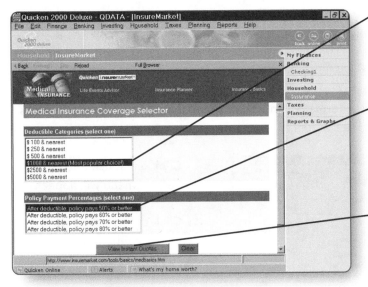

6. Click on the **deductible** that you wish to carry on the insurance policy. The deductible will be selected.

7. Click on the **percentage** the insurance policy will pay after the deductible amount. The payment percentage will be selected.

8. Click on the **View Instant Quotes button**. The Medical Insurance Price Comparison Report page will appear.

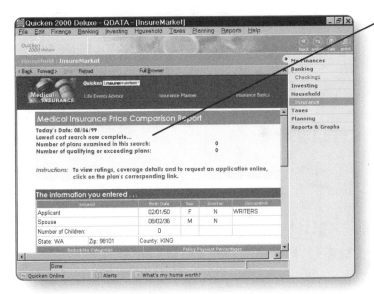

This page shows the information that you entered and a list of insurance companies that offer medical policies that meet your criteria and qualifications. If no quotes were found, the reason will be listed toward the bottom of the page.

Buying Life Insurance

As you've seen, shopping for insurance on the Quicken InsureMarket is a simple process. It's the same easy process when looking for life insurance. You may want to check out the informative links that discuss your options when it comes to life insurance.

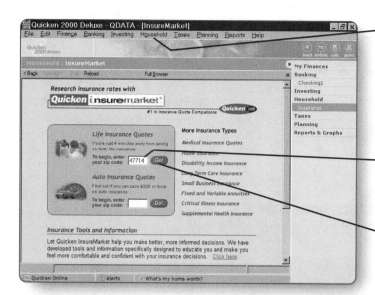

1. Click on **Household**. The Household menu will appear.

2. Click on **Insurance Research Online**. The Quicken InsureMarket page will appear.

3. Click in the **Life Insurance Quotes text box** and **type** the **zip code** in which you live.

4. Click on the **Go! link**. The Life Insurance page will appear.

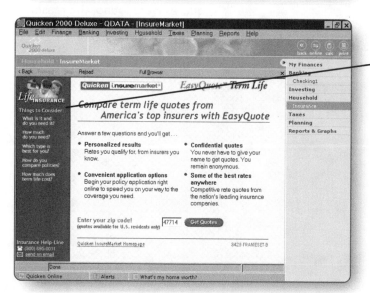

NOTE

Click on the navigation links at the left to learn more about life insurance.

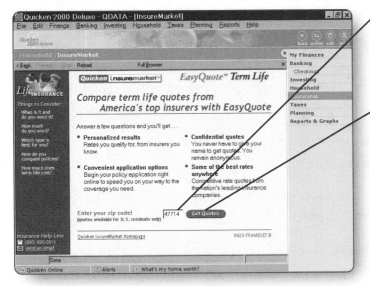

5. Click in the **Enter your zip code text box** and **type** the **zip code** in which you live. The zip code will appear in the text box.

6. Click on the **Get Quotes link**. You'll be asked to fill out a form that is several pages long. Read the questions carefully and at the bottom of each form, click on the Continue button. When you get to the end, a list of insurance companies that can meet your needs will appear showing options that are available in their life insurance policy.

Part IV Review Questions

1. Name the two different ways in which you can open the Quicken Home Inventory. *See "Starting the Home Inventory" in Chapter 17*

2. How do you add your belongings to the inventory list? *See "Adding Items to the Inventory" in Chapter 17*

3. Where is a good place to store a printed copy of your inventory reports? *See "Creating Inventory Reports" in Chapter 17*

4. What kinds of records can you track in the Emergency records organizer? *See "Getting Started with the Emergency Records Organizer" in Chapter 18*

5. How do you print an individual record in the Emergency Records Organizer? *See "Printing Records" in Chapter 18*

6. Which report would you print for someone who will be watching your home while you are away? *See "Viewing Emergency Reports" in Chapter 18*

7. Where can you go for one-stop insurance shopping? *See "Connecting to the Quicken InsureMarket" in Chapter 19*

8. What InsureMarket feature tells you just how safe your automobile is? *See "Finding Affordable Automobile Insurance" in Chapter 19*

9. Where can you go to find out about the different types of home insurance? *See "Determining Home Insurance Needs" in Chapter 19*

10. Where you can find a list of insurance agents who sell the type of insurance for which you are looking? *See "Looking for Medical Insurance" in Chapter 19*

P A R T V

Planning for the Future

20

Buying a Car

Dreaming about a new car can be fun, but if you base you car-buying decision on a dream, you may not be happy with the reality. If you think you've found the perfect car, do a little research and see if the car measures up to your expectations (and your pocketbook). Quicken has teamed up with Edmund's to provide car pricing, reviews, and other information to help you make your decision. Edmund's has been publishing vehicle prices and reviews since 1966. To pay for the car, you'll need to pay cash or obtain a loan. It also is a good idea to track your automobile expenses. In this chapter, you'll learn how to:

- Find a one-stop information bank for car shoppers
- Make a car financing decision
- Track car expenses

Making Car Purchase Decisions

How do you really know if you're getting the best car value for your money? Edmund's Web site is a helpful guide (**www.edmund.com**)—it's easy to navigate and contains a wealth of information.

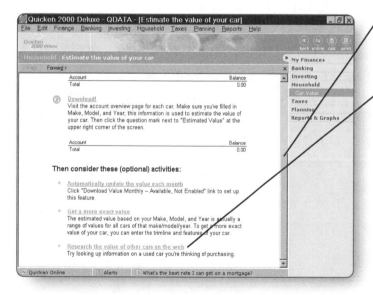

1. Click on **Household**. The Household menu will appear.

2. Click on **Car Values Download**. The Estimate the value of your car page will appear in the Household window.

3. Scroll to the **bottom of the page**. You'll see a list of optional activities.

4. Click on the **Research the value of other cars on the web link**. You'll be taken to Edmund's Automotive Information Source For Quicken page.

Edmund's is a good place to start car shopping because you can sit in one place and find loads of new and used automobile information.

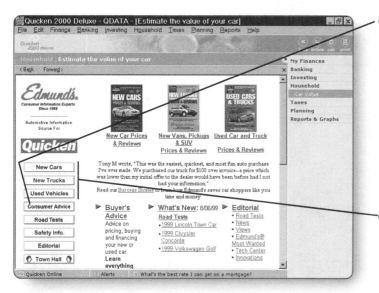

Consumer Advice. Before you start car shopping, check out the Consumer Advice link. You'll find help on how to shop for a car, advice on leasing a vehicle, and how to deal with used car salesmen. A search feature allows you to find the history of a particular car and much more.

New Cars, New Trucks, and Used Vehicles. These links provide specifications and prices, reviews, insurance estimates, warranty information, and directions to a car dealer near you.

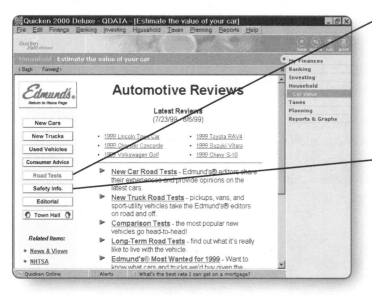

Road tests. If you really want to know about a car's performance, check out the Road Tests link. You can read a number of reviews and comparison tests and find Edmund's favorite picks.

Safety Info. Hang out with the crash test dummies at the Safety Info link. You'll find crash test data, manufacturer recalls, and other car safety information.

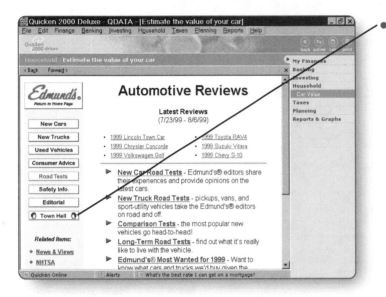

Town Hall. If you're curious about what others have to say about cars, sign up at the Town Hall and chat with other car owners about their cars and related issues.

Calculating Car Loan Payments

If you can't pay cash for a car, you need to consider financing options. Determine what the monthly payments would be and how they relate to your budget. Don't forget to consider other car expenses, such as gasoline, parking fees, car insurance, and maintenance.

Visiting CarFinance.Com

An Auto Loan Calculator appears at the bottom of each of the car information pages in Edmund's Web site. Another loan calculator is hidden away in Edmund's pages but if you don't want to search for these, you can use the Quicken loan calculator.

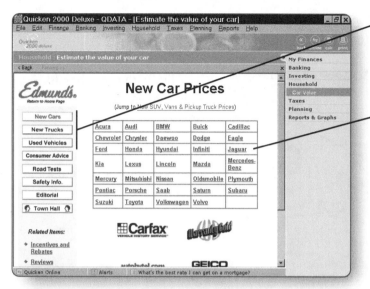

1. Click on the **link** for New Cars, New Trucks, or Used Vehicles. A list of car manufacturers will appear.

2. Click on the **manufacturer** of the car that you are interested in buying. A list of car models will appear.

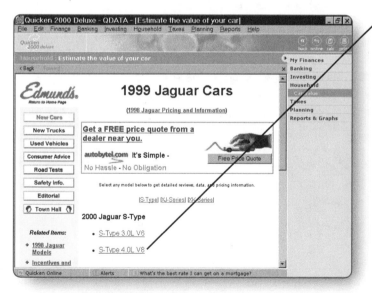

3. Click on a **model**. The information page for the automobile will appear.

4. Scroll to the bottom of the **page**. The Auto Loan Calculator will appear.

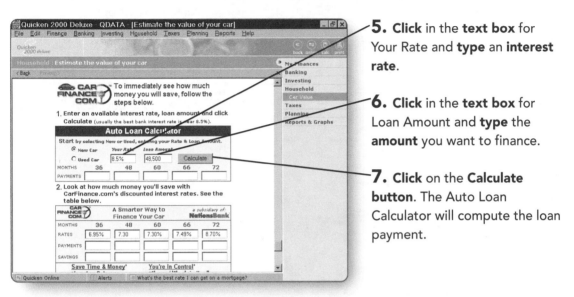

5. Click in the **text box** for Your Rate and **type** an **interest rate**.

6. Click in the **text box** for Loan Amount and **type** the **amount** you want to finance.

7. Click on the **Calculate button**. The Auto Loan Calculator will compute the loan payment.

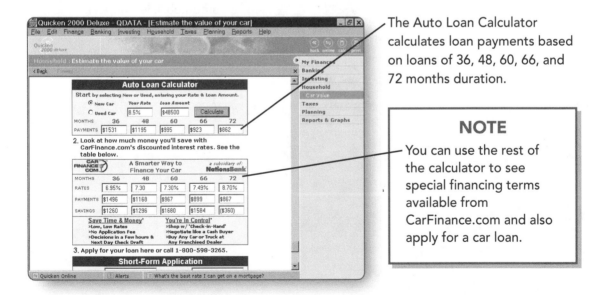

The Auto Loan Calculator calculates loan payments based on loans of 36, 48, 60, 66, and 72 months duration.

NOTE

You can use the rest of the calculator to see special financing terms available from CarFinance.com and also apply for a car loan.

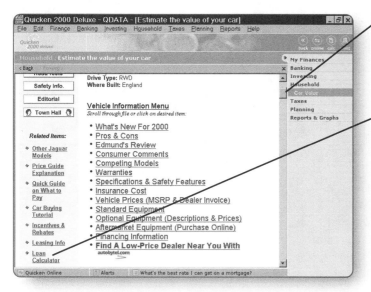

8. Scroll toward the top of the **page**. You'll see the navigation bar along the left side of the page.

9. Click on the **Loan Calculator link**. The Loan Calculator page will appear.

10. Click in the **text box** for Price of Car and **type** the **price** you expect to pay for the vehicle. Do not use commas.

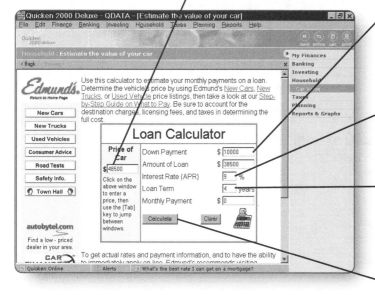

11. Click in the **text box** for Down Payment and **type** the **amount** you'll be paying out of pocket for the vehicle.

12. Click in the **text box** for Interest Rate (APR) and **type** the **interest rate** you expect to pay.

13. Click in the **text box** for Loan Term and **type** the number of **years** for which you want to finance the vehicle.

14. Click on the **Calculate button**. The monthly payment will be calculated.

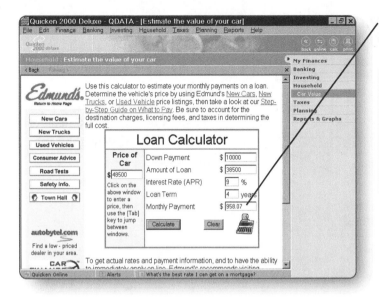

The car payment will appear in the Monthly Payment text box.

NOTE

If the monthly payment is too high, you may need to check for a better interest rate or loan term.

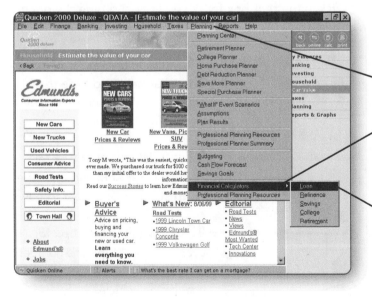

Using the Quicken Loan Calculator

1. Click on **Planning**. The Planning menu will appear.

2. Move the **mouse pointer** to **Financial Calculators**. A submenu will appear.

3. Click on **Loan**. The Loan Calculator will appear.

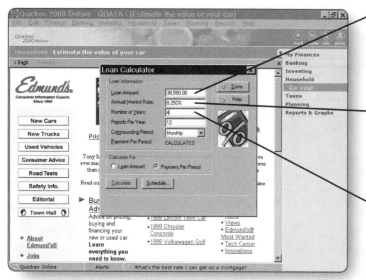

4. Click in the **text box** for Loan Amount and **type** the **amount** that you want to finance.

5. Click in the **text box** for Annual Interest Rate and **type** the **interest rate** you expect to pay.

6. Click in the **text box** for Number of Years and **type** the **number of years** that you will be paying on the loan.

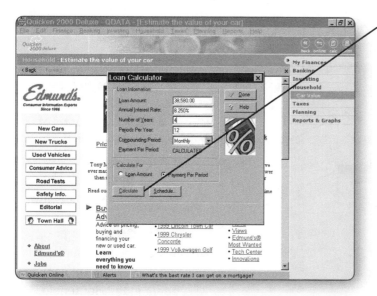

7. Click on the **Calculate button**. The monthly loan payment will be calculated.

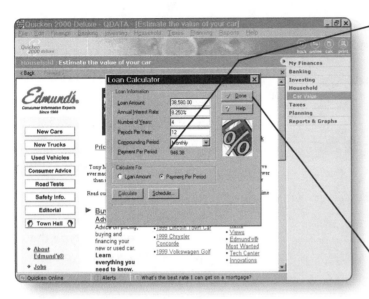

You'll find the monthly payment amount in the Payment Per Period field.

NOTE

You can try out other scenarios by changing the information in the text boxes and clicking on the Calculate button.

8. Click on **Done** when you are finished with the calculator. The calculator will close.

Tracking Car Expenses

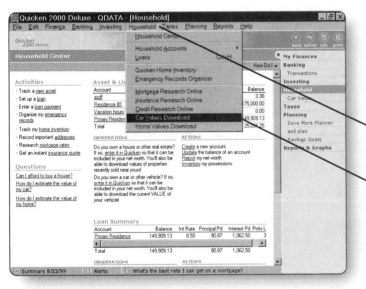

Quicken makes it easy to keep track of your car as an asset account and your automobile loan as a liability account. Let the wizard show you the steps.

1. Click on **Household**. The Household menu will appear.

2. Click on **Car Values Download**. The Find out how much your car is worth! page will appear in the Household window.

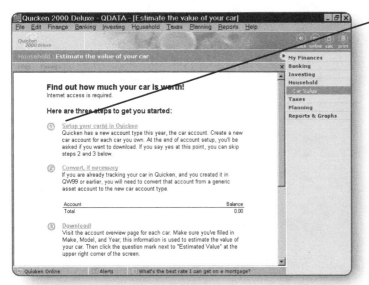

3. Click on the **link** for Setup your car(s) in Quicken. The Asset Account Setup wizard will start and the About this car/vehicle page will be displayed.

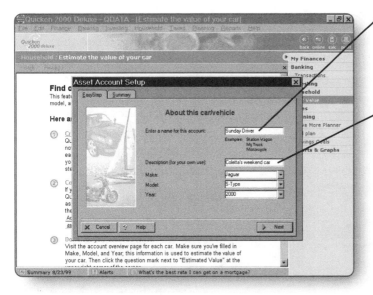

4. Click in the **text box** for Enter a name for this account and **type** a **name** for the car account.

5. Click in the **text box** for Description and **type** a **description** of the car or its use

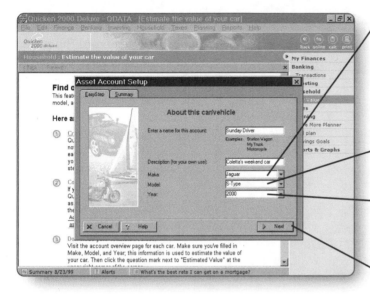

6. **Click** in the **text box** for Make and **type** the **manufacturer** of the car. The wizard will attempt to help you fill in this field. Keep typing until you see the correct name.

7. **Click** in the **text box** for Model and **type** the **car model**.

8. **Click** in the **text box** for Year and **type** the **model year** of the car.

9. **Click** on **Next**. The Enter the starting point information page will appear.

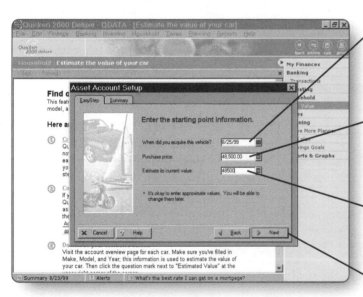

10. **Click** in the **text box** for When did you acquire this vehicle? and **type** the **date** on which you purchased the car.

11. **Click** in the **text box** for Purchase price and **type** the total **amount** you paid for the car.

12. **Click** in the **text box** for Estimate its current value and **type** the resale **value** of the car

13. **Click** on **Next**. The Is there a loan on this vehicle? page will appear.

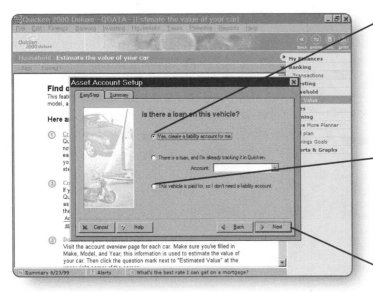

14a. **Click** on the **option button** for Yes, create a liability account for me (if you financed the car). The option will be selected.

OR

14b. **Click** on the **option button** for This vehicle is paid for, so I don't need a liability account if the car is paid off. The option will be selected.

15. **Click** on **Next**. The Summary page will appear.

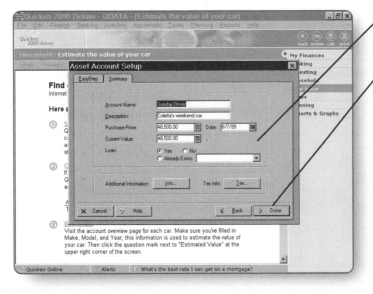

16. **Verify** that the **information** is correct.

17. **Click** on **Done**. If you financed the car, the Edit Loan wizard will start.

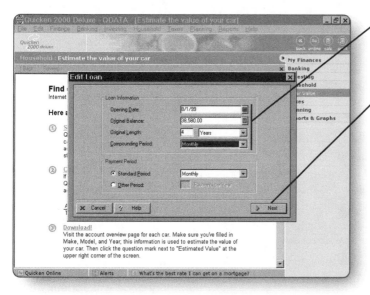

18. **Type** the **information** about the loan in the appropriate text boxes.

19. **Click** on **Next**. The next page of the Edit Loan wizard will appear.

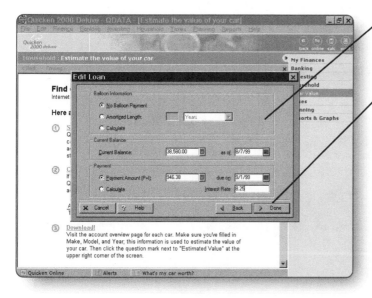

20. **Type** the **information** about the loan in the appropriate text boxes.

21. **Click** on **Done**. The Edit Loan Payment dialog box will appear.

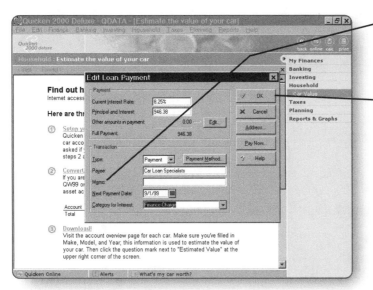

22. **Type** the **information** about the loan payment in the Transaction section.

23. **Click** on **OK**. A confirmation dialog box will appear.

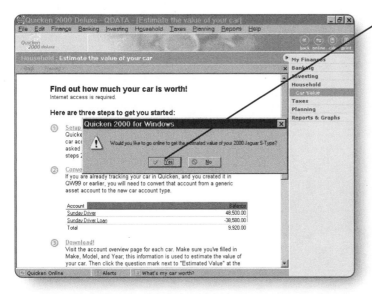

24. **Click** on **Yes**. The current market value for your automobile will be updated in your Quicken records.

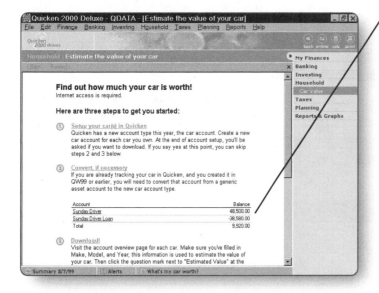

You now have everything you need to keep track of your car's value and your automobile loan.

21

Going to College

You're never too young or too old to think about going to college, junior college, business college, or a vocational school. To pursue your interests or gain skills to help advance your career, you'll want to plan for college tuition, books, housing, and other expenses. Quicken contains two tools that can help you make those important college financial planning decisions. The College Calculator is a simple tool if you're looking for some quick numbers to use for planning purposes. The College Planner provides some advice and information on how much college is going to cost and how to pay for it. In this chapter, you'll learn how to:

- Use the College Calculator to determine just how much you'll need to set aside to pay for a college education

- Work with the College Planner to build a long-term plan to finance a college education

Determining College Costs

The College Calculator is a great way to work out a number of scenarios to determine college costs and annual contributions to a college savings account.

Computing Annual Savings Amounts

If you know what a college education will cost, you can use the College Calculator to determine how much you will need to invest in a college savings account in one lump sum in order to be able to pay those college costs as they occur.

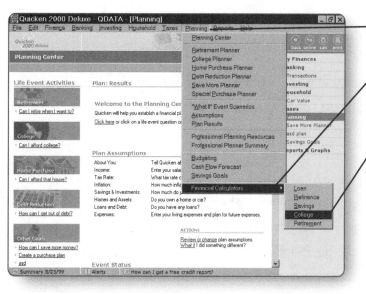

1. Click on **Planning**. The Planning menu will appear.

2. Move the **mouse pointer** to **Financial Calculators**. A submenu will appear.

3. Click on **College**. The College Calculator will appear.

4. Click on the **Current College Savings option button**. The option will be selected.

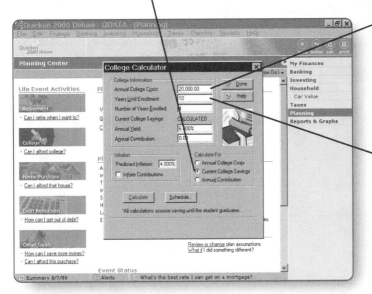

5. Click in the **Annual College Costs text box** and **type** the **amount** you estimate will be needed to cover college costs for a year. The amount will appear in the text box.

6. Click in the **Years Until Enrollment text box** and **type** the **number** of years it will be before the college education will start.

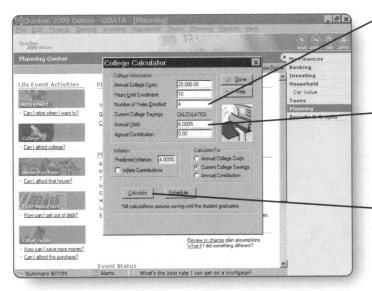

7. Click in the **Number of Years Enrolled text box** and **type** the number of **years** that the college education will last.

8. Click in the **text box** for Annual Yield and **type** the **interest rate** you expect to earn on the college savings account.

9. Click on the **Calculate button**. The starting college savings amount will be calculated.

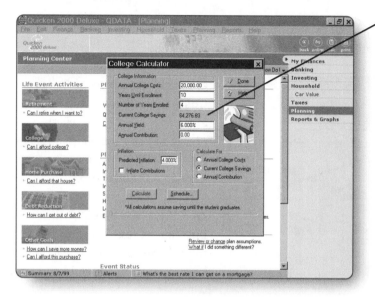

You'll find the amount you'll need to invest as a lump sum in order to be able to pay the estimated college costs in the Current College Savings field.

Computing an Annual Savings Amount

If you know how much the college education will cost, you can calculate how much to save each year to be able to pay those costs.

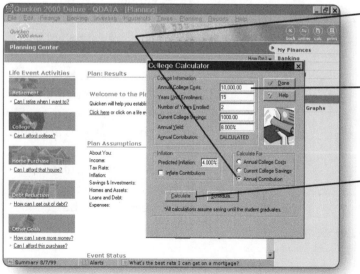

1. **Click** on the **Annual Contribution option button**. The option will be selected.

2. **Click** in each **text box**, in turn, in the College Information section and **type** the required **information**.

3. **Click** on the **Calculate button**. The annual savings amount will be calculated.

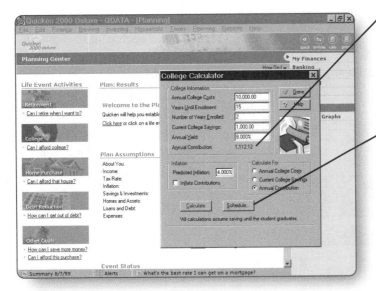

The amount that you'll need to save each year will appear in the Annual contribution field.

Determining College Spending Limits

If you have some money set aside and are able to set aside an amount every year for a college education, you can determine how much you will have when it comes time for you or your kids to go off to college.

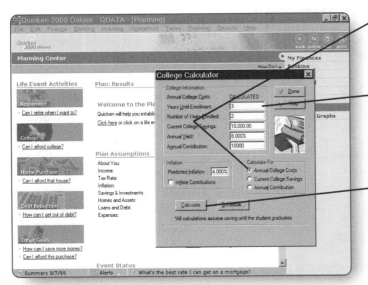

1. Click on the **Annual College Costs option button**. The option will be selected.

2. Click in each **text box,** in turn, in the College Information section and **type** the required **information** in the text boxes.

3. Click on the **Calculate button**. The annual college spending limit will be calculated.

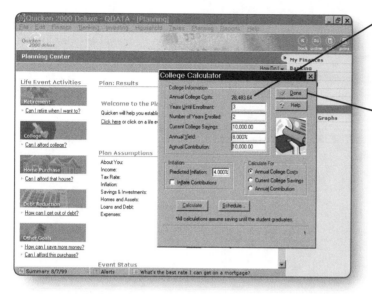

You'll find the amount that you can spend each year for college costs in the Annual College Costs field.

4. Click on **Done** when you are finished with the College Calculator. The calculator will close.

Using the College Planner

If you want to work out a long-term, flexible plan for funding a college education, but you don't want to pay a professional planner for assistance, use the services of the College Planner. The planner contains an abundance of guidance and ideas.

The College Planner is a powerful tool and the instructions that follow are just an introduction to get you started.

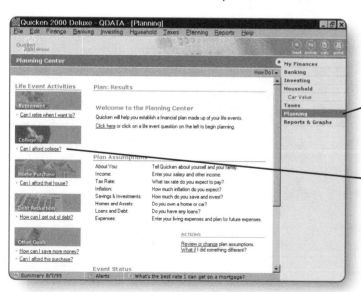

1. Click on the **Planning QuickTab**. The Planning Center will appear.

2. Click on the **Can I afford college? link.** The Welcome page of the College Planner will appear in the Planning window.

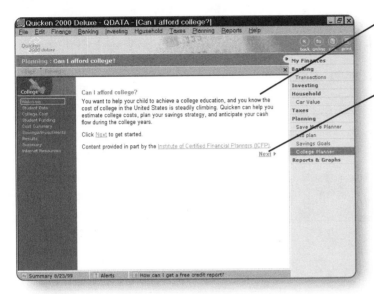

3. Read each **page** of the planner carefully before you proceed to the next page.

4. Click on the **Next link**. The Student Data page of the College Planner will appear.

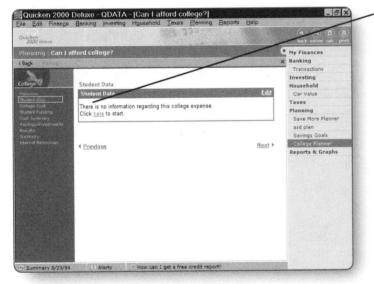

5. Click on the **Enter link**. A dialog box will appear.

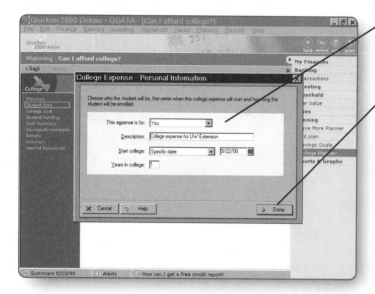

6. **Enter** the appropriate **information** in each of the text fields.

7. **Click** on **Done**. You will return to the College Planner.

8. **Continue** through the **College Planner**. Remember to read the directions, type the appropriate information, and click on the Next link to continue. You will come to the Results page.

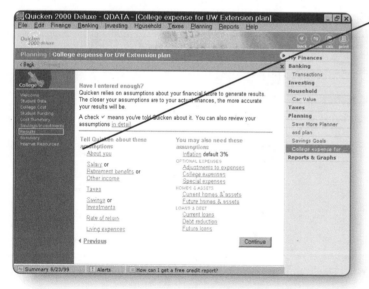

9. **Click** on a **link** in the Tell Quicken about these assumptions area. If Quicken has more information, it can better help you. A dialog box will appear.

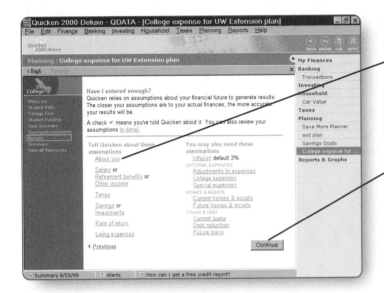

NOTE
For those assumptions that you've completed, a check mark will appear next to the link.

10. **Click** on the **Continue button**. The What if page will appear.

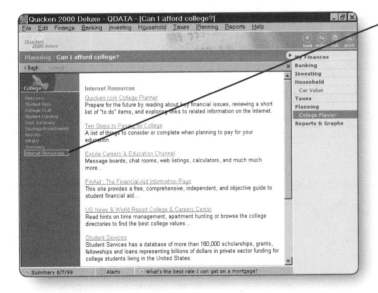

11. **Click** on **Internet Resources**. The Internet Resources page will appear. This page contains a number of resources for the college-bound.

22

Purchasing a Home

Buying a home is a major decision for most people. There are so many decisions to make just about the house itself—the location, number of bedrooms, the size of the yard, and that's only the beginning. Unfortunately, the major factor in deciding what kind of house to buy is usually the price. Before you go house hunting, check out Quicken's home purchase tools: a calculator to help you determine monthly mortgage payments, a planner to guide you through the home buying process, and even a Web site. QuickenMortgage.com can help you find a mortgage lender on the Internet. In this chapter, you'll learn how to:

- Calculate how much you can afford to borrow
- Find the services provided by the Home Purchase Planner
- Find mortgage information and lenders on the Web

Calculating Your Mortgage Budget

If you're looking for an easy way to do a few mortgage calculations, start with the Loan Calculator. The Loan Calculator can estimate a monthly mortgage payment based on the loan and interest rate you will be paying. It can also determine the maximum mortgage loan you can afford based on what you want to pay as a monthly payment.

Estimating Monthly Mortgage Payments

If you've found a house you really like, but aren't sure if you'll be able to afford the monthly payments, the Loan Calculator can figure the loan amount and your monthly payment.

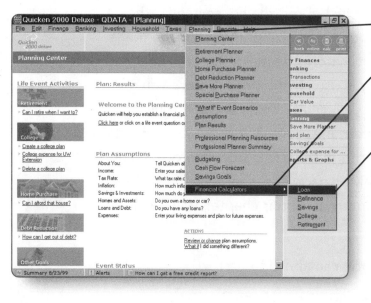

1. **Click** on **Planning**. The Planning menu will appear.

2. **Move** the **mouse pointer** to **Financial Calculators**. A submenu will appear.

3. **Click** on **Loan**. The Loan Calculator will appear.

4. Click on the **Payment Per Period option button** if it is not already selected. The option will be selected.

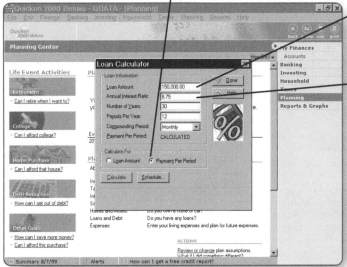

5. Click in the **Loan Amount text box** and **type** the **amount** of the mortgage loan.

6. Click in the **Annual Interest Rate text box** and **type** the **interest rate** you expect to pay on the mortgage loan.

NOTE

If you'll be working with an adjustable rate loan, enter the beginning interest rate.

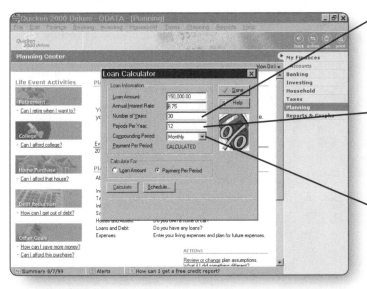

7. Click in the **Number of Years text box** and **type** the **number** of years you will be paying on the loan.

8. Click in the **Periods Per Year text box** and **type** the **number** of payments you'll make each year.

9. Click on the **Compounding Period down arrow** and **click** on the **frequency** at which interest will be compounded on the loan. The frequency will appear in the list box.

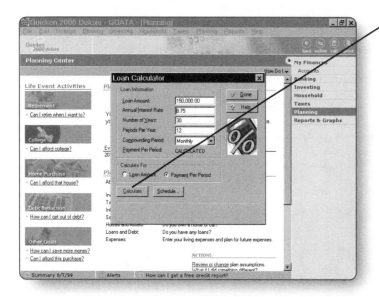

10. Click on **Calculate**. The monthly payment will be calculated.

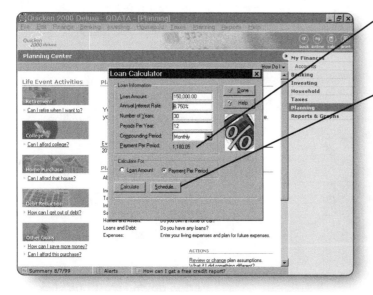

The amount of the loan payment will appear in the Payment Per Period field.

11. Click on the **Schedule button**. The Approximate Future Payment Schedule will appear.

The Approximate Future Payment Schedule shows the principal and interest payments during the life of the loan. You'll notice that after each payment, the balance of the loan is reduced.

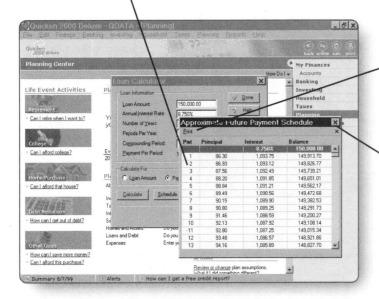

12. Click on the **Close button**. The Approximate Future Payment Schedule will close and you'll return to the Loan Calculator.

Estimating the Loan Amount

If you know how much you can afford to pay each month in mortgage payments, the Loan Calculator can determine a maximum loan amount.

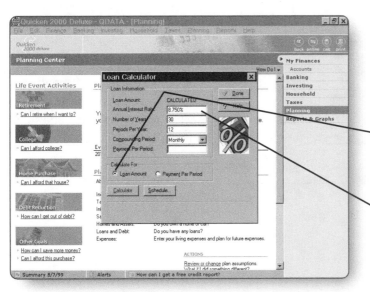

1. Click on the **Loan Amount option button**. The option will be selected.

2. Click in the **Annual Interest Rate text box** and **type** the **interest rate** you expect to pay on the mortgage loan.

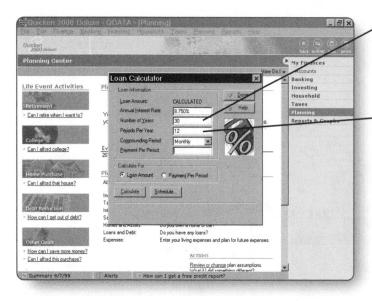

3. **Click** in the **Number of Years text box** and **type** the **number of years** you will be paying on the loan.

4. **Click** in the **Periods Per Year text box** and **type** the **number of payments** you will be making each year.

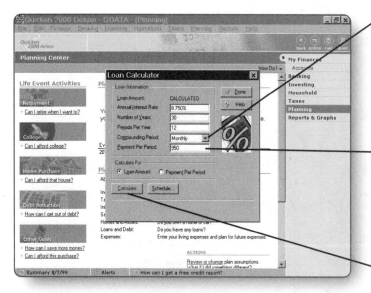

5. **Click** on the **Compounding Period down arrow** and **Click** on the **frequency** at which interest will be compounded on the loan. The frequency will appear in the list box.

6. **Click** in the Payment Per Period **text box** and **type** the **amount** you can afford to pay each month for a mortgage payment.

7. **Click** on **Calculate**. The loan amount will be calculated.

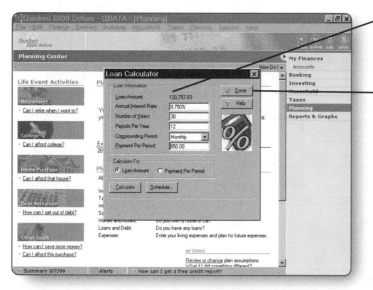

The amount of the loan that you can afford will appear in the Loan Amount field.

8. Click on **Done** when you are finished using the calculator. The calculator will close.

Consulting with the Home Purchase Planner

If you feel you need a guided approach to making a home purchase decision, the Home Purchase Planner is worth a look. You'll feel like you're working with a seasoned pro as you click your way through the planner.

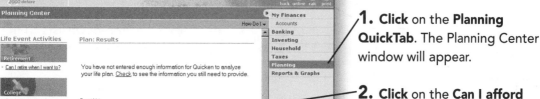

1. Click on the **Planning QuickTab**. The Planning Center window will appear.

2. Click on the **Can I afford that house? link**. The Home Purchase Planner will appear in the Planning window.

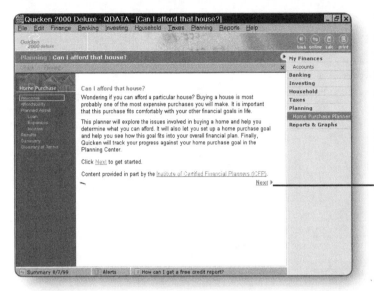

The Home Purchase Planner works like the other planners that you've seen used in this book. Take your time when working through the planner. There's a lot of information for you to read and many questions to answer.

3. **Click** on the **Next link**. The next page of the planner will appear.

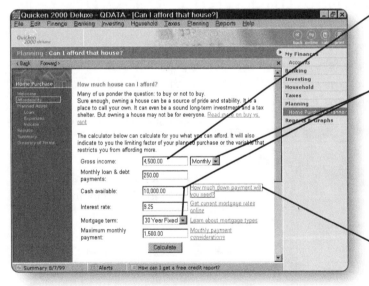

4. **Click** in the **text boxes** and **type** the **information** needed by the planner.

5. **Click** on the **list box down arrows**. Drop-down lists will appear.

6. **Click** to make a **selection** from the drop-down lists. The selections will be highlighted.

7. **Click** on a **link**. A page will appear that contains more information.

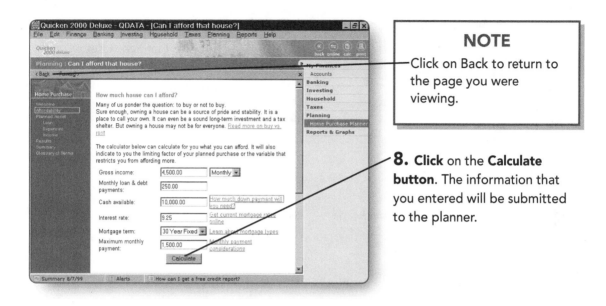

NOTE

Click on Back to return to the page you were viewing.

8. Click on the **Calculate button**. The information that you entered will be submitted to the planner.

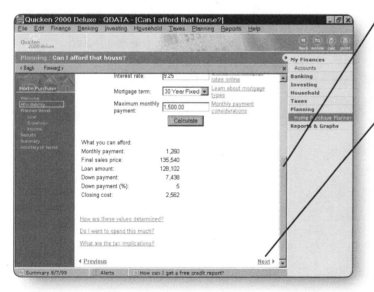

9. Scroll to the **bottom** of the page. You'll see the results of the information that you entered into the planner.

10. Click on the **Next link**. The Planned Asset page will appear.

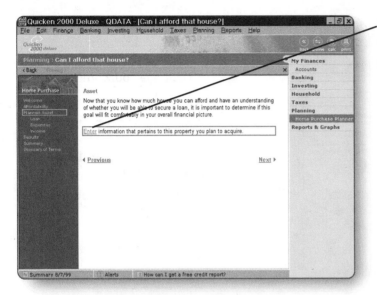

11. **Click** on the **Enter link**. The Add Planned Asset wizard will start.

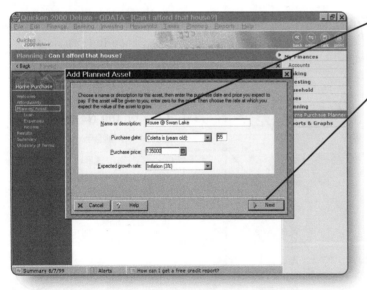

12. **Click** in the **text boxes** and **type** the requested **information**.

13. **Click** on **Next**. The next page of the wizard will appear.

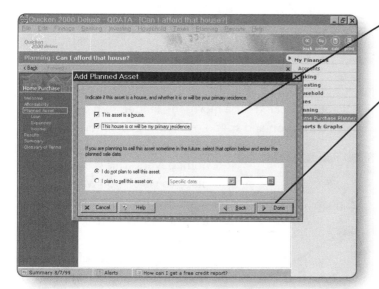

14. **Answer** each **question**. The options you choose will be selected.

15. **Click** on **Done**. You will return to the planner.

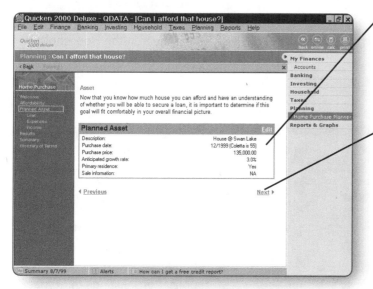

You'll see the information about the house you intend to buy in the Planned Asset section. If you want to change this information, click on the Edit link.

16. **Click** on **Next** and continue working with the planner. When you get to the Summary page, you'll see how well you'll be able to afford your planned dream home.

Researching Mortgage Rates on the Web

Well, it's time to do a little shopping from the comfort of your chair. If you're looking for a mortgage lender, turn on your Internet connection and speed over to QuickenMortgage.com. This site is not just for first-time homebuyers. This is also a good place to visit if you want to refinance your home or take out a home equity loan.

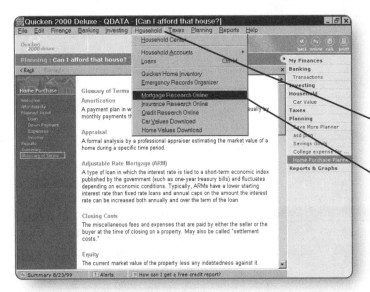

1. Click on **Household**. The Household menu will appear.

2. Click on **Mortgage Research Online**. The QuickenMortgage.com page will appear in the Household Center window.

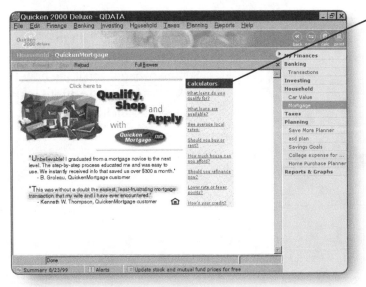

3. Click on the **links** to visit the different areas at QuickenMortgage.com.

You'll find an abundance of tools at this site: interest rate charts, loan comparisons, credit assessments, online applications, listings of homes for sale, and more. Have fun exploring and learning!

23

Planning for Retirement

If you want to enjoy a comfortable retirement with enough income to meet your needs, you need to begin planning early. The sooner you begin your retirement plan and start saving, the more money you'll have when you retire. At least that's the theory. Your retirement income level will depend on the soundness of your investment plan, how much money you invest, and how well you stick to the plan. Of course, you will need to adjust the plan along the way. Quicken contains two useful retirement planning tools. The Retirement Calculator can help you make some quick calculations, and the Retirement Planner can help you build a sound, long-term retirement plan. If you need professional financial help, Quicken can help you find a Certified Financial Planner. In this chapter, you'll learn how to:

- Perform some quick and easy calculations to determine how much you'll need to save to have the retirement income you want

- Enlist the professional help of the Retirement Planner to put together a comprehensive retirement plan

- Find a professional financial planner in your area to help you achieve your financial goals

Using the Retirement Calculator

You've seen many of the financial calculators in the last few chapters of this book. The Retirement Calculator works much the same way they do. You tell the calculator what to compute, type in a few numbers, and the calculator does its job. When you want to create a few quick retirement scenarios, the Retirement Calculator is the tool to choose.

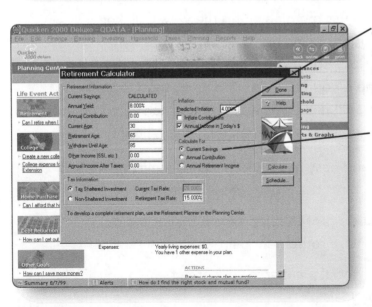

1. Click on **Planning**. The Planning menu will appear.

2. Move the **mouse pointer** to **Financial Calculators**. A submenu will appear.

3. Click on **Retirement**. The Retirement Calculator will appear.

4. Click on an **option button** to select one of the retirement calculations. The option will be selected. You can perform three different calculations.

- **Current Savings**. If you want to know how much money you need to have currently in savings in order to attain your retirement income goals, click on this option button.

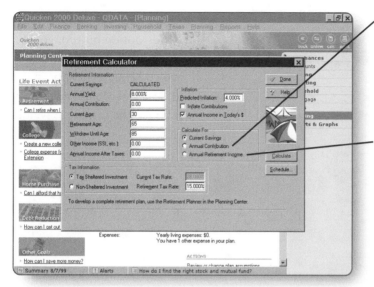

- **Annual Contribution**. To determine how much you need to save each year in order to reach your retirement goal, click on this option button.

- **Annual Retirement Income**. If you want to know how much retirement income your current savings will provide, click on this option button.

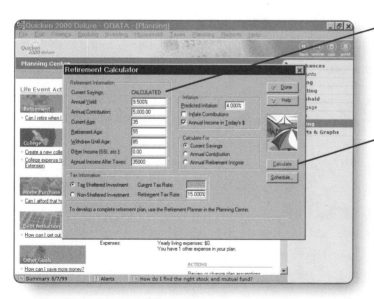

5. **Click** in each of the **text boxes** in the Retirement Information section and **type** the **information** needed by the calculator

6. **Click** on the **Calculate button**. The calculator will perform the math for you.

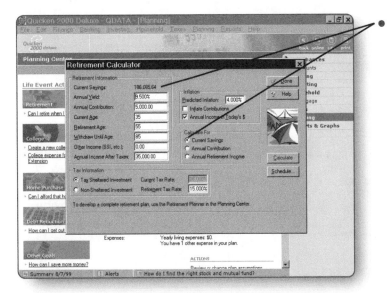

- If you selected the Current Savings option button, you'll see the amount you need to have currently in savings in the Retirement Information section in the Current Savings field.

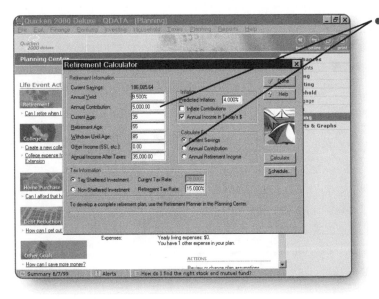

- The Annual Contribution calculation is found in the Annual Contribution field.

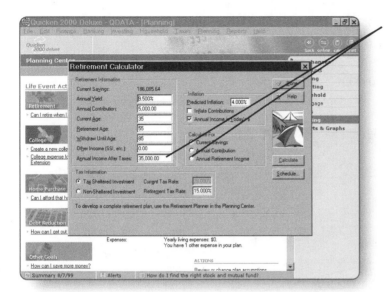

The Annual Retirement Income calculation is found in the Annual Income After Taxes field.

7. Click on **Done** when you are finished with the calculator.

Creating a Retirement Plan

You've already seen some of the planners that are found in Quicken. The Retirement Planner works the same way as other planners, but may take more time. If you've been keeping your records in Quicken, you'll see much of the information filled out for you. You can always add and edit information as needed.

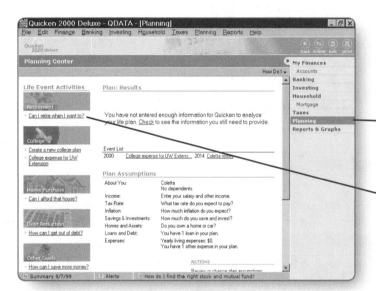

1. Click on the **Planning QuickTab**. The Planning Center will appear.

2. Click on the **Can I retire when I want to? Link.** The Retirement Planner will appear in the Planning window.

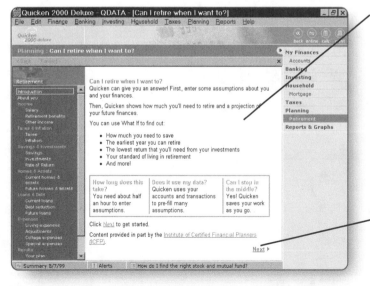

The Retirement Planner works like the other planners that you've seen used in this book, but is much more involved. Take your time when working through the planner. There's a lot of information for you to read, and the planner will ask many questions that you will need to answer.

3. Click on the **Next link**. The next page of the planner will appear.

You'll notice that some areas of the planner have been filled in for you. These figures were taken from information that you entered in other areas of Quicken.

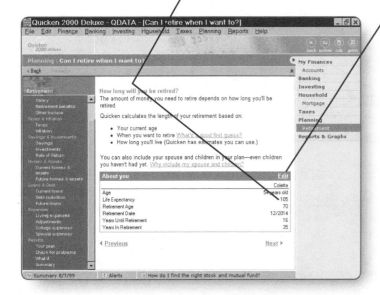

4. Click on the **Edit link** if you want to update the information. A dialog box will open, and you can change any of the information.

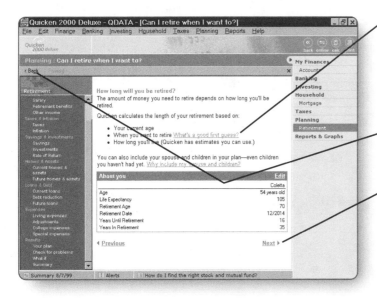

5. Click on a **link**. A page will appear that contains more information. You can click on Back to return to the page you were viewing.

6. Click on **Back** to return to the page you were viewing.

7. Click on the **Next link**. The next page of the planner will appear.

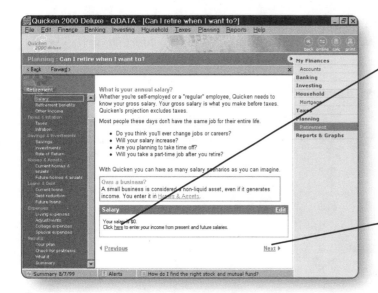

TIP

If Quicken does not have enough information, you'll see a Click here link. Click on the link to open a dialog box where you can enter the needed information.

8. Click on the **Next link** and work your way through each page of the planner.

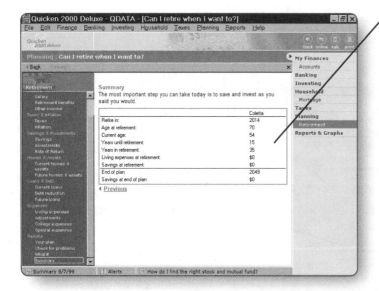

When you get to the end of the plan, you'll see a Summary page. You can print this page if you want to keep a record of this version of your plan.

NOTE

You can always come back later and revise your plan. Quicken will automatically save it.

Finding a Certified Financial Planner

If you don't feel confident managing your own finances, Quicken can guide you toward some professional help. Before you begin searching for a financial planner, you may want to fill out the Financial Planner Summary form. This is a good starting point for you and your prospective financial planner.

Filling Out the Financial Planner Summary

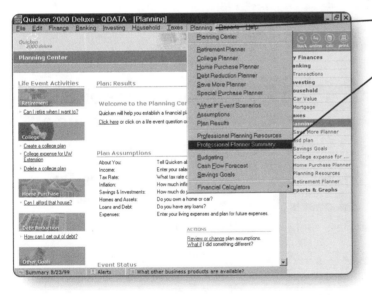

1. Click on **Planning**. The Planning menu will appear.

2. Click on **Professional Planner Summary**. The Financial Planner summary will appear in the Planning window.

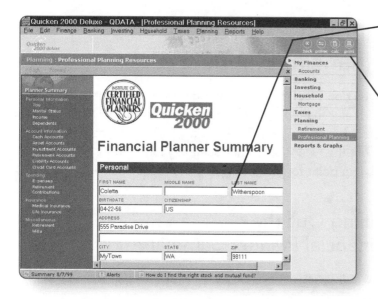

3. Click in each of the **text boxes** and **type** a **response** to the requested information

4. Click on the **Print button** when you have completed the form. The form will print.

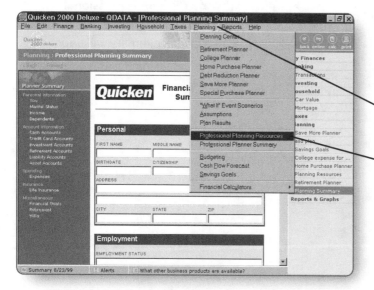

Searching for a Certified Financial Planner

1. Click on **Planning**. The Planning menu will appear.

2. Click on **Professional Planning Resources**. The Planning Resources page will appear.

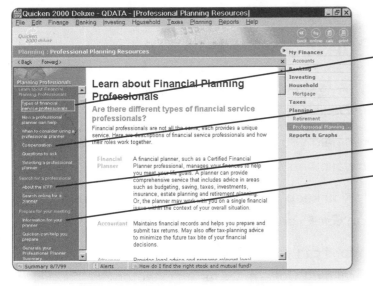

You'll find some good information at this site.

- Find some good tips on how to choose a financial planner.

- Learn how to interview a prospective financial planner.

- Search for a financial planner.

- Find out how to prepare for your first meeting with your new financial planner.

Part V Review Questions

1. Where can you go online to do car comparison shopping? *See "Making Car Purchase Decisions" in Chapter 20*

2. Which Quicken tool can help you calculate car loan payments? *See "Calculating Car Loan Payments" in Chapter 20*

3. How can Quicken help you keep track of your vehicle's value and car loan? *See "Tracking Car Expenses" in Chapter 20*

4. What different calculations can you perform with the College Calculator? *See "Determining College Costs" in Chapter 21*

5. Which Quicken feature can help you build a long-term college savings plan? *See "Using the College Planner" in Chapter 21*

6. How do you compute monthly mortgage payments on a mortgage for which you plan to apply? *See "Calculating Your Mortgage Budget" in Chapter 22*

7. What planning tool contains helpful advice about buying a home? *See "Consulting with the Home Purchase Planner" in Chapter 22*

8. Where can you find competitive mortgage rates on the Web? *See "Researching Mortgage Rates on the Web" in Chapter 22*

9. Which financial calculator can help you determine how much money you'll need to save in order to have a comfortable retirement? *See "Using the Retirement Calculator" in Chapter 23*

10. Where can you find professionals that can help you manage your finances and plan for future financial needs? *See "Finding a Certified Financial Planner" in Chapter 23*

PART VI

Appendices

A

Installing Quicken 2000

Installing Quicken 2000 is a quick and easy process. Just put the CD in your computer's CD-ROM drive and the setup wizard will walk you right through the process. As you move through the installation process, you'll find that there are several Quicken components that you can install. If you have the room on your computer's hard drive, you may want to give all of the components a try. This book assumes that you are installing Quicken 2000 with all the components. This appendix will guide you through the installation and help you get Quicken 2000 on your computer.

Installing Quicken

Before you begin the installation, you need to verify that your computer meets the minimum hardware configuration, which is a 486 processor running at 66 MHz with 16 MB RAM. For the full installation, you need approximately 85 MB of free hard disk space. You should close any programs that may be open and run Scan Disk and Disk Defragmenter before going any further.

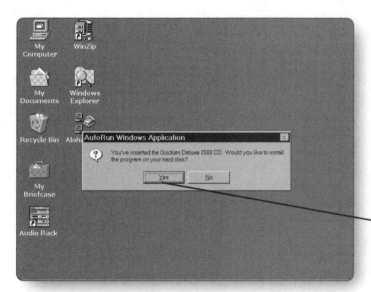

1. Place the **Quicken CD-ROM** in your computer's CD-ROM drive. The AutoRun Windows Application dialog box will open.

2. Click on **Yes**. The Quicken Deluxe 2000 Setup will begin and the Welcome screen of the setup wizard will appear.

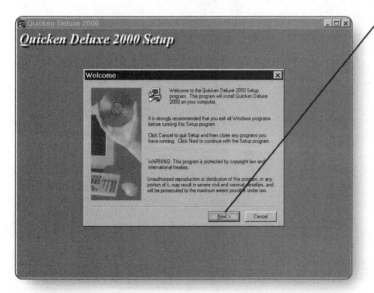

3. Click on **Next**. The Software License Agreement screen will appear.

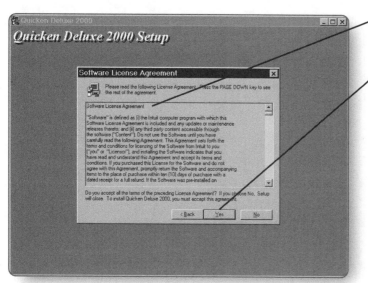

4. Read through the **License Agreement**.

5. Click on **Yes**. The Choose Destination Location screen will appear.

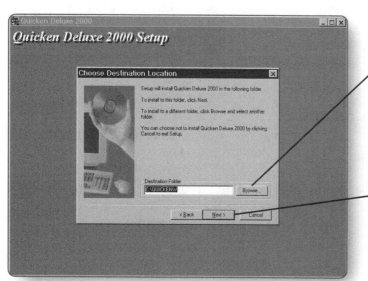

NOTE

Click on the Browse button if you want to change the destination folder. However, it is suggested that you accept the default folder.

6. Click on **Next**. The Confirm New Directory dialog box will open.

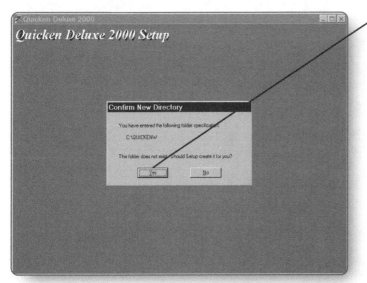

7. Click on **Yes**. The Type of Installation screen will appear.

8a. Click on the **Express option button** if you want to install the default Quicken components.

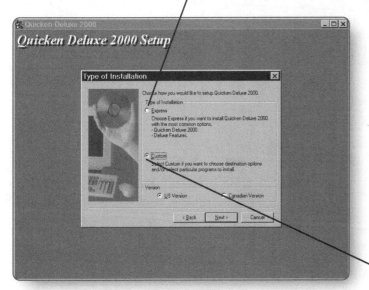

NOTE

The Express option button will not install the 128-bit SSL version of Microsoft Internet Explorer—you'll need a 128-bit browser to do online banking, which you can install as a Custom option.

OR

8b. Click on the **Custom option button** if you want to select which components to install. The option will be selected.

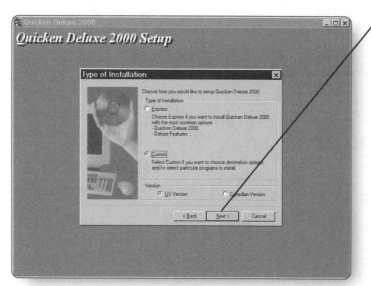

9. Click on **Next**. The Select Installation Components screen will appear, if you selected the Custom option. If you selected the Express option, the program will begin installing on your system.

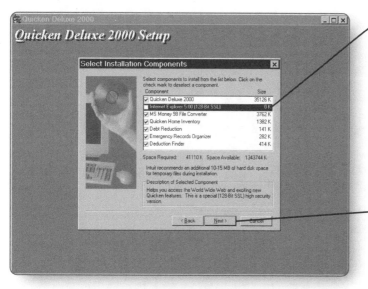

10. Click on the **Internet Explorer 5.00 (128-Bit SSL) check box** if you will be using online banking.

11. Clear any **check boxes** next to those components that you do not want to install. The check boxes will be blank.

12. Click on **Next**. The Select Program Folder screen will appear.

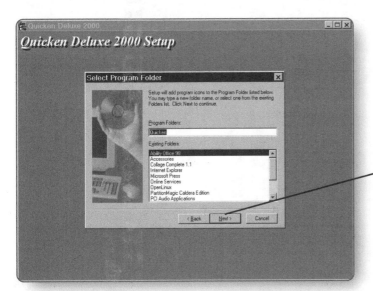

13. **Click** on **Next**. The Check Settings screen will appear.

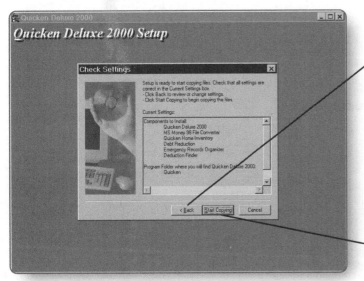

14. **Click** on **Start Copying**. The installation will begin.

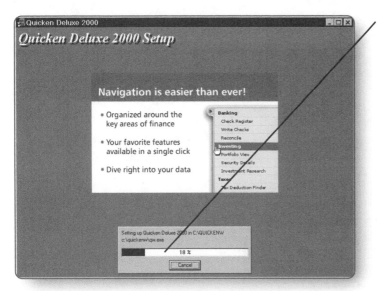

Wait while Quicken installs the software. When the setup is complete, the AOL Offer screen will appear.

NOTE

You'll need a modem with an attached phone line before you can use the AOL offer.

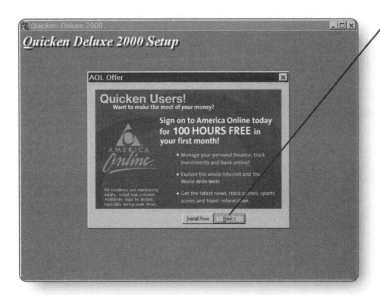

15. Click on **Next**. The Setup Complete screen will appear.

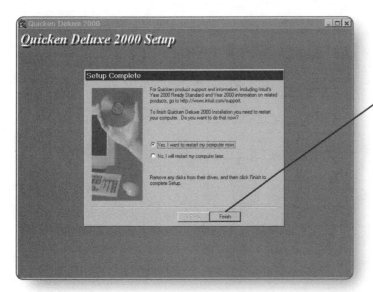

16. **Remove** the **Quicken CD-ROM** from your computer's CD-ROM drive.

17. **Click** on **Finish**. Your computer will restart and the Quicken program will finish the installation process.

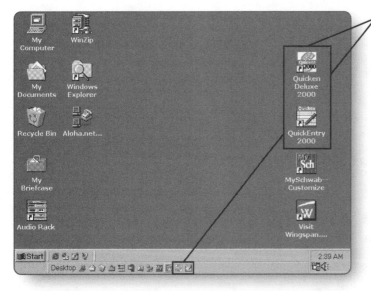

You'll notice that two icons have been added to your desktop, the Quicken Deluxe 2000 icon and the QuickEntry 2000 icon.

B

Using Shortcut Keys with Quicken

You may have noticed the keyboard shortcuts listed on the right side of the Quicken menus. You can use these shortcuts to execute commands without using the mouse to open the menus. Not only do these shortcuts speed up your productivity, but they also help decrease wrist strain caused by excessive mouse usage. Keep these shortcut guides close at hand and practice using these keyboard shortcuts. You'll find that with a little time, you'll be using the keyboard as naturally as you once used the mouse. In this appendix, you'll learn how to use shortcut keys to:

- Move around the Quicken window
- Work with the Registers
- Use the Financial Calendar and budgets

Moving Around Quicken

The following table shows you some common keyboard shortcuts to use when navigating between open windows that you have been viewing in Quicken.

To execute this command	Do this
Move backward between previously displayed windows	Press the Alt and Left Arrow keys simultaneously (Alt+Left Arrow)
Move forward between previously displayed windows	Press Alt+Right Arrow
Display the Quicken Home Page	Press Alt+Home
Print the page you are viewing	Press Ctrl+P
Get Help on the window you are viewing	Press F1

Working with Quicken Files

It's easy to open and back up any data files with these shortcuts

To execute this command	Do this
Open a new data file	Press the Ctrl and O keys simultaneously (Ctrl+O)
Back up a data file	Press Ctrl+B

Using the Register

You'll probably spend most of your time in Quicken working with the various account registers. Here are a few simple keyboard shortcuts you can use while you're working in any of them.

Navigating the Register

To execute this command	Do this
Open the register	Press the Ctrl and R keys simultaneously (Ctrl+R)
Go to the first transaction in a register	Press Home three times
Move to the last transaction in a register	Press End three times
Go to the first field in a transaction	Press Home twice
Go to the last field in a transaction	Press End twice
Move to the next field or column	Press Tab
Move to the previous field or column	Press Shift+Tab
Go to the beginning of a field	Press Home
Go to the end of a field	Press End
Move to the next transaction	Press Page Down
Move to the previous transaction	Press Page Up

Entering Transactions in the Register

To execute this command	Do this
Select an account	Press Ctrl+A
Select a category	Press Ctrl+C
Go to a new transaction	Press Ctrl+N
Enter a transaction	Press Enter
Open the Split Transaction window	Press Ctrl+S
Close the Split Transaction window	Press Ctrl+Enter
Pay a scheduled transaction	Press Ctrl+J
Memorize a transaction	Press Ctrl+M
Recall a memorized transaction	Press Ctrl+T

Editing Transactions in the Register

To execute this command	Do this
Decrease the selected date or check number	Press – (Minus key)
Increase the selected date or check number	Press + (Plus key)
Find a transaction	Press Ctrl+F
Cut a field in the register	Press Shift+Del
Copy a field in the register	Press Ctrl+Ins
Paste a field in the register	Press Shift+Ins
Delete a transaction	Press Ctrl+D
Void a transaction	Press Ctrl+V

Working with Planning Tools

Two common planning tools are the Financial Calculator and the Budget. It's possible to maneuver your way through these tools without the aid of a mouse.

Moving Around the Financial Calendar

To execute this command	Do this
Open the Financial Calendar	Press Ctrl+K
Select the current date	Press t
Go to the first day of the current month	Press m
Go to the last day of the current month	Press h
Display the first day of the current year	Press y
Display the last day of the current year	Press r
Go to a specific date	Press Alt+G
Add a note to the calendar	Press Alt+N

Creating a Budget

To execute this command	Do this
Go to the first row in the budget	Press the Ctrl and Home keys simultaneously (Ctrl+Home)
Go to the last row in the budget	Press Ctrl+End
Move to the right in a row of budget items	Press Tab
Move to the left in a row of budget items	Press Shift+Tab
Go to the row above the currently selected row	Press ↑
Go to the row below the currently selected row	Press ↓
Go to the first cell in the current row	Press Home+Home
Go to the last cell in the current row	Press End+End
Scroll the budget one page to the left	Press Ctrl+Left Arrow
Scrolls the budget one page to the right	Press Ctrl+Right Arrow
Scroll up the budget to display the previous group of categories	Press Page Up
Scroll down the budget to display the next group of categories	Press Page Down
Undo the last amount just entered	Press Esc

C

Quicken Product Feature Comparison

Quicken 2000	Basic	Deluxe	Home & Business	Suite
Organize & Make the Most of Your Money				
Streamlined User Interface	NEW	NEW	NEW	NEW
Bank Account & Credit Card Tracking	X	X	X	X
Easy Bill Paying	X	X	X	X
Receive Bills Online*	X	X	X	X
Fast Checkbook Balancing	X	X	X	X
Online Banking & Online Payments*	IMPROVED	IMPROVED	IMPROVED	IMPROVED
One Step Update*	IMPROVED	IMPROVED	IMPROVED	IMPROVED
Background Downloading	NEW	NEW	NEW	NEW
Reports & Graphs	30 IMPROVED	60 IMPROVED	70+ IMPROVED	60 IMPROVED
Budgets & Loan Tracking	X	X	X	X
My Finances Home Page	IMPROVED	IMPROVED	IMPROVED	IMPROVED
Financial Activity Centers	NEW	IMPROVED	IMPROVED	IMPROVED
Support Pocket Quicken for Palm® Organizers	X	X	X	X
Track in Multiple Currencies	X	X	X	X
One-stop Shopping for Auto & Life Insurance*	IMPROVED	IMPROVED	IMPROVED	IMPROVED
One-stop Shopping for Mortgages*	IMPROVED	IMPROVED	IMPROVED	IMPROVED
Address Book	IMPROVED	IMPROVED	IMPROVED	IMPROVED
Account Overviews		NEW	NEW	NEW
Enter Transactions When Away from Home via Web (WebEntry)*		X	X	X
Quick Entry		X	X	X
Download Car Values**		NEW	NEW	NEW
Download Home Values**		NEW	NEW	NEW
Alerts		IMPROVED	IMPROVED	IMPROVED
Personal Credit Report		X (Free until Dec. 31, 2000)	X (Free until Dec. 31, 2000)	X (Free until Dec. 31, 2000)
Invest Smarter				
Investment Tracking	basic	complete	complete	complete
Downloading Investment Account Information*	X	X	X	X
Online Trading*	X	X	X	X
Track Against Market Indexes	IMPROVED	IMPROVED	IMPROVED	IMPROVED
Track Using "Average Cost" Method	X	X	X	X
Track Employee Stock Options		NEW	NEW	NEW
401(k) Tracking		X	X	X

Quicken 2000	Basic	Deluxe	Home & Business	Suite
Invest Smarter, *continued*				
Current News, Quotes & Research*		IMPROVED (Free until Dec. 31, 2000)	IMPROVED (Free until Dec. 31, 2000)	IMPROVED (Free until Dec. 31, 2000)
Stock Screener*		X	X	X
Mutual Fund Finder*		X	X	X
Stock Evaluator*		NEW	NEW	NEW
Download Historical Stock Quotes-Up to 5 years*		X	X	X
Download Asset Classes*		IMPROVED	IMPROVED	IMPROVED
Compare Your Asset Allocation to a Target Portfolio		NEW	NEW	NEW
Estimate Capital Gains		X	X	X
Portfolio Value vs. Cost Graph		NEW	NEW	NEW
Multiple Security Charting		NEW	NEW	NEW
View Quicken Portfolio Away from Home Via Web*		IMPROVED	IMPROVED	IMPROVED
Plan for the Future				
Integrated Retirement Planner		NEW	NEW	NEW
Integrated College Planner		NEW	NEW	NEW
Home Purchase Planner		NEW	NEW	NEW
Improved Debt Reduction Planner		IMPROVED	IMPROVED	IMPROVED
Save More Planner		NEW	NEW	NEW
Special Purchase Planner		NEW	NEW	NEW
Professional Planner Summary		NEW	NEW	NEW
Find a Financial Advisor Online		NEW	NEW	NEW
Plan for and Prepare Taxes				
Tax Categorization	IMPROVED	IMPROVED	IMPROVED	IMPROVED
Free Web TurboTax* (with rebate)	X	X	X	X
Frequently Asked Questions	X	X	X	X
Final Review Checks Your Taxes for Accuracy	X	X	X	X
Automatic Import of TurboTax file		NEW	NEW	NEW
Estimate Itemized Deductions		NEW	NEW	NEW
Estimate Tax Withholding		NEW	NEW	NEW
Shared Tax Profile		NEW	NEW	NEW
Easy-Step Interview to Prepare Taxes		X	X	X
Free Electronic Tax Filing +		X	X	X

Quicken 2000	Basic	Deluxe	Business	Suite
Plan for and Prepare Taxes, *continued*				
Find and Track Tax Deductions		X	X	X
Tax Activity Center		X	X	X
Automatically Track for Possible Tax Deductions		X	X	X
Tax Planning & Estimates		IMPROVED	IMPROVED	IMPROVED
Proactive Tax Alerts		NEW	NEW	NEW
Onscreen Tax Library				X
IRS Publications On-screen				X
Expert Video Advice				X
Tax Q&A				X
Prepare for Emergencies				
Emergency Records Organizer		X	X	X
Home Inventory		X	X	X
Estate Planning	online only	online only	online only	X
Prepare Over 100 Legal Documents				X
Manage Your Business Finances				
Create and Track Invoices			X	
Email Invoices*			NEW	
Print Custom Statements			X	
Integrated Payroll*			NEW	
Accounts Receivable Capabilities			X	
Accounts Payable Capabilities			X	
Track Reimbursable Expenses			X	
Complete Business Tax Tracking			X	
Contact Manager Import/Export			NEW	
Manuals				
Making the Most of Your Money with Quicken 2000		X	X	X
Business User's Guide			X	

*These features and online transactions services require Internet access. Online transaction services may be subject to application approval and certain service charges. Services and fees may vary by financial institution.

+ Refer to the Quicken 200 Fast Fact Sheet for pricing information.

** Home values may not be available in all areas; car value may not be available in all models.

Glossary

A

Accounts. Quicken organizes your financial information into separate categories that resemble your real world accounts for your assets and liabilities. Using these accounts you can track your checking and savings activities, your mortgage and credit card transactions, and all of your other financial activities.

Accounts list. This is Quicken's quick overview of your accounts.

Accrual-basis accounting. This is an accounting method that recognizes obligations when they occur, and income when the customer is billed.

Adjustable rate loans. These are loans with a variable interest rate. When the interest rate of your adjustable rate loan changes Quicken can calculate your new payment amount using the new interest rate.

Amortize. To write off a regular part of an asset's cost over a specified time period.

Assets. Items that you own: your car, real-estate, investments, etc. A business definition of an asset is something that has a probable future economic benefit, is controlled by the business, and came about from a prior transaction or event.

Asset depreciation range. This is the defined range of depreciable (amortizable) lives allowed by the Internal Revenue Service for each class of asset. This was replaced by the Accelerated Cost Recovery System (ACRS) but was later revived in the 1986 Tax Reform Act and is used to determine class lives.

B

Balance. The difference between total debits and total credits to an account, as in loan balance or bank balance.

Balloon payment. The last payment on a loan if it is significantly larger than previous payments. These kinds of loans are also called partially amortized loans.

Billminder. A list of upcoming financial actions, bills to pay, payment instructions, etc. It appears each time Quicken opens.

Blue Chip. A high-quality common stock with a long history of consistently paying dividends. These are very attractive long-term investments.

Budget. A plan of actions and programs expressed in assets, liabilities, revenue, and expenses, that directs financial planning and activities to meet the requirements for obtaining a specific operational objective.

C

Cash flow. This is the net result of cash receipts less cash disbursements for a particular operation or asset over a specified period of time.

Categories. A method of identifying transactions by placing them in related groups. An example would be an income category to keep track of deposits and an expense category for automotive repair costs.

Classes. Quicken identifies transactions by assigning them to classes based upon details supplied by you specifying where, when, whom, and to what the transactions apply.

Credit. (1) The entry made in the right-hand column of an account. In double-entry bookkeeping credits are an increase in the liabilities, equity, and revenue accounts, but they are a decrease in the asset and expense accounts. (2) The ability to borrow money or buy things with a promise to pay later.

Credit analysis. A process used to determine the suitability of a potential creditor to receive credit and how much credit should be given.

D

Debit. The bookkeeping entry made on the left side of the account. In double-entry bookkeeping a debit is an increase in the asset and expense accounts and a decrease in the liabilities, equity and revenue accounts.

Demand deposit. This is an account where funds may be withdrawn, or transferred on demand to another person, by means of a check. A checking account is an example of a demand account.

Disposable income. This your income less income tax and all other government deductions. Disposable income is what most people think of as their take-home pay.

Dividend. Money paid to shareholders of a money market fund, a stock, or mutual fund.

E

Embezzlement. The theft of money or property from a business by a person responsible for its safekeeping.

Encumbrance. A lien on assets used to secure a loan.

Ending balance. The balance of all transactions in the account register.

Exchange rate. The ratio at which one currency or commodity can be exchanged for another.

Expenditure. A payment made with cash or property (or a promise to pay later) to obtain an asset or service.

Expense. Something paid out to obtain revenue in the current period. One example is the depletion of an asset through depreciation. Another example is to incur an obligation to which regular payments are made, like in an equipment lease.

Excise tax. This is a tax levied on specific goods or services to collect money for a specified purpose. The excise tax on gasoline is an example—the money is used to build and maintain the road system.

F

Factoring. The sale of a firm's accounts receivable at a discount and without recourse to avoid having to wait until the accounts mature, or to avoid collection costs.

Financial statement. A report containing a snapshot financial representation of the organization. It usually contains a balance sheet, an income statement, and a statement of changes in financial condition.

Fixed asset. An asset, purchased for the use of the organization and not intended for resale, with a life of more than one year. Property, plant, and equipment are first considerations.

Fixed cost. Costs that remain constant as expenses regardless of changes in operation. Rent, insurance, and licensing are examples of fixed-cost expenses.

G

General partner. The partner who is liable for all debts and obligations incurred by the partnership.

Graph. A visual representation of data, such as a pie chart or bar chart that might represent the distribution of your salary.

Gross income. The amount of money received from the sale of goods or services less the cost of those goods or services. Gross income less the operating expenses of the company is called net income.

Gross sales. This is the total of all sales before the adjustment for returns and discounts. It is the total number of units sold multiplied times the unit sales price.

Growth stock. This is a group name applied to companies that have no earnings record from past operations. The value of the company is based on speculation about future earnings. These stocks may have a potential for high return because they do have a faster than usual rise in the market and industry. Because they are speculative in nature and the expected gains may not materialize at all growth stocks have a high risk associated with them.

H

Hidden accounts. These are accounts that Quicken uses to keep track of accounts that are obsolete or have a zero balance. By hiding accounts you can remove an account and its balance from your list of accounts but still retain the transaction information.

I

Income. This is money earned during a specific period that increases total assets. This can come from salaries, rent, interest earned, gifts, commissions, etc. Any excess over expense is called net income.

Individual Retirement Account (IRA). A special account for the investment of money for retirement that meets the government regulations for an account that does not generate any taxable income as long as the funds remain in the account.

J

Joint stock company. A group of individuals joined together to form and operate a business. Similar to a corporation except that the investors are not given limited liability.

Joint tenancy. An arrangement in which property or real estate is deeded and held by two or more persons who hold an undivided interest in the property. Should one of the members die, the property will revert to the control of the remaining member(s) without the need to go through the estate of the deceased.

K

Keogh plan. A retirement plan for self-employed persons who meet certain requirements. A Keogh plan member may make an annual contribution up to 25% of income or a maximum amount of $30,000.

Kiting. The illegal practice of concealing a cash shortage by taking advantage of the time that it takes for a check to clear through the banking system.

L

Lead time. This is the number of business days from the time you send online payment instructions until the payment is received by the payee. Quicken automatically calculates this number when you enter payment instructions.

Liability. An amount payable in dollars or services. The party having the liability is called a debtor.

Lien. The right of a second party to take control over or possession of the property of another to satisfy a debt or duty obligation.

M

Maturity date. The date by which the principal of a debt must be paid.

N

Net worth. Total assets minus total liabilities. This represents an individual's personal equity; in a business this would be the shareholders' equity.

Non-profit organization. An organization that meets a need for goods and services that is structured so that no one involved in the organization may benefit from or share in the profits or losses. These organizations are exempt from taxes and donations to them are tax deductible.

Non-taxable gross income. Money received by a taxpayer that is not taxed like a gift.

O

Owner's equity. The owner's interest in the assets of the business. These are represented by capital contributions and retained earnings.

Operating loss. The amount of money by which the business' operating expenses added to the cost of goods sold exceeds the operating revenue.

Operating revenue. This is net sales plus all other regular business income.

Operating risk. The risk encountered because of a fluctuating operating revenue stream. The higher the risk the more unstable the company.

P

Paid-in capital. The results of donations to the company or sale of treasury or capital stock at a price above par value.

Par value. The arbitrary value assigned to one share of stock by the company charter. This is the amount printed on the certificate.

Patent. An exclusive right to manufacture and market a product or a process for 17 years without interference or infringement. Patents are issued by the government to companies and individuals.

Q

Quicken. Personal finance software by Intuit, Inc.

QuickTabs. A Quicken feature that keeps the most-used windows open and provides a tab at the right of the screen to facilitate switching back and forth from one window to another one.

Quickzoom. A Quicken feature that enables you to get a detailed display of a graph or report.

Quoted price. The last transaction price of a commodity or a listed security.

R

Recession. A downturn in the economy as indicated by a drop in the Gross National Product.

Reconcile window. This window displays cleared transactions that occur before the statement end date for reconciling an online account to a statement.

Reconciliation. Ensuring that there is agreement between your account register and the statements you receive from financial institutions.

Retirement accounts. These are accounts in which the income generated by the deposits does not incur a tax liability as long as it remains in the account.

S

Short-term debt. Money owed to a creditor with a repayment term of less than one year.

Shrinkage. The difference between inventory on the books and the actual inventory on hand.

Simple interest. Interest that is based on the original principal and not compounded.

Speculation. The method of investment that puts money in high-risk investments to increase the chance of higher capital gain.

Stock quotes. Continuously updated prices of stocks and securities. Quicken provides access to these prices through Internet access.

T

Tax credit. A reduction in taxes payable where the basis for reducing the taxpayer's obligation is dollar for dollar for the amount of the credit.

Transaction. Any action or item that affects the balance of an account, including checks, fees, service charges, deposits, deposits, etc.

Treasury bill (T bill). An actively-marketed, low-risk short-term obligation of the government. These are sold without interest at a discount and redeemed in 91 or 182 days at face value. There are some T bills that are sold for nine or twelve months occasionally. The T Bill amounts range from 10,000 to a million dollars.

Treasury bond. (1) A long-term obligation of the Federal Government with maturities of ten years or more that is sold in minimum amounts of $1,000. (2) A long-term obligation sold by a corporation and then repurchased (retired) by the corporation at a later date.

Treasury certificate. A debt security of the federal government bearing coupon interest, with a maturity date of one year or less.

Treasury notes. Actively marketed obligations of the federal government with maturities of one to ten years.

U

Unappropriated retained earnings. Funds in the retained earnings account that are available for disbursement as dividends.

Unaudited statement. A statement that was not prepared by an accountant according to the Generally Accepted Auditing Standards (GAAP).

Unit trust. A mutual fund whose only investments are in bonds.

Unlimited liability. The liability that applies to owners of sole proprietorships or general partnerships. Shareholders in corporations have limited liability which limits their risk of loss to the investment they made in the stock.

V

Variable costs. These are costs that vary in direct proportion to changes in activity. Examples are vehicle operation expenses or the costs of overtime hours.

Variable annuity. An investment through an investment or insurance company in which the periodic annuity payments are dependent on the performance of the portfolio.

Venture capital. A potential funding source for new or restructured businesses where the potential for high return is great, but so is the risk. Often wealthy individual investors or investment clubs and small investment companies participate in venture capital because of the big potential for return.

Vested. A description of an employees paid-up rights to retirement benefits. These are benefits not contingent on the employee's remaining in the employ of the organization.

Voucher check. A business check with additional voucher space on the side to allow for more detail about the transaction.

Vouching. The recognition of obligations and the authorization of cash disbursements.

W

Warranty. The agreement of a seller or manufacturer to settle any grievances over the quality or performance of an item for a specified amount of time.

Windfall profits. Unexpected unearned income not usually a result of the investment or effort of the person benefiting.

Worker's compensation. A program of compensation to a worker injured on the job made without consideration for negligence.

Index

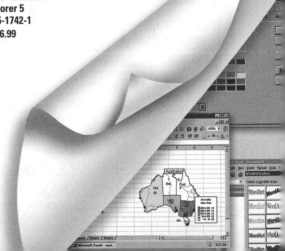